Creative Flower Arrangement

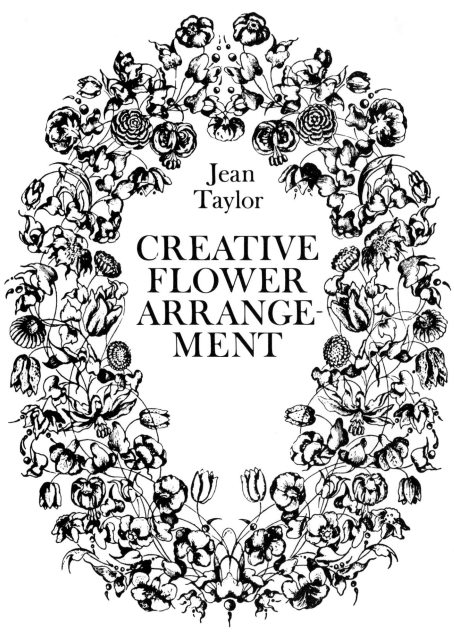

Jean
Taylor

CREATIVE
FLOWER
ARRANGE-
MENT

Stanley Paul

London Melbourne Auckland Johannesburg

Stanley Paul & Co. Ltd

An imprint of Century Hutchinson Ltd

Brookmount House, 62–65 Chandos Place, Covent Garden, London WC2N 4NW

Century Hutchingson Australia (Pty) Ltd
PO Box 496, 16–22 Church Street, Hawthorn, Victoria 3122

Century Hutchinson New Zealand Limited
PO Box 40-086, Glenfield, Auckland 10

Century Hutchinson South Africa (Pty) Ltd
PO Box 337, Bergvlei 2012, South Africa

First published 1973
Reprinted 1974, 1978, 1980, 1983, 1984, 1986
Copyright © Jean Taylor 1973
Illustrations copyright © Stanley Paul & Co. Ltd 1973

Set in Baskerville

Printed in Great Britain by Ebenezer Baylis and
Son Limited, The Trinity Press, Worcester and London

ISBN 0 09 113631 8

Contents

Acknowledgements

The drawings are by Malcolm Drake and Amanda Cobb.

The photographs are by the courtesy of the following, except where credit is given under the photograph.

The National Association of Flower Arrangement Societies of Great Britain
Pages: 29 *left*, 39, 81 *top left*, 88 *left*, 91 *left*, 100 *left*, 120 *top right*, 180, 184, 232, 244.

The Flower Arranger
Pages: 32 *top right*, 48 *right*, 67, 89 *right*, 117 *lower left*, 146 *left*, 210 *top right and lower left*, 212 *lower right*, 264 *top left*.

Thames Television
Pages: 71 *left*, 81 *top right*, 85, 89 *left*, 101, 260.

D. Rendell Esq, AIIP, ARPS
Pages: 26, 48 *lower*, 53, 69 *lower*, 76 *right*, 79, 103, 139 *left*, 141, 144, 152 *top* and *lower left*, 154, 160 *right*, 165 *left*, *right lower* and *lower*, 171 *left*, 208, 241, 246 *top*, 264 *right*, 270 *lower*, 287, 288.

The Trustees of the Tate Gallery
Pages: 37, 58, 96 *lower*, 142, 152 *right*, 163, 165 *top right*, 183, 212 *top right, lower left*, 223 *right*, 226 *lower right*, 230 *top*, 243 *top left*, 264 *lower*, 277, 283, 285 *right*.

Garden News
Pages: 15, 17 *left*, 25, 28, 32 *left*, 45, 55, 57, 75 *right*, 81 *lower*, 90, 98, 100 *right*, 120 *lower*, 157, 169, 212 *top left*, 230, 235.

The National Gallery
    Pages: 10, 156, 243 *above right,* 243 *lower.*

The Victoria and Albert Museum
    Pages: 96 *right,* 167, 205, 206, 226 *top right,* 245, 285 *left.*

The British Museum
    Pages: 69 *top,* 71 *right,* 226 *above left,* 226 *lower left.*

S.P.A.D.E.M.
    Page: 96.

Mansell Collection
    Page: 139.

Topix
    Page: 223.

The Colour Circle on page 181 by courtesy of The National Association of Flower Arrangement Societies of Great Britain.

My thanks to:
My family for their encouragement and understanding; my students who have always taught me more than I have taught them; the many flower arranging friends who happily lent photographs; Mr. D. Rendell for his generous gift of photographs; the following friends who kindly read the script and gave advice—Mrs. Dulcie Brunskill, Mrs. Dorothy Cooke, Mrs. Ella Forrester, Mrs. Catherine Hastings, Mr. Eric Hillidge, Mrs. Renée Mottershead, Mrs. Sylvia Pullan, Mrs. Rosemary Stille and Mrs. Iris Webb.

Publisher's Note: We would like to thank Mrs Daphne Vagg for ensuring that all information in this book is up to date for the fifth and sixth editions.

PART 1

Creative Flower Arrangement

'Flowers in a terracotta vase and fruit.' Jan Van Huijsum (1682-1749)

INTRODUCTION

'If of thy mortal goods thou art bereft
And from thy slender store, two loaves alone to thee are left
Sell one and with the dole
Buy hyacinth to feed thy soul.'

Moslih Saadi, Persian poet 13th century.

For more than 4,000 years beautiful flowers have been an inspiration to Man. They have been written about in poems and literature, painted, carved in wood, modelled in clay and stone, woven into fabrics and embroideries, copied in mosaics. Since civilisation began they have been arranged in containers of water to enhance Man's surroundings.

In the present day, more people enjoy arranging flowers than ever before and have awakened also to the beauty of foliage, branches, roots and bark, so that plant material of any variety has become the medium of a distinctive visual art called 'flower arrangement', even though flowers may not be included in the design. It is certain that this can be an exciting and highly creative art, but the flower arranger needs confidence, which develops when she understands the nature of her materials, learns to discipline her creative impulses and to conform with the design principles. It also comes from seeing her work in relation to other art forms and to history, which gives a broader vision and so greater perception.

'It is ordained that never shall any man be able out of his own thoughts to make a beautiful figure, unless by much study he hath stored his mind.' *Albrecht Dürer*

'Those who are enamoured of practise without science are like a pilot who goes into a ship without rudder or compass and never has any certainty where he is going.'

Leonardo da Vinci

The final form created by the flower arranger is the sum total of her inspiration, selection, technical skill and artistic ability. It includes the setting of the design and also its function. It includes the style and manner of presentation. This gives infinite variation which is not always pleasing to everyone as perception, taste, sensitivity and knowledge vary from person to person. However, the infinite variation in the final form and the differing assessment by critics are what make all art a constant challenge. It is always exciting, often original, ever-changing and usually controversial.

I

Creativity

Creativity implies open thinking, originality and a different approach. A creative person is one who breaks away from convention and tries something new. He or she challenges accepted concepts, is inquisitive and usually adventurous, has divergent ideas and thinks constructively.

What is creative and what is conventional differs from culture to culture and from time to time. Creative thought *now* may be conventional thought in fifty years time, but without it there would be no progress at all. There were those who laughed when Columbus said the world was round and not flat, but his *was* creative thought!

The term 'creativity' is a popular one in education today. Comprehensive studies are being made of creative people and of their parents and environment. Creativity's relationship with intelligence is being queried. Many teachers are being encouraged to teach in a way that fosters creativity in their students but its exact meaning has yet to be clearly defined. A dictionary definition refers to 'the action of bringing into existence a work of thought and imagination'. By usage generally, it also implies a certain amount of originality and distinction. A. J. Cropley writes 'Although the concept of creativity is a difficult one to employ with precision because of its impreciseness, the term is coming to be accepted by many psychologists and educators as referring to an intellective mode characterised by thinking of the divergent kind'.

Students in all subjects are being urged to think and discover for themselves and not to sit and be told, to try new things and to refrain from conforming for the sake of conformance (and because it is easier).

In the visual arts there has been a great upsurge of interest in creativity. The whole approach is now much more personal with greater freedom for the individual and tolerance of new ideas. This does not mean that tradition is obsolete for classical art will live for ever, but it does mean that there are new attitudes and aspirations leading to new trends.

Period and traditional flower arrangements will always be admired and enjoyed, but many arrangers now appreciate more freedom to experiment with different approaches to the art. In flower arrangement creativity comes through having an open mind and a well developed 'seeing eye'. It implies knowledge of design and its application to flower arrangement since the design principles are basic to all forms and styles of art; technical skill and an awareness of the potential qualities for design in plant material; a study of the other arts to broaden the approach; experiments in related activities, such as painting, drawing, collage, modelling and so on.

This does not mean that there should never be any imitation of previous styles—most flower arrangers have an imitative period at some stage in their careers as they learn the art—but imitation should be approached in an enquiring manner. What is good about this traditional style? Which of its qualities could be adapted to a new style? If a flower arranger wishes to be creative it is important that she tries new ideas (for her) *at the same time* as imitating other styles, so that a spontaneous approach is not entirely lost forever, which often happens with continual conformance to set styles or shapes.

In trying something different there is often failure. All designers, great and not so great, experience failure as well as success and not only at the beginning of their careers. This is part of being creative and should not be depressing or discouraging. The creative person tries something new and experiments with extending the present limits or boundaries

14

'The Wave' by R. E. Langridge. Green arums, variegated aspidistra leaves with a modelled accessory.

Opposite: Wall plaque by Edna M. Cordon. Tree bark with eucalyptus, poppy and gonnal seedheads and pods.

Above left: 'Spring Rain' by Joan Lutwyche. Golden mitzuhiki and daffodils.
Above right: Simple plant materials with original composition. Arranged by Margaret Punshon.

of her art, as she knows it. She has to find out for herself what will work and what will not—to retract and advance alternately—which is all part of the creative process. In flower arrangement the action of originality may be in using a new plant, or including an unusual object, or assembling the plant material in a different way, or an unusual final effect, or a combination of any of these.

Practically speaking, creativity in flower arrangement involves:

1. Challenging 'the rules' and questioning their validity and use.
2. Trying new methods of composition based on the good use of design principles and not always conforming to the usual ways of assembling plant material.

17

3. Trying out new techniques—perhaps borrowed from other crafts—in creating new surfaces, textures and appearances.
4. The use of new plant materials and searching for the unusual and untried at home and abroad.
5. The use of different accessories instead of the conventional ones—such as waste glass, plastic, rusty wire, tow rope, nylon thread, strips of metal—anything with design potential.
6. Trying to find new 'containers'—some homemade, others adapted from plant material, machinery or spare parts—with new techniques applied to them.
7. The use of interesting backgrounds instead of drapery, clearly integrated with the design so that arrangements can be well displayed.
8. Experimenting continually to find out and learn.
9. A collection of likely objects, related and unrelated to flower arrangement, with which to experiment.
10. Roving about with an enquiring mind in cities, shops, art galleries and museums, in the country, seashore, garden and nursery and absorbing ideas from the environment.

A creative flower arranger must be prepared for criticism but needs to settle for being 'true unto herself'. It is this creative approach which will keep flower arrangement vital, provocative, controversial and most of all, absorbing.

'I call a man an artist who creates forms—and I call a man an artisan who imitates forms.'

André Malraux

SUMMARY

Creative people challenge accepted concepts.
They are divergent thinkers.
Progress happens from creative thinking.
Creativity implies originality and distinction.
It plays a large part in modern education.
A creative person experiences failure and success.
In flower arrangement, creativity means challenging rules, experimenting, collecting, roving.
It means trying out new methods of composition, techniques, plant material, accessories, containers and backgrounds.

CREATIVE STUDY

Observe:

New styles in art of all kinds—needlework, painting, sculpture, window dressing, photography, set designing, architecture, weaving.

New thinking and ideas from other people in books, on television, in newspapers and magazines which challenge and consider old concepts.

New techniques and materials in the other arts.

Collect:

Experiences everywhere from the environment.
Objects of all kinds which might be useful.
Fabrics, different textures, colours, qualities.
Stones, glass, coral, metal of all sizes and types.
Wire in many gauges, plastics, rope.
Bases of all kinds.
Accessories.
Containers of unusual shape.
Books and pictures, newspaper cuttings.
Driftwood, branches, fungi.
New plants to grow.
New plant material from abroad.

Make:

Containers.
Backgrounds of varying designs.
Bases.
Experiments in other fields of art.

Flower Arrangement:

Try new styles for yourself.
Try composing in a different manner.
Try colour schemes not tried before.
Use unusual materials for accessories.
Use unusual plant material and combinations of plant material.

2

Inspiration

Inspiration is one of the most beautiful words in the English language, it is lovely to say and promises so much that is exciting in its meaning. It is the spark which kindles imagination and is at the heart of all creative talent, Carl Sandberg wrote:

'Nothing happens unless first a dream.'

A well-executed flower arrangement without inspiration pales in comparison with one created when the arranger has been inspired. Yet, when most needed, inspiration often eludes us and we need something or someone to stimulate and impel us, to enliven our minds and make them fertile, to 'inspirit' us.

The great masters of art and the famous composers were sometimes utterly inspired and at other times their work is artistic and well-executed but lacking in inspiration. What is this needed spark that sets creative talent aflame? What are the sources of inspiration to stimulate beautiful and moving self-expression? Inspiration means more than just enthusiasm, for it implies energy and confidence, even a touch of something magical. It is said that genius is 1% inspiration and 99% perspiration but it is that 1% which starts the work in motion as the switch starts a motor or the yeast causes the bread to rise. Usually inspiration is the result of a personal aesthetic experience.

'In truth I have painted by opening my eyes day and night on the perceptible world and also by closing them from time to time that I might better see the vision bloom and submit itself to orderly arrangement.'

Georges Roualt

In this quotation is perhaps the key to finding inspiration —our eyes must be open day and night on the perceptible world and we need to develop 'a seeing eye', to absorb and experience the nature of things so that anywhere at any time we may be inspired. The art of observation and perception needs constant practice, and we all have so little time. Inspiration comes not by waiting for it but by looking at things, experiencing things and being in a stimulating atmosphere. So many ordinary things have beauty if we have time to look —the texture and colouring of an old brick wall, the iridescent shine of petrol on a road, a water-worn pebble, a skeletonised leaf.

'It is as if Substance said to Knowledge; My child, there is a great world for thee to conquer, but it is a vast and ancient, and a recalcitrant world. It yields wonderful treasures to courage, when courage is guided by art and respects the limits set to it by nature. I should not have been so cruel as to give thee birth, if there had been nothing for thee to master; but having first prepared the field, I set in thy heart the love of adventure.'

George Santayana

NATURE

The world of nature has given inspiration to designers in all the arts for centuries. Cicero said 'Art is born of observation and investigation of nature'. Many resemblances to natural things can be found in man-made objects; the pagoda is similar to the native pine of the Orient; the Egyptian column to the lotus plant of the Nile; the tower of Pisa to the ancient plants of Horsetail (*Equisetum*); the Pharaohs' pyramids to mountains; Gothic cathedrals' tall pillars and vaulting ribs to forests. More recently Frank Lloyd Wright took the

shell of the nautilus as inspiration for the Guggenheim museum in New York. T. E. Brown wrote 'Nature is the art of God'.

There seems to be an intuitive and persistent tendency which endures through all time to take inspiration from nature. It may be because nature is familiar, near at hand, an inescapable part of our life and a powerful environment. It seems that almost everything in nature offers some unique quality from which designers can gain ideas. It also invokes strong emotional experiences. Many of us are deeply moved at the vision of a flaming sky at sunset, huge waves pounding on the rocks, the stillness of a moonlit night, the grandeur of the Alps, the majesty of the stars, the unexpected sight of a glorious rainbow, even the dark clouds of a storm. These experiences usually remain with us to offer inspiration when needed, often adding up to a deep perception and a way of looking and feeling. Although much of what is observed and experienced may not appear specifically in a design it becomes basic knowledge to be stored for later use.

The world of nature is of first importance to flower arrangers as their medium brings them closer to it than the medium of any other artist. They make collections of such things as dried materials, stones and shells not only for the sheer joy of possessing them but also for their inspiration in beginning new work. Ideas can spring from the sight of Autumn leaves against a grey sky, the many whites on a snowy day, the brilliant colour harmony in a bird's feathers, lichen growing around a tree trunk or grasses leaning in the wind. There are the centres of flowers, a spider's web, waves breaking on the shore, flotsam in the sand or a misty November evening; a dandelion clock, the pattern of a flower of Queen Anne's lace, the sheen on the inside of a buttercup, lacy pink seaweed in a pool, a butterfly's wings. Looking at a heather clad mountain we can see a colour harmony but we can also perceive a way of interpreting strength, grandeur and solitude.

Opposite: An Egyptian vase, Dynasty XVIII (c. 1450 BC), inspired by the flower of the lotus. *(Photographie Giraudon)*

'The study of basic design is deeply concerned with the infinite variation of natural phenomena. To live in wonderment and to recognise this phenomena as his birthright is the artist's role.'

Kenneth F. Bates

THE VISUAL ARTS

To see the work of artists in other fields can be very stimulating.

'All the arts are brothers; each one is a light to the others.'

Voltaire

'All the arts appertaining to man have a certain common bond and areas as it were connected by a sort of relationship.'

Cicero

'All arts are one, howe'er distributed they stand. Verse, tone, shape, colour, form are fingers on one hand.'

William Wetmore Story

In sculpture the interplay of form and space, the treatment of heavy masses and the challenge of using only one type of material are lessons to us. It is inspiring to look at the weaver's skill in blending textures and colours in tweed, silk and nylon and creating the beauty of velvet and lace. Embroidery, pottery and photography have so much to offer and of course painting gives an unending supply of inspiration. Gauguin's symbolism and use of rich colours, Van Eyck's exquisite detail, Picasso's power of expression, the rhythm of Van Gogh, and Gainsborough's subtle colourings are but a few examples. Not the least are Turner's paintings of light and it has been written that someone once said to him 'I never saw any such light and colour in Nature as you put on your canvas'. Turner replied 'Don't you wish you could? As for me, I never can hope to match with pigment the glory in the sky.'

Many artists have themselves been inspired by the very plants that we use as our medium in flower arrangement and have found natural things their greatest source of inspiration.

Opposite: 'Dream of Florence' in pink, gold and white. Arranged by Jean Taylor.

'CONTAINERS ARE AN INSPIRATION'
Above left: Antique, bronze, Chinese.
Above right: Stoneware by Staite Murray.
Below left: A copy of an Etruscan cup (c. 500 BC).
Below right: Alabaster, Edwardian.

Graham Sutherland said 'In nature lies the key . . . I am lost without nature . . . I can't invent unless I've got something to invent from. But I CAN carry it further,' and 'I find that all natural forms are a source of unending interest—landscapes, cloud formations, tree trunks, the texture and variety of grasses, the shape of shells, of pebbles, etc. The whole of Nature is an endless demonstration of shape and form and it surprises me when artists try to escape from this. Not to look at and use Nature in one's work is unnatural to me.'

Sometimes artists copy Nature realistically, as for example Constable, but there is always a degree of selection and often the aim is to catch the mood of a landscape rather than to record every detail of twig and leaf. Sometimes artists take inspiration from Nature but without realism, so that there is a sensation rather than a naturalistic scene, which conveys a special meaning the artist wishes the viewer to understand. At times this can go to the extent of distortion, but Nature can still be the source of the original stimulus to work, whatever the style. Henry Moore said 'Observation is part of an artist's life, it enlarges his form knowledge, keeps him fresh and from working only by formula, and feeds imagination.'

HISTORY

There is much to be gleaned from the past; the style of flower arrangements in former times and their settings; the. wood carvings of Grinling Gibbons, the Flemish flower paintings, beautiful containers and accessories of taste and discrimination; the buildings in Venice, and many other old and lovely things.

THE WRITTEN WORD

There is often a thought in poetry which may start our ideas flowing:

> 'Tis the noon of Autumn glow
> When a soft and purple mist
> Like a vaporous amethyst
> Or an air-dissolved star . . .
> Fills the over-flowing sky.'

Shelley

or

'When men were all asleep, snow came flying
In large white flakes falling on the city brown.'

LONDON SNOW
R. Bridges

and in literature:

'The oaks alone, the flower with light tassels of greenish
yellow are most glorious; the young beech leaves, almost
transparent are wonderfully tender and brilliant in the sun,
the May itself lies on the hedges in thick clouds of cream.

Opposite: 'Inspired by a Cock' by Jean Taylor. Strelitzia flowers, grasses
and dried palm.

Below left: 'Old Master.' Inspired by a Chinese painting. Arranged by
Miss Peggy Lovell.
Below right: 'Inspired by Metal Sculpture' by Margaret Punshon. Dried
buddleia with a section from an old blackcurrant bush.

The lilac and the chestnut are in bloom. . . . In gardens there is a perfect union between spring and summer so that roses and tulips bloom together and pinks and primroses. And in the fields there is a glory of moondaisy and campion and . . . clover that never comes again and everywhere one's feet are dusted with gold.'

H. E. Bates' description of May 18th
from THE ENGLISH SCENE

MUSIC

For some, inspiration can flow from music, for example, from Beethoven's *6th Symphony,* the *Pastoral,* composed in the wooded environs of Vienna, Debussy's *La Mer,* and Mozart's *Eine Kleine Nachtmusik.*

SEASONS AND EVENTS

The simple, cold beauty and freshness of spring, the heat and perfumes of summer, the abundant colourings of autumn and the starkness of winter all offer different inspiration.

At Christmas time carols, frosty trees, and decorations give ideas and the Christmas story itself is a source of continuing and beautiful inspiration. Events such as May-day folk festivals, and bonfire night are all stimulating in their way.

THE SEEING EYE

A 'seeing eye' develops from looking and observing, from peeping inside things, turning things over and regarding objects for their factual appearance not necessarily connected with use or association. It comes from a constantly enquiring and inventive approach to everything in the environment, so that remarkable and unusual things are noticed afresh in familiar objects. From an interplay of inspiration *without* and of discovery *within,* the imagination stays lively and fertile. Children have an enquiring approach which is very refreshing but as we get older, familiarity causes us to pass over so many things and we do not find time to look and wonder as a child and so to develop perception.

Opposite: Wood carving by Grinling Gibbons. Petworth House. (By courtesy of *Country Life*)

Left: 'Inspired by Grinling Gibbons.' A swag of dried plant material with the head of a cherub. Arranged by Mrs. K. M. Gasser. *Above:* 'Inspired by Andrea Della Robbia'. Arranged by Miss Olive Wilson.

Opposite: 'Inspired by a Roman Garland.' Arranged by Mrs. Renée Mottershead.

'Today I visited that place where the garbage men dump their rubbish. God, how beautiful that was! Tomorrow they are sending me a few worthwhile objects collected from that heap—among others broken street lanterns to be looked at or used as a model—if you wish. The whole thing was like an Andersen fairy tale. What a collection! All these old objects which have resigned their services—baskets, kettles, bowls, oil cans, metal wires, street lanterns, clay pipes . . .'
Vincent Van Gogh to Anthon Van Rappard 1883

It has been suggested that to express an emotion one must feel it, to express a scene one must have seen it and to express an atmosphere one must experience it. Certainly inspiration comes from feeling, seeing and experiencing and we need to go into the world as seekers and collectors with eyes and minds open to the world around us. In 1842 Joseph M. W. Turner painted a picture of a snowstorm at sea which could have been done only after a close study. To experience a storm, Turner went aboard a ship and although a fierce storm arose which threatened to sweep him overboard, he ordered the sailors to lash him to the mast so that he could watch it for hours and the result was a magnificent painting.

SUMMARY

Inspiration is the beginning of creative composition.
A seeing eye helps perception and therefore inspiration.
Many seemingly ordinary objects have beauty when closely studied.
Nature is, and has always been, the greatest source of inspiration.
Flower arrangers can be inspired by the work of other artists, history, the written word, music, seasons, and events.
An artist needs to feel, see and experience.

CREATIVE STUDY

Observe:
The moods of music.
Design in many fields and analyse the inspiration.
Everything closely in your environment.
Under a microscope—crystals, shells, stones, coal, wood graining, flower petals, tree bark and so on.
The things around you on a walk and record some of them.
Absorb and record the atmosphere of various scenes—woodland, cave, city and so on. Write down the characteristic colours, forms, textures, components.

Collect:
Driftwood, shells, coral, stones, cork, glass, bones, sea urchins, lacy seaweed, skates' egg-cases, feathers, limpets, loofah—while beachcombing.
Containers, bases and accessories which might inspire.
Pictures or paintings which could inspire a flower arrangement.
Gravel, bricks, rusty metal, glass, wire, corrugated iron, lumps of cement—from the town or city.
Lists of impressions, ideas, poems, writings.
Skeletonised leaves, moss, fungi, bare branches, bark, stones, cones, feathers, curled dried leaves, snail shells, seeds—from a woodland.

Make:

Visits to art galleries, museums, theatres, stately homes, libraries, design centres, craftsmen's studios, shops stocking goods from other countries, gardens, nurseries.
Diagrammatic sketches in a record book of inspiration.

3
Composition

DEFINITION

Composition is the art or practice of so combining the parts of a work of art as to produce a harmonious whole. To compose means to form by putting together; to make-up; to arrange artistically; to design and execute or to put together; to place shape, texture and colour in ordered relationships.

Composing or designing brings order out of chaos and is an aesthetic and physical need in man. Order is necessary to living but the word implies more than making order out of disorder; the order can be such that the end result is something beautiful.

IN DESIGN

Composition brings together in practice the various aspects of design, the skill, colour, texture, form, setting and function, to give underlying order and a sense of fluency and unity.

There are two ways of composing. Either the design can be previously thought out to the last detail which can sometimes produce a static design, or there can be no previous plan and the designer works with his particular medium until a pleasing and rhythmical grouping emerges. Sometimes this method brings chaos. Good design usually results from a

Left: 'Project for a Family Group.' Henry Moore, 1944, Bronze.
Right: 'Hylas and the Water Nymphs.' John Gibson, 1826, Marble.

combination of two methods, a certain amount of planning to give order and to start the design, and then some 'playing' with trial and error. This has flexibility, and a design may eventually be quite different from the original plan, and yet lead to order with a degree of freedom of expression.

Basically it can be said that composing is *choosing* and then arranging. Consequently the importance of choice cannot be overestimated. Careful discrimination is needed to choose one thing in preference to another, because of the object's appearance and usefulness in a particular context. This discrimination is vital to good design for it involves selecting an object because of its separate characteristics and with regard to its underlying relationship with the other components in the design. Informed or knowledgeable choice becomes second nature as the designer becomes more familiar with his medium.

It is essential to think of the design as a whole and not as a number of separate parts, consequently all the shapes,

37

colours, textures and spatial relationships need care and thought so that every part of the design is part of the total effect and yet keeps its own importance. Composition is necessary for every style. The end result of composing or designing does not have to be naturalistic and the act of composition relates as much to abstract art and to surrealism as to naturalism. It is impossible to give formulas for composition as every situation is different. A design grows from the first intent, the choice of components and the action of combining them. To think too much about the principles of design as one works is probably inhibiting. These are certainly tools of expression but they are more useful in assessing the finished form than as conscious disciplines while working. It is better to work spontaneously and enjoyably, as a laboured design is rarely as good as a spontaneous one.

IN FLOWER ARRANGEMENT

The word flower in this context has come to mean more than literally 'flower' and this is often confusing to some people. It has taken on the broader meaning of 'flora' with consequently more interest and scope for creativity. 'Flower arrangement' now means the composing of plant material of *any* stage of growth and of any type, with or without associated objects. Flower arrangers work with forms already created bringing together sometimes uncohesive and diversified materials from our environment into meaningful order whereas architects, painters and sculptors create their own forms. Also the medium of plant material is normally used unchanged except for cutting, grooming and sometimes a little polishing, painting or preserving. Selection of suitable objects, then, plays a major part in flower arrangement composition, since so few changes are made in the medium as found. It is necessary for the flower arranger to select many objects, often of a widely differing nature. These objects include plant material and, when used, containers, bases, accessories, drapes and backgrounds. The selection must be made from many thousands of colours, forms and textures in each component. After selection, they must be assembled and

TWO WELL-COMPOSED INTERPRETATIONS OF 'BAZAAR'
Left: Arranged by the Epsom Mayday Flower Club.
Right: Arranged by the Penzance Floral Club.

co-ordinated into a pleasing whole and although the source of forms differs in sculpture and flower arrangement, the following description by Henri Laurens applies to both. 'Sculpture is essentially occupation of space, construction of an object with hollows and solid parts, mass and void, their variations and reciprocal tensions and finally their equilibrium.'

SELECTION OF MATERIALS

This is not always easy as the desired material may not be readily available but this is one of the challenges offered by flower arrangement.

Composition starts either when some beautiful plant material is discovered by an arranger and she wishes to share its beauty with others and place it in a position where she herself can often regard its beauty, or when plant material is a gift and needs arranging in water, or when a design is made

39

to fulfil a certain function. This function can be the decoration of a home, church, hospital and so on, or it can be a class at a flower show. In the first two the initial plant material sets the path of the composition, in the third the *function* of the design dictates the form of the composition. Fortunately this helps to limit the field which can otherwise be endless. The following are helpful in selecting the materials of flower arranging:

1. *Scale*
Think of the size of the setting—either the position in a room, or the niche or space at a show. This will suggest the size of the container and consequently of the plant material. All the components need to be related in scale.

2. *Function*
Think of the reason for the design—if it is to be decorative, then beautiful plant material must be selected. If it is to cheer up a dark corner then luminous colours will be necessary. If the arrangement is for a wedding in a church then it must suit the colours of the bridal party. A dinner table arrangement must decorate, and interest the guests, without being an impediment. A cocktail party may need a striking design, a hot day may require cool colours. Hospital arrangements need to be both beautiful and restful. Designs for a class in a show, requiring the interpretation of a theme, idea or story, must fulfil the requirements of the schedule and be expressive of the theme and not necessarily decorative.

3. *Compatibility*
Think of the colours, textures, shape, style, lighting, quality and formality of the setting so that the design will be compatible with its surroundings in every way. The individual components must also be selected for their compatibility with each other.

With regard to designs created for a flower show class in which the decorative quality is not so important as the interpretation of an idea, mood or story, then the components must be compatible with the theme portrayed and be chosen for their associations with it in addition to being suitable for each other.

Opposite: A plaque of dried plant materials with unusual composition, by Mrs. Sylvia Pullan.

4. *Design*

Think of the necessary qualities which make good design. Although the individual components may be compatible and related to each other, it is also essential to select them for the part they are to play in the design itself. For example a rough stoneware container may suit the rugged plant materials used and the simple modern style but if the textures are all similar —that is dull and rough—then a container with a slightly shiny glaze could be more suitable. Contrasts of texture may be needed, variation and repetition of colour, and changes of form. It is necessary to think of the needs of the design as the plant material is selected. The materials should be chosen for the particular qualities they offer not because 'they might come in', which is confusing and wasteful. Much time and work is saved by bearing in mind the design qualities needed when making the first selection of materials.

5. *Quantity*

Few people design well when there is so much plant material that selection becomes difficult. The best designs are often made when plant material is in short supply, such as in the winter or when a few pieces of plant material are 'left over' from a bigger design. Fewer materials give clearer cut design and eliminate fussiness and the feeling 'it is picked so I cannot waste it'. It is always easier to design with too little material than too much.

6. *Containers and other related objects*

These need to be selected with as much care as the plant material as a design is no better than any of its parts. They need to be related in scale, colour, texture, shape, quality, style and often association or idea.

PLAYTIME

After selecting a group of plant materials and other components it is necessary to 'play' with them to find out their nature and how they combine together. 'Playing' in this context means handling the materials, looking at the shapes, textures, colours, finding out the limits and possibilities, exploring and probing. Often the actual composition is very quick to assemble if there has been no preliminary rush to put it together. Height can be tried and combinations of colour and texture. The habit of growth of each plant can be studied so that it can be used in sympathy with its nature and not against it. For example, a straight growing piece of plant material will not easily bend into a curve for a crescent design and either the idea of a crescent must be discarded or naturally curved material must be found. Plant material is not malleable as clay and other media and its qualities must be understood before arranging it.

Roger Fry in 'Vision and Design' writes of one child's definition of drawing as 'I think then I draw a line around my think'. In flower arrangement one 'plays' and then assembles the plant material.

BEGINNING THE COMPOSITION

After the plant material has been handled and enjoyed, the form of the design roughly planned and the mechanics secure, the actual composition can begin. It does *not* matter in the slightest where the design begins. Some arrangers may like starting with a 'backbone', others with the main flowers at the centre of the design or where they are needed for emphasis. Some people prefer to start with a framework if they are following a distinct geometric shape and in modern work a side placement may be the best start. Physically it is easier to start towards the back of the mechanics. However, there is no right or wrong way of beginning.

The very first placement does condition the choice of other materials as there will be a desire for harmonious relationship between this and the further plant materials used. No formula should be given for the order of placements, as a set order is inhibiting and not always suitable for every type of plant material. The design should evolve as plant material is added and the arranger observes each new relationship, visually weighing one piece of plant material against another.

A time comes when it is difficult to know where to add the next placement and it is then wise to stop, even if one beautiful flower is left over (it can go in a specimen vase). The design has probably 'jelled' and needs little more attention. This is the time to see if anything can be removed and it usually can.

Major alterations to a design are not sensible in flower arrangement. It is better to work quickly and not labour the design. Spontaneous arranging is often much more successful and less contrived than one that takes hours and ends up tired in appearance (as the arranger). Many people regard the short life of a flower as a disadvantage but it can also be regarded as an advantage; if the design is poor the flowers are short-lived and will be thrown out. A bad flower arrangement does not hang around as a bad painting or book. The transient quality of plant material gives much of its charm and makes flower arrangement a fascinating art for one is continually inspired to capture its fleeting beauty.

After the design is finished, leave it and return later to assess its qualities. Alteration does little good as in fact one major move can lead to many others and the design goes completely wrong. It is better to assess faults but to leave the arrangement alone, the faults will probably be naturally righted when the next arrangement is created.

SIMPLICITY

'. . . simplification is essential to all art. Without it art can-not exist; for art is the creation of significant form and simplification is the liberating of what is significant from what is not.'

Clive Bell

In this context 'simplicity' refers to being uncomplicated, clear and plain, but not necessarily to being few in numbers. If a design is to communicate to an observer it should not be lost in extraneous and non-essential elaboration. A good design is one to which no more can be added but from which nothing can be subtracted without causing a feeling of emptiness or lack of completion. Quintilian, a first century Roman orator, said 'The perfection of art is to conceal art' and H. F. Amiel wrote 'The great artist is the simplifier'. At an exhibition of children's art, Picasso said to a friend 'As a young man I could draw like Raphael, it has taken me years to learn to draw like these children'.

A simple design is one that appears effortless in effect, the final form not being contrived in its impression. It uses too few

Opposite: 'Shelter' by Joan Lutwyche.

44

materials rather than too many and every item functions for the good of the whole and has a reason for its inclusion in the design. There is of course naïve simplicity that has no skill or knowledge, which is quite different. The Japanese word 'shibui' describes sophisticated simplicity and refers to the highest most serious artistic expression, implying imaginative insight and clarity that permits uncontrived simplicity and repose. Paul Klee said 'If a primitive impression is sometimes given by my work, this primitiveness is to be understood by my discipline, which is to reduce things to a few steps. It is only economy, a final professional perception, and thus the opposite of real primitiveness'.

Michelangelo said that 'if a carved figure was rolled down a steep hillside, what arrived at the bottom in one piece would be sculpture; the rest would be superficial elaboration'.

In flower arrangement simplicity can be difficult. Flowers picked need to go in water and it is tempting to add one too many to a design. The enjoyment of arranging such beautiful things as flowers is often so great that one does not want to stop. Accessories can be fascinating and too many may be added. It is true to say that one leaf which is turning colour can suggest Autumn, a trickle of sand suggest the shore, a small amount of moss suggest the woodland. The imagination often carries these 'suggestions' further, and the complete picture need not be spelt out by the arranger. Restraint is subtle and infinitely more interesting and stimulating to the imagination

'To gild refined gold, to paint the lily,
To throw a perfume on the violet
To smooth the ice or add another hue
Unto the rainbow or with taper-light
To seek the beauteous eye of heaven. To garnish
Is wasteful and ridiculous waste.'
William Shakespeare

AREAS OF EMPHASIS

All designs need areas of heightened interest and areas of lesser interest. This makes a good composition as it is in conformance with the principle of dominance, and it gives unity to the design. A room looks better when there is an interesting feature in it such as a good picture; a garden may have an ornamental pool or a specimen tree for accent; a painting may have a dominant figure and so on. In flower arrangement the area of greater interest is called the focal point or the centre of interest or where there is more than one area, the emphasis points.

Although an area of emphasis needs to be a dominant feature of the design, it must not be so strong that the eye is held rigidly to it, unable to travel to any other part of the design. Neither should it be so weak that it does not catch the eye or hold it.

The dominant feature can be made from a variety of things depending on the other materials in the design. It is relative as plant material that is dominant in one situation may not be dominant in another. Most flower arrangers agree that it should be plant material and not any of the related objects. If it is not plant material, then another field of activity, art or craft, is entered.

One certain quality or a number of qualities may make a dominant area of greater interest, such as:
1. A larger flower than the others in the design.
2. A round flower which attracts the eye and holds it.
3. A more brilliant colour or a more luminous colour than others in the design.
4. A group of flowers densely packed.
5. An enclosed space.
6. Something shiny in texture.
7. A dominant feature combined with plain surroundings such as one or two round, brilliant red flowers surrounded by some plain green foliage, which enhances the flowers.
8. A number of the above combined.

Usually the question of whether an area of heightened interest is present in the design must be assessed after completion. However, while 'playing' with the plant material before composing it, an assessment can be made of which is the most dominant plant material in the assembled group by reason of size, shape, colour or texture.

The *position* in which the area of greater interest should be placed depends on the style of the design. In traditional triangles and geometric designs, it is usual for it to be placed

Above left: Traditional pedestal with roses forming an area of greater interest in the centre. Arranged by Mrs. Elsie Lamb.

Above right: Free-form design with strelitzia flowers as the dominant attraction, although their placement is not central. Arranged by Jean Taylor.

Below: A branch (Line), leaf (Transitional shape) and flower (Point).

No interest

A little interest no resting place

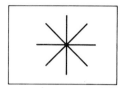

A central resting point but no variety

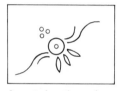

A central resting point with more variety

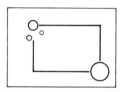

Two resting places or emphasis areas

in the centre of the complete design (including the base and container) depending on the visual attractions either side of the horizontal axis. It becomes the pivot of the design and this is a satisfying style as the eyes, seeking equilibrium, find a target area in the appropriate centre of the composition. In modern arrangements it is placed in any position which suits the balance. In more abstract designs there may be areas of interest in more than one place equated through the design and not centralised.

COMBINING SHAPES

Very generally speaking plant material can be classified into three basic shapes or forms:
Lines—such as bare branches, bulrushes, delphiniums, iris

49

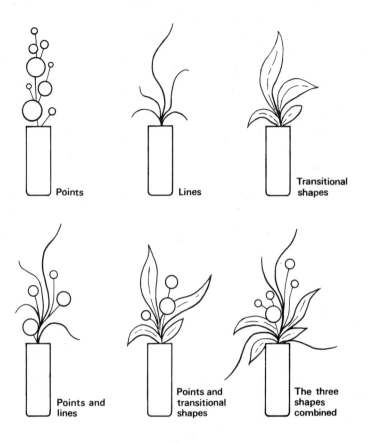

Points

Lines

Transitional shapes

Points and lines

Points and transitional shapes

The three shapes combined

leaves, all of which move the eye at varying speeds *along* rather than holding it.

Points—or near points such as open round flowers seen full on, oranges, rosettes of houseleek, gourds. These forms hold the eye momentarily giving emphasis and rest.

Transitional Shapes—such as many leaves, oval shaped fruit, half-open flowers or turned flowers.

Arrangements can be made of any one of these forms alone or can be a combination of two or often all three. The latter can be more satisfying to the eye in that it uses variety of form and gives movement as well as rest. Beginners will find it helpful to choose one variety of plant material for each basic shape.

One's eye movements when looking at a design are interesting for they usually go first to a large round form or point and temporarily rest there. They then start travelling around the design stopping at various resting places, or emphasis points, throughout the design. These may be an interesting shape, bright colour, shiny texture, something that is more dominant and eyecatching than other things in the design. In other words the eyes are attracted to various elements in the design and travel from one to another. It is reasonable then that a design should be combined of forms which hold the eye, and forms which help movement. If a soft rhythmic movement is desired then a transitional shape gives a gentler movement. Some plant material has all three shapes in the same plant. For example, an open rose is a point, a half-open rose and the leaves are transitional shapes, the tight buds and stems are lines. Roses are well suited to an arrangement of one type of flower. The same applies to gladioli and arums.

WORKING IN THREE DIMENSIONS

A painter works on canvas which has two dimensions and creates a sensation of depth with his use of forms and colours. Flower arrangers, as sculptors, work in three dimensions using height, width and depth, and the resulting form may be solid or volumetric.

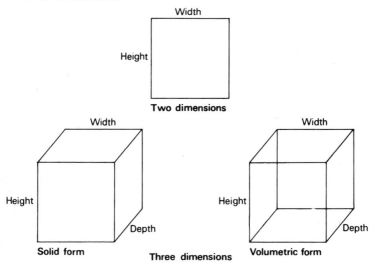

Plant materials are nearly all three dimensional—few varieties being completely flat (or two dimensional) and they can be assembled into solid forms as a cone design, or into forms with space within the design.

PLANE

A plane is any two dimensional area enclosed by an actual line or by imaginary line. It can be of any shape and can be flat or have a textured surface, even a slightly bumpy one. Another plane occurs when there is a different directional movement—in other words a corner is turned.

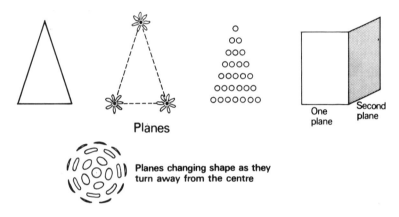

Planes

Planes changing shape as they turn away from the centre

Everything referred to as a shape or a form consists of one plane or a combination of planes. A solid box has six planes— the top, the bottom and the four sides. A painting on flat paper has one plane, but a sculpture has many, assembled round a central axis. These planes by their directional movement create depth in the design. They are detected through a change in shape and by light and shadow. As a plane moves away from the immediate field of vision, less and less of its surface is seen and part of it may be in shadow. A number of planes are seen circling around the central stem in an allium where the rounds seen in the front gradually appear as ovals and then as lines as they turn away from the centre.

An orange is solid and circular with one clear plane in front but as the walls of the orange turn away, new planes are entered. Each piece of plant material often has many planes.

In addition, the flower arrangement can have many, if the arranger creates them by turning flowers or other plant material to give a sensation of depth. A flower arrangement, either a solid or a volumetric one, should consist of many planes assembled around a central axis and not one, as a painting. A flower arrangement composed on one plane with all the flowers at the same level (on the same plane) is an uninteresting flat creation. Turning flowers creates new planes and gives depth.

A sculptural quality or sense of depth is very attractive in a flower arrangement and gives greater interest. The plant materials themselves, being three dimensional, contribute to the effect but the eye can be tricked into seeing more depth than actually exists:

Below left: Boulders—the planes detected by light and shade.
Below right: Cone—the planes detected by a change of shape.

1. *Composition*

A greater sense of depth is created by turning plant material around a central axis so that the flowers, for example, are seen from the side-view and eventually back-view towards the rear of the design. This way of composing plant material also follows the natural growth of many plants. As they emerge from a central root system they divide in all directions so that every part of the plant receives rain, sun and air. (It is also of interest to see the flower from all angles.)

If plant material is recessed, which means that some of it is tucked behind other plant material, there is a greater feeling of depth than if the flowers are all on the same plane which gives a solid appearance. Recessing is a particularly useful way of giving depth in a mass design.

Small details such as a tiny grouping of flowers tucked into the back of a landscape design, seen only on a second look, are another way of creating an illusion of greater depth. The composition can be solid or volumetric but in either case planes should be created and assembled around a central axis.

2. *Plant Materials*

Some appear more three dimensional than others and have sculptural quality of their own. These include flowers such as acanthus, arum, gladiolus, delphinium and tulip, also foliage such as eucalyptus (the spiral kind), carnation, aspidistra, echeveria, and houseleek. Many seed-pods and fruits are like sculpture, including pine cones, fungi and berries. Although not deeply three dimensional, branches which have twigs reaching in different directions give a sensation of depth. Transparent material such as skeletonised leaves can give a similar illusion when other plant material is placed behind. Driftwood in itself is often exactly similar to a piece of sculpture.

3. *Colour*

The use of advancing and receding colours is helpful. For example, orange placed against light blue gives a sense of separation of the colours and therefore a feeling of spatial quality. A dark value of a colour used behind a light one has a similar effect. This is useful in a mass arrangement where

An anemone is beautiful from any angle (*Syndication International*)

dark colours can be used behind bright or light ones to give a shadowy depth.

4. *Textures*

To a lesser extent shiny textures which tend to advance can be placed next to dull ones to give the same effect.

5. *Lighting*

This gives greater depth to a design when it comes from one source so that shadows are deeper.

6. *Containers, Bases and Accessories*

If any of these are placed so that more than one plane is seen, a stronger three-dimensional effect results. Bases placed across the diagonal of a niche or a table are a very good example. Containers can be placed so that more than one plane is seen as can accessories.

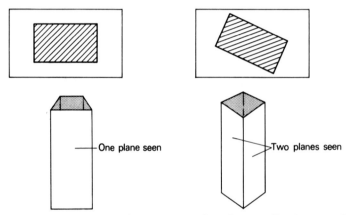

A base or container with a pedestal or legs to lift it and give space below also helps to give a three dimensional quality.

DRAWING

Drawing can be a supreme art in itself but it is also fundamental to all kinds of art. It is a useful servant for all forms of design activity and a very valuable aid to composition.

Many great painters and sculptors have sketched their ideas on paper as a preparatory step to their great works of art. The sketch of preparation sets the mind on a path and puts ideas into visual order. It also helps the discard of unessentials and reveals gaps in the designer's knowledge so that 'homework' can be done. It greatly assists the selection of materials for a

'Inspired by Sculpture,' by Mrs. Sylvia Pullan.

Metal Sculpture 14,
Dûsan Džamonja, Iron,
1960.

design so that the designer can begin composing with less clutter around her.

In addition to being a useful preparation for composing a design, drawing is a means of storing ideas seen at odd moments and is a help to poor memory. A sketch book can be carried around for odd jottings of forms, ideas and so on. It can be made to work well for the designer as a record of things seen and experienced for future use in a design. Memory may be short and a few pencil lines can act as a reminder. In addition, awareness of an object's qualities is increased because of the concentration and keen observation needed to draw it, and unexpected discoveries may be made.

The thought of making sketches is very inhibiting to some people who have previously regarded drawing as an end in itself, to be critically assessed. Many of us find it difficult and our inability to draw what we see, artistically and accurately is an embarrassment to be avoided. However, if it is regarded not as an end in itself but as a means to the end of good design, then it need not be an embarrassment, particularly as the sketch book need not be shown to others.

Broadly speaking, drawing includes sketches with pencil, pen, felt-tip pen, brush or crayon. It can also include torn or cut paper. It can be in the form of diagrams and need not be at all realistic. It can also use symbols for objects instead of pictorial imitations of them. Usually a quick impression is more useful and appropriate for preparation and for recording purposes than a laboured effort. The drawings should be simple and direct without any extraneous detail. It is helpful to practise drawing simple things like furniture and fruit but these need not be pictorial representations. Most subjects can be related to a square, rectangle, straight line, triangle, circle, oval or part of a circle or oval. These symbols can also be combined to make other forms:

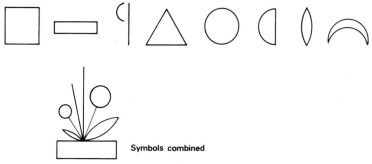

Symbols combined

Basic symbols.

It is surprising how very helpful such simple jottings can be in preparation for composition, and drawing is almost essential when several arrangements are grouped together and seen as a composition and not in isolation. The actual drawing process also increases the sense of design and the drawer begins to think 'design' in regarding objects and to analyse and simplify things seen into basic shapes, which are useful for definite purposes in a design. Drawing not only complete objects but sections and parts can be useful in giving ideas, such as the radiating lines on a *Begonia rex* leaf, the markings on a shell or its spiral, the graining of wood or the parts of a flower.

59

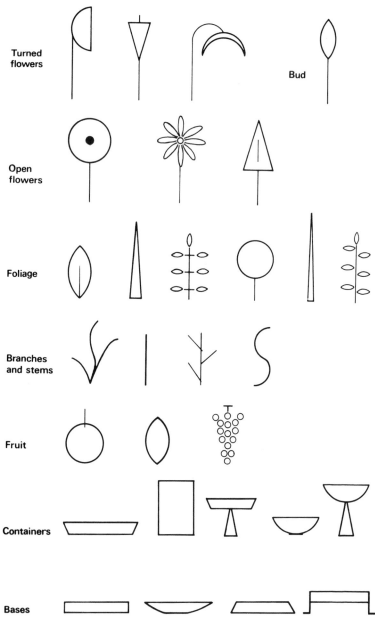

Turned flowers

Bud

Open flowers

Foliage

Branches and stems

Fruit

Containers

Bases

Symbols for use in drawing.

SUMMARY

Composition is the art or practice of combining the parts of a work of art.

It brings order from chaos and is a physical need in man.

A design can be previously planned, or quite unplanned or a combination of the two. The latter is most often practised.

Selection of components is of great importance in composing.

There can be no set formula for composition.

Flower arrangers compose forms already created.

The medium of plant material is used almost unchanged.

Selection of components must include consideration of scale, function, compatibility, purpose in design, quantity, related objects, appreciation of materials.

Preliminary playing with the materials is of importance.

The first placement may be anywhere in the design but governs the choice of other materials.

Too much can be placed in a design and often material can be removed.

Major alterations are impractical with short-lived plant material.

Simplicity of form is needed so that non-essential elaboration is avoided which can confuse the design.

A good design is one to which nothing can be added or subtracted.

Areas of emphasis

Designs need areas of heightened interest which should not be too dominant or too weak to hold the eye.

They can be created with larger flowers, round flowers, more brilliant colour, dense grouping, enclosed space, or combinations of these.

The position of the area of greater interest depends on the style of the design. It can be called focal point, centre of interest, emphasis point.

Combining shapes

The three basic shapes can be used in design either combined or separately.

61

The beholder is usually satisfied when there are forms which hold the eyes and others which move them along.

Depth

Flower arrangement is a three dimensional art.
Plant material is usually three dimensional.
A plane is a two dimensional area.
Forms whether solid or volumetric consist of many planes.
Planes are observed by the change in shape and by lighting.
Depth can be 'created' with maximum effect by the use of careful composition (turning flowers and recession); the use of certain plant materials; the use of colour, texture and lighting; the placement of containers, bases and accessories.

Drawing

Drawing is a useful preparation for composing.
It can also be used for recording and aiding memory.
The drawings can be diagrammatic and not realistic.
Symbols can be used.

CREATIVE STUDY

Observe:

The composition of paintings, photographs.
The aesthetic and design qualities of various containers, bases and accessories.
The most beautiful quality in a piece of plant material.
Photographs of flower arrangements to see if anything can be eliminated from the design.
The effect of a spotlight moving over a design, watching the sense of depth and looking at the shadows.
The component that is of greatest interest in flower arrangements and painting and analyse the quality that makes it dominant.

Collect:

Prints of paintings with good composition.
Photographs of flower arrangements similarly.
Groups of plant materials in the three basic shapes.

Groups of plant material and choose the most dominant for an area of greater interest.

Plant materials which are strongly three dimensional.

Make:

Photographs in black and white of your own arrangements to see if things can be eliminated from the design.

Preliminary drawings of possible designs with suggestions for plant materials.

Groupings of plant material arranged in the hand.

Tracings with tracing paper of the 'paths of movement' in photographs of flower arrangements and in prints of paintings.

Flower Arrangement:

Using foliage only.

Using a pair of containers.

Interpreting 'contrasts' 'sculpture' 'simplicity'.

Interpreting a picture.

Using one accessory.

Using a pair of figurines.

A design using components from one habitat.

Use a turntable and look at the sides and back of the design.

Using one type of flower turned in every direction.

Using a grouping of receding colour in the centre of a design.

Using a centre of interest and then removing it.

4
Style

The word style comes from the Latin 'stylus' meaning a metal pencil for writing on wax and other tablets. It came to mean the characteristics of a person's handwriting and by extension it is now used to describe manner of expression in many things—writing, deportment, works of art. It can refer to the manner of construction, as, for example, 'Victorian style', or to the general distinction of a design—a design with good style meaning that it has a distinctive character and mode of presentation.

IN DESIGN

Many artists have their own recognisable style but when certain characteristics keep recurring through the work of many designers, it may be said that they conform to a certain general style, for example, surrealistic. This does not mean that there is no diversity within the particular style. No two leaves of the same tree are precisely alike, each is individual and yet every one conforms to a recognisable pattern, characteristic of the species. Works of art broadly fit into styles, for example, realistic, geometric and abstract.

Style is usually more easily recognisable in retrospect

because a general trend takes some time to be recognised. It may start with an individual designer whose work is sufficiently divergent to create excited interest so that other artists emulate him. If eventually his style meets with popular approval, it settles down to being a generally accepted style. Alternatively a new style may be a general trend seen in the work of many designers stimulated or influenced by social conditions, scientific discoveries, new materials or environmental changes. In flower arrangement, for example, these could be the discovery of water retaining plastic foam; the availability of foreign plant materials; the use of weedkiller on plants which causes strange distortions in form.

Trends in one art may influence styles in another.

Dr. Thomas Munro commented:

'. . . trends in artistic style are never independent but parts of still larger cultural trends embracing all forms of thought and behaviour, social, political, economic, religious, scientific . . . we see the artist as never entirely original, never a bolt from the blue, always responsive to the currents about him and therefore different from what he would have become in another cultural setting. . . .'

Some styles become classics and every generation enjoys them while other styles are short-lived.

Style is not fashion, which is superficial change, widely but temporarily popular. Fashion refers to the popularity of certain things, for example, in flower arrangement, bleached broom or the use of fabric covered bases. The *basic style* still underlies each fashion change and is not capricious, being the fruit of the social and technical conditions of the age that produces it. The particular design has a definite, visual relationship to when and where it was made, the available materials and the ideas dominating the life of the society. A style of design for one historical period, even if it is only for one or two decades, seems to be out of place in another. Style changes as an idea arises and develops. Eventually it may become boring and be replaced by a new style. Alternatively it may be continued with less vigour and new trends may appear at the same time. The existence of traditional styles alongside modern movements can be of great benefit to artists as the traditional styles act as a break and the new ideas act as a spur to creative efforts and balance is achieved.

IN FLOWER ARRANGEMENT

With the increase in popularity of flower arrangement, new styles have arrived with great rapidity. The following gives a broad description of some of those recognised by flower arrangers with their main characteristics, but within each one there are many variations. There are also 'hybrids' which may fit into more than one classification.

Mass arrangement with flowers turned for interest and to give a sense of depth. Arranged by Mrs. Doris Starling.

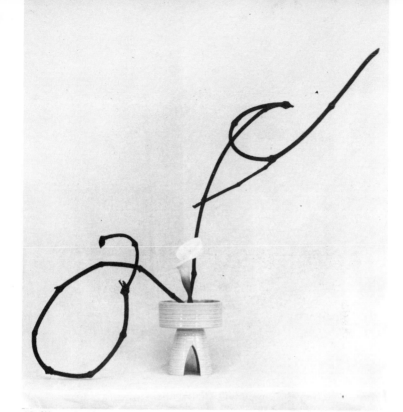

'Calligraphy' by Mrs. Constance Webb. The wild clematis vine is the dominant feature in this line arrangement.

MASS AND LINE

This is a broad classification but, generally speaking, flower arrangements fall into one of these two groups. A mass arrangement depends on a larger quantity of plant material for its beauty and can be likened to a bouquet of flowers gathered from a summer garden. Within the design itself there is little space and the effect is more of a solid mass. Period, traditional and geometric mass designs using many flowers fit into the classification of 'mass'.

Line arrangements use more space *within* the design itself, there is restraint in plant material and lines are a dominant feature. Their beauty can be likened to that of a single branch of apple blossom.

Bronze flower bowl, Egyptian XVIII Dynasty (c. 1450 BC), Thebes. The stems were placed under the band on which stands a cow with the horns and disk of the goddess Hat-Hor. (*The Metropolitan Museum of Art, Theodore M. Davis Collection*)

There are designs which clearly fall half-way between the line and mass classification. An American term for these hybrids is 'massed-line'.

1. *Period Arrangements*
These make a fascinating and rewarding study as they reflect the prevailing social conditions of the time. They are usually considered to be pre-World War II and go back to the beginning of civilisation as flowers have been placed in containers of water since about 2800 B.C. In ancient Egypt beautiful vases were made for flowers, in particular the lotus, sacred flower of the goddess Isis. In Japan flower arrangement has been practised for over a thousand years and for even longer in China. Some periods in history—usually those which had a

Right: Stella of a priestess
worshipping Rehorakhty. New
Kingdom, 1250 BC. Lotus flowers
may be seen in the centre.
Below: 'Inspired by Egyptian Art'
by Jean Taylor. Cut palm with lotus
seedpods and bulrushes.

settled atmosphere—produced more flower arrangements than others and there were dark ages when there were none at all.

Flower arrangements in history were influenced by the environment of the age in which they were made, the social atmosphere, religious thought, and the culture of the time. The available containers, plant material and mechanics also had an effect upon the design. Each period has a distinctive style, revealed through its art and sometimes its literature, and certain characteristics are apparent which enable flower arrangements to be made today in the manner of a past time. For example, it is clear that the Egyptians liked clarity and order above all else and their designs were highly stylised. The Greeks preferred flowers arranged in garlands and wreaths with which they crowned their gods and heroes. Early Chinese arrangements showed a great love for nature and simple restraint. Flemish paintings of flower arrangements show the feverish interest which prevailed in the seventeenth century in horticulture and the natural sciences. Eighteenth century French designs are distinctive for exquisite containers and soft colouring but the Victorians, who also showed tremendous interest in flowers and flower arrangement, used harsher colour schemes, symmetry and tight bunching of wired stems. These are only a few of the periods of flower arrangement which can be studied. The following are of interest:

Ancient Egyptian	2800 BC–AD 28
Greek	600 BC–146 BC
Roman	AD 28–AD 325
Byzantine	AD 325–AD 600
Chinese	AD 960–AD 1912
Gothic	AD 1200–AD 1425
Persian	AD 1300–AD 1700
Renaissance	AD 1400–AD 1600
Japanese	AD 586–present day
Dutch and Flemish	17th and 18th Centuries
Baroque	AD 1600–AD 1700
American	AD 1620–present day
Rococo	AD 1715–AD 1774
Georgian (Late), Regency	AD 1759–AD 1830

Left: Inspired by a Byzantine cone, by Molly Duerr. A modern adaptation of an ancient form of flower decoration.
Right: Stoneware vase with floral design painted in brown slip under a white glaze. Chinese, Sung Dynasty (AD 960–1279).

French	18th and early 19th Centuries
Victorian	AD 1830–AD 1890
Art Nouveau	AD 1890–AD 1910
Art Deco	AD 1920–AD 1940

It is possible to create compositions that express the spirit of these periods in history even though correct plant material is not always possible as some varieties are no longer in existence. Victorian containers are easily found but it is often not possible to use authentic vases from other periods because of scarcity or value. However the manner can still be caught with modern copies or containers of similar style.

A study of illustrative material is necessary before attempting to copy a period style. There are many sources—paintings,

71

engravings, tapestries, mosaics, wood carvings, rugs, coins and illuminated manuscripts, but no photographs, as the camera was unknown. Most museums and art galleries have postcard reproductions of historical flower arrangements which are invaluable for study. The questions which need to be asked when studying source material are:

1. What was the environment like at the time? The culture, religious thought, social atmosphere, wealth? Was the civilisation settled?
2. Was there a purpose in the use of cut flowers? Decorative, symbolic, for gifts?
3. What was the style in furnishings? Where were flowers placed? In a room, temple, around statues, on the ground?
4. Was there a characteristic style in composition?
5. What were the containers like in material, shape, colour? Were bases used?
6. How were the flowers supported in a container?
7. What plant materials were used?
8. Which colours were popular and how were they combined?
9. Were accessories, or associated objects, placed near flower arrangements?
10. Is there a distinctive spirit which can be captured?

Period designs are most helpful to study in order to broaden the outlook and to realise the development of present day flower arrangement in the context of history. Previous styles are also stimulating and give ideas for present day designs. Books which are helpful for studying period flower arrangements are: *The History of Flower Arrangement* by Julia Berrall published by Thames and Hudson; *Period Flower Arrangement* by Margaret Marcus published by Barrows (o.p.); *The Art of Flower Arrangement* by Beverley Nichols published by Collins (o.p.) and *Guide to Period Flower Arranging* published by the National Association of Flower Arrangement Societies (NAFAS).

2. Traditional
This term usually refers to the style of flower arrangement created in Great Britain from Edwardian times to the 1939–45

Opposite: In the Art Nouveau Style, by George Smith.

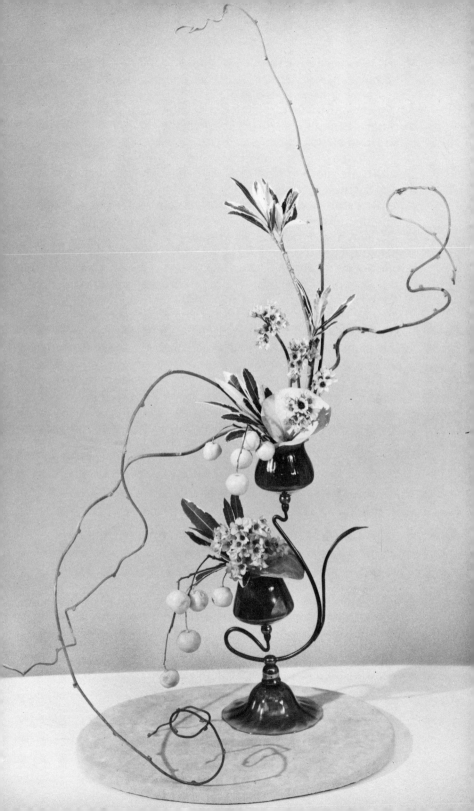

war. This style is still practised more than any other and has become a classic. It originated in Europe with the arrangements of garden material placed in large containers in the bigger country homes and the smaller bouquets placed in cottage homes. These were somewhat shapeless in style with a massed effect.

By usage the term 'traditional' now applies to arrangements which are more ordered and stylised. Characteristically they display mass groupings of flowers and foliage, often from the garden and using many varieties of plant material. The outline shape is often a triangle, sometimes an oval or circle but there are many variations within the traditional style including stiff, formal designs with a clear outline and soft flowing ones.

The words 'triangle', 'oval', 'circle' are misleading and tend to suggest a two-dimensional figure whereas these designs, which use three-dimensional plant material, should also have a total three-dimensional effect with interesting side-views and an increased effect of depth created by the recessing of flowers and by the use of colour.

Traditional arrangements can be of any size from a miniature of a few inches to a massive pedestal fifteen or more feet high but the characteristic manner of composing always uses a mass of plant material and little space within the design. The outline of the mass is of greater importance than the internal grouping of the plant material and colourings tend to be soft and harmonious. Transition of size in the individual pieces of plant material is usual, with smaller material being placed on the outside and larger flowers in the centre. Horticultural interest and variation is also a feature, rather than the design qualities present in the plant material.

Containers are varied but often deep to hold the quantity of water necessary for the large amount of plant material, for example, urns of metals or china. In recent years new types of mechanics such as candle-cups have enabled many stemmed and pedestal types of containers to be used, including figurines and candlesticks.

With the wealth of plant material in this country it is likely that this traditional style will retain its popularity. It is highly decorative, often restful because of its static type of balance

74

Left: A traditional arrangement by Sheila Macqueen.
Right: A traditional pedestal in the shape of a triangle by
Mrs. Elsie Lamb.

and well-suited to many homes, churches, cathedrals and to
special occasions such as weddings.

3. *The Geometric Style*

The need for variety and the desire for experimentation
brought the geometric style into existence in post-war years.
Flower arangements began to have a more streamlined
appearance and a definite geometrically shaped and recognisable outline. These shapes are often referred to as crescents,
Hogarth curves, verticals, and diagonals. This more streamlined style probably resulted from the desire for more order in
the chaotic world immediately after the war. There was a need
to tidy up everything and just as in history the social atmosphere influenced style, so it did in these post-war years.

With the British heritage of mass design, geometric arrangements were at first packed with flowers but have tended to
become looser and softer over the years. By trial and error it

Left: A plaque of dried plant material in a 'Hogarth' curve, arranged by Jean Mawdsley. (By courtesy of *Lancashire Life*).
Right: A crescent-shaped design by Jean Taylor.

was found that some flowers could not be used in every geometric shape. For instance, daffodils with their straight stems are not suitable for a curved geometric shape such as a crescent and curving stems are not suitable for straight-line shapes. These geometric styles are often popular with new flower arrangers as the geometric shape is known and can be recognised and copied with comparative ease.

Transition of size with smaller plant material at the extremities and larger in the centre is used, as in traditional styles. There is normally a well-defined centre of interest. The space around the geometric shape is important to show up the outline. Any type of container may be used. It is normally effective to use curved containers with curved shapes and angular ones with straight shapes.

Geometric designs need not be in mass style, they can also be made with less plant material and with lines being dominant, still following the geometric symbol. These can be termed

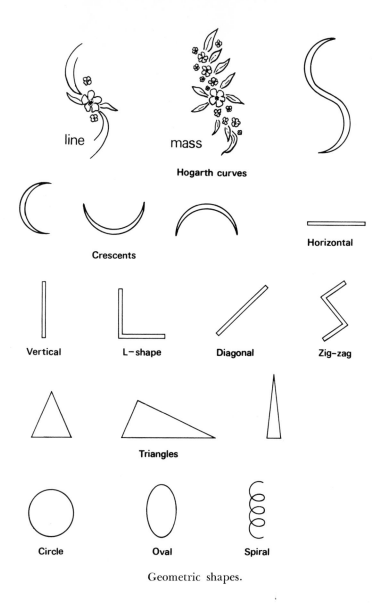

line

mass

Hogarth curves

Crescents

Horizontal

Vertical

L–shape

Diagonal

Zig–zag

Triangles

Circle

Oval

Spiral

Geometric shapes.

'line designs with geometric shape'. In the past the term 'line' (defined in Chapter 9) has been used to describe all geometric styles whether mass or line, but the geometric form can be followed in either mass or line style. It is the quantity of plant material used, the amount of space and the presence of dominant line plant material which determines whether a flower arrangement is a line or a mass design and not the presence of a geometric symbol.

The term 'traditional' with reference to flower arrangement styles, changes with the years and designs once thought new, have become, through familiarity, traditional in appearance. This is already beginning to refer to the geometric style.

4. Free-Form

This term covers a very wide range of designs without a definite geometric shape—that is free (of geometric) form. The term sometimes used for these designs is 'free-style', but this infers lack of style of any kind (even individual) and so 'free-form' is more descriptive and accurate.

Reaction from the stiffness of the geometric style was inevitable, together with a social atmosphere of growing freedom and self-expression. The interest in design also increased and in the qualities of individual plant materials. Rapid communications of the present day brought many pictures of Japanese and American styles both of which have revealed more interest in the use of space in design than the British styles. This combined with a growing trend all over the world to value space in the environment led to designs using far more space within the design itself, less plant material and no particular geometric outline.

Free-form designs are often very beautiful as they depend on the qualities of individual plant material for effect such as the fascinating curve of a piece of driftwood, a brilliant colour, an unusual shape or a lovely texture. The natural growth of plant material is regarded and the design normally follows it, with restraint in composition so that the plant material's beauty is clearly seen. Less plant material is normally used so there are strong contrasts of form and texture and colour is often striking. Theoretically there can be free-form mass designs as well as line designs but mass tends to

A free-form design of proteas and driftwood by Jean Taylor.

need a more definite shape for good effect.

The chief difference between traditional and geometric designs and the newer free form styles is in the type of balance. The former tends to depend on symmetry with a more static type of balance and the latter on balance created by the assembling of objects of equal eye-pull either side of the vertical and horizontal axes (see Chapter 12).

Any type of container may be used with the exception of those which have strong period or traditional associations. There is a wide scope of interesting and unusual plant materials which tend to be bolder in form and less fussy than some of the ones used in previous styles.

Free-form designs are very creative as there is less rigidity in the approach to composition. The basic design principles, as always, must be regarded for good work, but no 'rules' in assembling plant material.

5. *Landscape Designs*

This is a realistic style developed in recent years. It is completely naturalistic and the least abstract of any style. A moment from nature is captured, such as a scene from a woodland, lakeside, seashore, stream, mountain or moor, which is relatively easy as the scene portrayed can usually be studied in life and copied. Garden 'landscapes' can be created as well as wild scenes.

The secret of composing a good landscape lies in the use of restraint for one or two brown leaves suggest Autumn, a trickle of sand—the beach, a little moss—woodland, and there need not be piles of any of them strewn across the design, which can be kept tidy and restrained. Viewers of an arrangement usually enjoy using their imagination, which 'completes' the scene for them from the smallest suggestion in the design.

Formal containers that can be seen are not normally used as they look unnatural, hidden containers being used for water. However 'water' arrangements depicting a lake or stream must have a large container to feature the water and in this case shallow containers made of glass, pottery, lead, or metal are suitable.

Bases are often used with a non-manufactured appearance such as cross-cuts of wood, slate, and stone which look natural. Accessories too should not appear manufactured as the natural appearance of the design can so easily be lost. Any accessories used should look very realistic in colour, texture and form and this is why natural accessories such as stones and shells look effective. Scale is also important and should be close to the natural scale which is why small china animals which are not life-size appear incorrect when placed next to a flower in a naturalistic landscape design. Drapes used as a background or base are quite unsuitable as a piece of fabric is not seen in the woods or by a stream in nature.

Plant material should if possible be as in the natural scene portrayed, for example, reed-mace, iris, and rushes are suitable for a lake or stream design. Plants with similar appearance can be used at home but for show work the plant material should be correct.

Landscape designs have great charm and are easy for beginners in flower arrangement. Simplicity should be the

'LANDSCAPE DESIGNS'
Above left: 'The Garden' by Mrs. J. E. Coxhead.
Above right: 'The Waterside' by Jean Taylor.
Below left: 'The Fells' by Jean Taylor.
Below right: 'The Mountainside' by Jean Taylor.

guide together with observation of natural scenes. It is worth taking time to look at such things as the way moss grows over a stone, how a tree leans with the prevailing wind, how a shrub grows from under a rock or a feather peeps out of the soft sand.

6. Abstract

DEFINITION. To refine, condense, separate or withdraw from. In art 'to abstract' means to present, or characterise, non-representational designs depicting no recognisable thing, only geometric figures or amorphous creations. An abstract is that which concentrates in itself the essential qualities of a large thing or several things. It represents the essence. An abstraction is defined as a visionary notion, a withdrawal from worldly objects and as a composition or creation suggested initially by a concrete object but transformed by the artist into a non-representational design.

IN ART. The influences of the twentieth century have led to abstraction which has become a universal phenomenon and language, very different from the representative art of the past. Artists inevitably belong to their own time and consciously or not are influenced by the thought, behaviour and discoveries of the age in which they live and with such a world wide movement no single art escapes its influence.

Abstract is not an entirely new style as can be seen from the drawings of the cavemen who expressed so much in a few lines on the walls of their caves, but this was not conscious abstraction as now. Liberty and free-expression are of our time and with the artist's release from being the world's recorder due to the invention of the camera, this new approach to painting arrived.

Although artists have painted in the abstract style for around seventy years it has been slow to reach flower arrangement, probably because plant material is the medium closest to nature and difficult to alter or manipulate at will.

Opposite: 'Inspired by Mondrian'—a non-objective abstract with glixia flowers and black wood. Arranged by Marjorie Wilson.

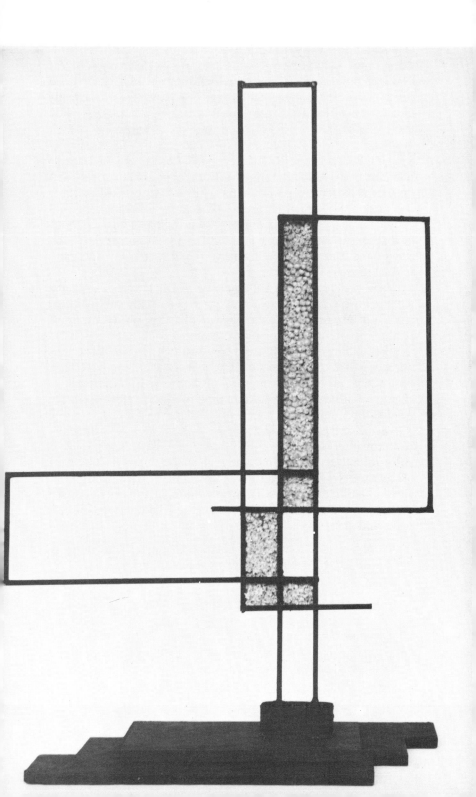

FLOWER ARRANGEMENT. With the exception of land-scape designs which are copies of naturalistic scenes, all flower arrangement is to a certain extent abstract in that the plant material has been taken from its natural environment and re-assembled in a different manner in a container. But there are degrees of abstraction and an arrangement which follows the natural look of plant material growing, that is with radiation from a centre, turned flowers and a natural flow can only be termed semi-abstract. The further the design departs from using plant material in a naturalistic manner the more abstract is the design. The term 'abstract style' has come to apply to those designs which have little or no trace of reality or naturalness and are at the other end of the imaginary scale from the landscape designs which reproduce nature as exactly seen.

Abstract flower arrangements use plant material only for texture, form and colour from which, with the addition of space, patterns can be created bearing little or no resemblance to the natural growth of plant material.

Abstract flower arrangement has developed in two directions and the same trends can be seen in other arts, non-objective, which has no subject matter, and objective, which has a theme or subject matter and is described with interpretative designs in Chapter 5.

Non-objective Abstract
This refers to the organisation of space, form, colour and texture to convey order without subject matter. Plant material is used for its design qualities only, to form patterns *in* space and *with* space. Traditional methods of composing are not necessarily regarded.

'What I dream of is an art of balance, of purity, and serenity devoid of troubling or depressing subject matter.'

Matisse

'I do not now intend by beauty of shapes what most people would expect, such as that of living creatures or pictures but, for the purpose of my argument, I mean straight lines and curves and the surfaces or solid forms produced out of these by lathes and rulers and squares. . . .

84

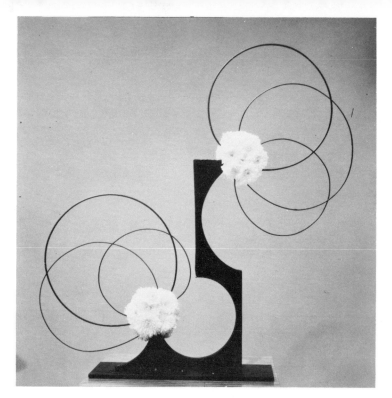

Yellow chrysanthemums and blackened cane in plastic foam with old iron. A non-objective abstract by Jean Taylor.

'For I mean that these things are not beautiful relatively, like other things, but always and naturally and absolute. . . .'

Socrates in
THE PHILEBUS OF PLATO (*4th Century* B.C.)

Characteristics
1. Emphasis points equating interest throughout the design and not necessarily one centre of interest.
2. Simplification and the use of much space within the design.
3. Strong contrasts.
4. A sense of pattern, without subject matter.
5. Unity without necessarily using radiation.
6. If a container is used it is part of the overall design and not just a receptacle of water. It is part of the total expression.

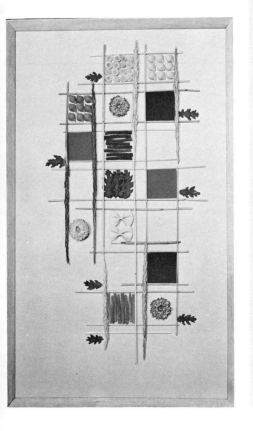
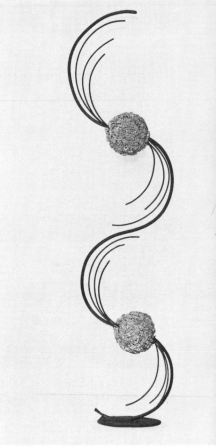

Left: Abstract plaque of dried plant material; shells, felt and macaroni on a framed and covered board by Pat Haigh.
Right: Black painted cane and orange painted dried *Achillea* with iron. A non-objective abstract by Beryl Gordon-Davies.

7. The plant material may be changed but is not used naturalistically. It may be cut, twisted, or tied but this is not a necessary characteristic of abstract designs and is only justified when the end result is good design.

As in all styles the use of good design principles is a necessity and plant materials should predominate over all other components. Mechanics are not easy in simple uncluttered

86

designs such as these and a flower arranger needs technical skill to know how to hold the plant material in place without showing the mechanics.

Abstract designs suit modern settings very well and are in keeping with abstract paintings and sculpture, both of which are useful to study before attempting this style in flower arrangement.

7. Pot-et-fleur

This is a decoration of growing plants, in or out of pots, arranged in a large container with cut flowers. It is useful for winter months when flowers are scarce as it is economical. The plants will often live and thrive together for years and can have cut flowers added or not, so maintenance is easy.

The container should suit the setting but should be chosen mainly for its ability to hold plenty of compost and to take water without overflowing.

The care of a pot-et-fleur is the same as for pot plants but plants should be combined which like the same amount of water, temperature, light and humidity. For example, a sansevieria plant likes little water and should not be put with a hydrangea which likes a lot, unless its roots are first wrapped in polythene.

The same principles of design apply as in flower arrangement and plants should be chosen which have contrast or variety in form, colour and texture; there should be a rhythm through the design, the plants should be in scale with the container and each other, and the design should be balanced. Proportion may alter as the plants grow and if plants do overgrow they should be removed and replaced. The flowers often provide the need for a dominant feature in the design.

The container for flowers can be inserted in the compost using the normal mechanics, or flowers can be added in tubes taped to the stem of large plants at different heights. Accessories such as shells, stones and coral are effective for hiding mechanics. Driftwood blends very well with plants and can give needed height and a change of texture.

If the plants are left in their pots a larger container than normal is necessary and watering is not as simple, but it has advantages: easy re-positioning of pots, poor plants can be

Left: Day-lilies with plants placed in coconut shells fixed to driftwood. Arranged by Kay Wallington.
Right: A pot-et-fleur in tones of red. Arranged by Violet Stevenson.
(By courtesy of Leslie Johns).

easily removed and plants with differing water requirements can be used together. The 'bottom-heavy' appearance of this type of pot-et-fleur is difficult to avoid. It can sometimes be counteracted by using a very tall plant.

This method of using flowers with growing plants is suitable for centrally heated houses and busy people, as it needs the minimum of attention for maximum decorative effect. It is very economical as it needs few flowers. It is also well-suited to plants, which thrive when growing together.

8. *Plaques, Swags, Pressed Flower Pictures*
A plaque is defined in the dictionary as a thin piece of wood, metal or the like, displayed as on a wall for ornament. This can be used as a background for plant material either

fresh, dried, or combined. The background is visible and may be framed or not but is usually unglazed. It may be covered with fabric, paper or paint, and should be chosen to show up the design of plant material.

A swag may be mounted on a background but this is not part of the design and is not visible. Swags may use any type of plant material, be of any shape or size, and are normally made to be hung up, as a plaque. Both use three dimensional plant material.

A pressed flower picture uses two dimensional plant material which has been pressed flat. This is normally placed under glass to protect the plant material. It shows a background and it may or may not be framed.

These three styles are particularly attractive for preserved plant material. The same principles of design apply as to all other styles of flower arrangement. They can be excellent practice in design as they can be arranged and 'played with' before securing. The design may be abstract, naturalistic, geometric and so on.

The term 'collage' refers to any mounted composite and for show purposes is regarded as being the same as a plaque.

Above: Pressed plant material under glass in a frame, by Mrs. Ivy Israels.
Right: Traditional plaque of dried plant material on wood, by Mrs. Doris Starling.

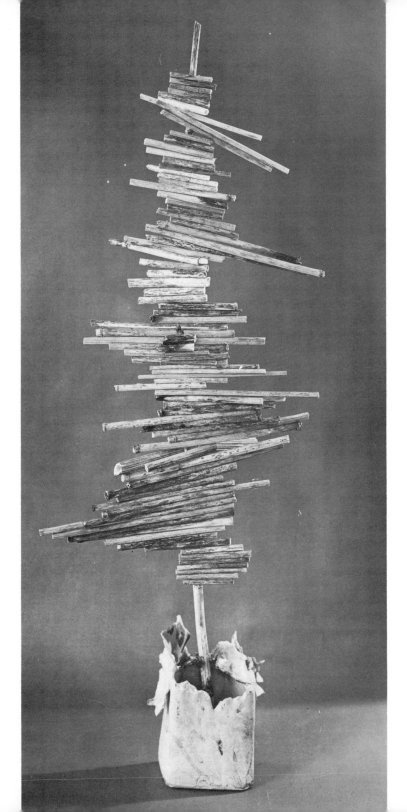

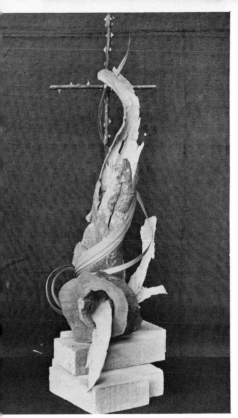
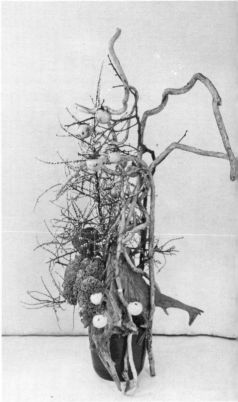

Opposite: A non-objective abstract design of cow-parsley stalks
by Marian Aaronson.
Above left: 'For the Consecration of Coventry Cathedral'—bark,
a crosscut of wood, rose stems and palm, by Mrs. Dorothy Woolley.
Above right: Exhibit at the Sogetsu Exhibition, 1965, by Joan
Lutwyche.

9. *Individual Style*

General classifications have been described but with a
creative approach to flower arrangement, individual style can
be developed and a sense of a strong individual 'personality'
can be shown through all one flower arranger's work. This
is excellent and can often lead to a new style being developed
through the whole movement although sometimes an artist
can have such a distinctive and personal style that it cannot
be copied. Often the manner of an artist's work can be
described, the technique analysed, but the certain 'personality'
which gives individual style is elusive and can defy description.

It is not possible to teach individual style, for it comes from a creative approach, from experimenting and from experience which develops through years of slow growth and maturity. Each artist will differ from another in his or her work as style is an individual reaction to a given task. Varying outlook, experiences, powers of observation, discrimination and perception, environment, technical and artistic ability will contribute to a differing end result, which may be in a recognisable style or in an individual one.

It is helpful during the learning process to imitate the style of others but maturity can bring individual style through constant experiment to find out the limits and possibilities of both materials and design principles and in composition and technique. Many individualists need to be able to withstand strong criticism but it is reassuring to realise that great painters, composers, sculptors, writers and poets have not always been popular in their lifetime!

SUMMARY

Style refers to manner of expression.

It can refer to the type of construction and also to distinctive character

General styles or trends can be seen in all art.

There is great diversity within the general style.

A style is usually more obvious in retrospect.

It is influenced by the environment, social conditions, culture, religious thought, discovered materials and scientific developments of the time in which it is created.

Style is never independent or entirely original as it is part of still larger trends. Trends in one art influence another.

Flower arrangements fall generally into broad styles.

There are many variations within the styles and some hybrids.

Mass and line are broad classifications.

Mass has a larger quantity of plant material and little space within the design.

Line has a restrained use of plant material, space within the design and dominant line plant material.

Period arrangements are usually considered as pre-1939.

Some periods in history produced more interest in flower arrangement than others.

Source material should be studied to capture the distinctive spirit of the time.

Traditional usually refers to designs made post-Edwardian and up to the 1939–45 war. They are usually mass designs, in particular triangles.

Geometric designs follow the outline of a known geometric shape.

Free-form designs are free of geometric form.

Landscape designs are the most naturalistic.

Abstract designs are the opposite—unrealistic.

A pot-et-fleur is a combination of growing plants and cut flowers.

Plaques, swags and pressed flower pictures are hanging decorations.

Individual style can be developed.

CREATIVE STUDY

Observe:

Style in the other arts and attempt classification.

Style in pictures of flower arrangements and classify.

Style in interior decoration, fashion.

The objects displayed in The Design Centre.

Compare general styles in design now and ten years ago.

Scenes in nature.

Collect:

Pictures of varying styles in the arts.

Pictures of varying styles in flower arrangement and mount together in groups.

A list of the characteristics observed in each style.

For landscape designs, lists for each season and for each scene of: colours, fauna, weather, flora.

Do this for river, stream, lake, moor, mountain, meadow, beach, sky, cliff, downs, roadside, cornfield.

Any reproductions (postcards, photographs, cuttings) showing flower arrangement and containers in history.

Make:

A pressed flower picture.

A swag of dried plant materials.

A swag of fresh plant materials.

A plaque of dried plant materials.

A plaque of fresh plant materials.

A collage of many materials including plant material.

Try the above in different styles, e.g. naturalistic, abstract, geometric.

Flower Arrangement:

Arrangements in the style of various periods in history.

Traditional triangle, oval and circular designs.

Geometric designs—a crescent, a Hogarth curve, various triangles, and what are known as verticals and diagonals in both line and mass style.

A Hogarth curve and a crescent shape with horizontal movement.

Landscape designs.

Free-form designs.

A pot-et-fleur.

Abstract designs without subject matter concentrating on pattern and design. They can have titles such as:

Play on a circle (rectangle, square and so on).

Linear construction.

Motion.

Calligraphy.

Contrasts.

Space conscious.

Nature's patterns.

A style never tried before.

5
Interpretative Designs

DEFINITION

This is the name given to flower arrangements which have subject matter. They translate or elucidate to the viewer the designer's feelings about the specific subject matter. These designs can use *any* style, accepted or original, and beauty in the 'prettiness' sense is not a criterion of their quality. The important consideration is the message they convey. This type of design has appeared since about 1950. Although symbolism has been used for centuries no other age has produced interpretative designs in this manner.

FLOWER ARRANGEMENT

All flower arrangements can be described as expressive in that they say something to the viewer—it may be prettiness, elegance, dignity—in other words a decorative quality, but interpretative designs do not depend on, or of necessity use, decorative qualities in expressing a mood or feeling, an observation on life, a philosophy or a story. For example, a pedestal arrangement at a wedding is decorative and expresses the loveliness of the flowers, but it has no subject matter. An interpretative design expressing 'anger', possibly in red and black with darting angles of plant material, may or may not

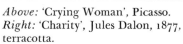

Above: 'Crying Woman', Picasso.
Right: 'Charity', Jules Dalon, 1877,
terracotta.
Below: 'The Unknown Political
Prisoner' ('Defiant and
Triumphant'), T. Roszak, 1952.
Steel brazed wih nickel-silver.

be beautiful in effect, but is intended primarily to give the viewer the impact of the subject matter 'anger'.

'To evoke in oneself a feeling one has experienced, and having evoked it in oneself, then by means of movement, lines, colours, sounds or forms . . . so to transmit that feeling that others experience the same feeling—this is the activity of arts.'

Count Leo Nikolaevich Tolstoi

These designs offer a challenge and stimulate thought and research. They are also valuable as an exercise in controlling design and selecting materials. Many people can tire of doing the same type of design in the same place and container in their homes. The interpretative designs which form the major part of flower arrangement shows offer a different approach. They induce the arranger to study the subject matter and to strive for the fullest possible communication so that the viewer is able to understand the interpretation. This is excellent for stretching the imagination and for carrying the flower arranger, as she does her 'homework' on the subject, into new and interesting fields. It may lead her to the library to look up something about an ancient civilisation she has to portray, to experience and study a sunset she intends to interpret in flowers or to read poetry to find a few lines to express in plant material. It is rare for subjects to be interpreted in the same manner by two people, which is fascinating, as each designer has a different experience of life, a different environment, sees different things as important and uses different materials to represent the idea.

SUBJECT MATTER

There is an infinite number of subjects which can be interpreted, although not all subjects can be expressed *well* with plant material as the medium of expression. Themes suggesting abstract ideas are often more suitable than subject matter which illustrates a fact. For example, 'Flight' is better than 'Aeroplane' as the latter is too literal and flowers are not seen at their best formed into the shape of an aeroplane.

The theme can be the title of a book, play, ballet, opera, piece of music or film. It can be a proverb, quotation, prose

97

or poetry. It can ask for an interpretation of a scene, a landscape, a season, atmosphere or event. It may require the arranger to depict sculpture or painting. It can be abstract in that it requires the interpretation of a mood, feeling or concept. In flower arrangement shows themes are usually provided by the show committee and the exhibitor makes a choice from a list in the show schedule. At home the designer can depict anything she wishes and an interesting 'exercise' is to make an arrangement and then to give it a name.

COMPOSITION

The method of composition is the choice of the designer and any style which is felt suitable for the subject can be used. Communication to others is important unless the design is only for self-expression. In a flower arrangement show, the clarity of the 'message' is the basis for the judge's assessment of the design. Selection of materials, both plant material and related objects, to convey this message is the most important consideration.

First hand experience of the subject matter is ideal to help selection and decide the manner of representation; for example if a scene is to be interpreted, it is best to see it and to absorb the atmosphere. Van Gogh said '. . . when the thing represented and the manner of representing agrees, the thing has style and quality.'

To use as few materials as possible is one of the secrets of good interpretative work. A clutter of materials tends to hide the interpretation and often suggestion is more effective than exact illustration or pictorial representation. Most people like to use their imagination when they look at a design and having received a strong suggestion from the arranger, prefer to imagine the rest.

APPROACH TO INTERPRETATIVE WORK

A suggested approach to interpretative work is to choose

Opposite: 'The Pipes of Pan' interpreted with a bronze figure, a tree root and plant material, in pale pink, blue-green and beige. Arranged by Jean Taylor.

Left: 'Extravaganza'—ostrich feathers with pink and lime green plant materials. Arranged by Gwen Kitching.
Right: 'The Garden of Eden', arranged by Mrs. Elsie Lamb.
Opposite: 'Apprehension,' arranged by Jean Taylor.

first from the show schedule a class which can be personally enjoyed and which has a stimulating title. After the entry for the class has been accepted by the Show Secretary, decisions must be made by the exhibitor about the selection of materials and the manner of interpretation. Often this field is so wide that limitation is difficult. It is suggested that words are written down which are associated with the subject matter. If, for example, 'Norway' is to be interpreted, associated words can be put down opposite a standard list of headings.

Norway
  Plant materials: Evergreens, driftwood, simple flowers, conifers.

Style of design:	Landscape.
Spirit of design:	Naturalistic, unsophisticated, simple.
Container:	A hidden receptacle for water.
Base:	Natural wood, stone, slate.
Colours:	Brown, blue, green, white, grey.
Mechanics:	Pinholder.
Accessory/ies:	Not man-made. Pine cones, rocks, drift-wood.
Background:	Painted grey-blue.
Drape:	None.

The headings on the left can remain constant for any subject. The associated words on the right hand list will vary according to the flower arranger and to the subject matter for interpretation. For example if Persia and not Norway had been the country, very different words would be appropriate, as they also would for themes like 'Anger' or 'Tranquillity'.

This method of preparation is very helpful, as it sets the mind on a path and provides a check list for the components. It can also show where research is needed, for example, the type of plant material that grows in Norway.

First hand experience is the most valuable but occasionally

this is not possible and books must be consulted. This preparation list shows where such 'homework' is necessary.

THE USE OF ACCESSORIES

Accessories are normally considered to be objects which are not made of plant material or, if made of plant material such as wood, have been altered from their natural state and perhaps carved or moulded. These objects include such things as plates, candles, jugs, figurines and so on. Reference should be made to any handbook of definitions designated for show work before entering a flower arrangement show. This should give an exact definition of an accessory.

Accessories may be placed either in the actual container used for the flower arrangement or beside the container.

Accessories present problems because they should suit the design in many ways including style, colour, theme, scale, form and texture and this is a lot to expect. They must then be incorporated or integrated into the design so that they do not 'stick out like a sore thumb' or an afterthought. They must also be a part of the overall balance. To find out if the accessory has been well integrated, remove it and see whether it is missed in the design or if the arrangement can stand alone without it. Accessories are useful for interpretative work and one well chosen object may be enough to 'tell the story' and can be invaluable, if it can be found, borrowed or bought. A stock is useful since the correct one is rarely at hand at the right moment.

More than one accessory, with the exception of such things as stones, can give an overstatement. For example, when interpreting Spain—black lace, castanets, a black bull and a Spanish dancer may all be suitable accessories but the use of all of them in one design leaves nothing to the imagination and can detract from the plant material which should be the dominating feature in the design.

When it is not possible to find a suitable accessory, it is

Opposite: A bronze figurine draws attention to the camellia flowers, arranged by Jean Taylor.

better to do without one as plant material itself can be inter-pretative without the use of other objects. Sometimes the subject matter calls for an accessory which is not particularly suitable but conveys the message. This should be used with care and discrimination as plant material is often of such beauty that it does not easily harmonise with objects of less taste. The use of accessories is not a necessity in interpretative work and has in fact led to some poor designs when an arranger has become carried away by her theme. The use of tasteless and unsuitable accessories has also led to accusations of the use of 'gimmickry' in flower arrangement which is not surprising.

Natural accessories are the easiest to use as they harmonise with the plant material so well, for example, rocks, stones, shells, coral and fruit. The Flemish and Dutch flower paintings of the seventeenth and eighteenth centuries show remarkable sensitivity in the use of accessories and make a valuable study.

SYMBOLISM

This has been used in connection with flowers and plants for centuries. Symbolism is a universal tendency as it is natural to let one thing stand for another. It may be association or it may be tradition that selects certain flowers to represent ideas and to send messages.

For example certain plant materials from damp regions, such as reeds, marsh grasses and lotus, were offered with prayers for rain to the gods of the early Egyptians. Grapes, figs and fruit with many seeds were symbolic of fertility in this civilisation. Early Chinese flower arrangers often used symbolic flowers to give messages to the viewers of their arrangements—the narcissus stood for happiness, the plum blossom for endurance and the bamboo for humility, but there were many other symbols. Lady Mary Wortley Montague wrote in 1763, 'There is no colour, no flower, no weed, no fruit, herb . . . that has not a verse belonging to it and you may quarrel, reproach or send letters of passion, friendship or civility or even of news without even inking your fingers'. Later symbolism was practised to a great extent by the early Victorians who conducted long courtships by sending and receiving nosegays containing flowers with special meaning. They owned small books called 'The Language of Flowers' giving the meaning of hundreds of flowers; acacia stood for a secret love, foxglove for insincerity, French marigold for jealousy and so on.

Today such symbolism is rare although white heather is still used for weddings to bring good luck in the future and red roses are expressive of love. There is however a symbolism in colour, form and texture which is helpful in interpretative designs and a mood can be invoked as the result of the use of certain colours, forms and textures. For example, vigorous lines give a living active quality whereas drooping ones give a feeling of dejection. Any mood can be suggested through this type of symbolism and the manner in which the arrangement is made. To give an example a sansevieria leaf which has tall, rigid growth can symbolise dignity. It gives such a feeling or sensation because of its appearance. Most people associate dignity with something vertical such as a man standing upright in a 'dignified manner'. In other words a vertical line is symbolic of dignity and the appearance of the sansevieria leaf is easy to associate with it. The leaf, a vertical line, man standing upright and dignity have a common feeling. A weeping willow tree has downward movement and could better represent sorrow or grace.

This use of plants, which imagination can associate with certain subjects, is a most helpful way to communicate with viewers without using words. The feeling or association is transferred and the sensitivity of the designer is communicated through the flower arrangement so that others may understand. To accomplish this a selection must be made from many thousands of forms, colours and textures to find those most suitable to represent the subject matter concerned. The following is a general guide.

Forms

Lines
All lines have direction which can be vertical, horizontal or diagonal. They can also be straight or curved. Each direction and type of line has a distinct and different effect upon the observer.

Vertical

This suggests poise or balance and can symbolise uprightness, integrity, aspiration, dignity, exaltation.

Horizontal

This suggests the horizon and a man lying down and is associated with rest, calm, repose, stillness.

Diagonal

This suggests unbalance, something falling over, a man leaning forward in running and so may be associated with insecurity, restless activity, speed.

Zig-Zag

Associated with lightning, this is a very fast line. It is active, nervous, jerky and agitated.

Straight Lines

These are precise and rigid compared with curved lines. They can be stiff and unyielding, sparse and strong.

Curved Lines

Can be associated with wandering streams and gentle movement when the curves are slow and easy. They may represent grace, playfulness, leisure, continuity, flexibility, looseness and also laziness, slowness, femininity, voluptuousness and aimlessness. More vigorous spirals are active and thrusting as a spiralling rocket.

OTHER FORMS

Solid forms are symbolic of weight, airy ones of delicacy. Larger forms seem more masculine, smaller ones, feminine. Curved shapes are more graceful, angular ones can be harsh. Simple forms are quieter than broken-up ones which are restless. Points are more solid than transitional shapes which have more movement.

Texture

This is not as expressive as form and colour as it is not such a strong element but fine silky textures are associated with elegance, wealth, femininity and rough ones with informality, masculinity, strength. Downy and velvety textures are leisurely, civilised, and opulent, prickly ones are aggressive, shininess is sophisticated, happy, gay, modern and so on.

Colour

Colour is strongly symbolic although people may vary in their associations because of their differing environment and traditions. The chroma and value of the colour concerned also changes the effect. For example, dark red is 'rich', scarlet might be 'danger', pink (a light value) femininity. All colours have both negative and positive aspects and make both a mental and an emotional impression on man's receptive nature. Various authors have contributed the following associations:

Red

Aggression, passion, anger, danger, excitement, hatred, joy, strife, virility, fire, heat, courage, Christmas, femininity (tint), pageantry, richness (shade), strength, torture, love, cruelty, lust, destruction, friction, courage, martyrdom, the devil.

Yellow

Sunshine, candlelight, springtime, cleanliness, cheerfulness, cowardice, lightness, visibility, youth, wealth (gold), wisdom, deceit, optimism, luminosity, liveliness, sickness.

Blue

Space, peace, transparency, cold, cleanliness, inspiration, depression, introspection, calm, rest, healing, truth, spirituality, clarity, sea, sky, serenity, passivity, tranquillity, enchantment, nothingness, loneliness, boundlessness, fidelity, piety.

Orange

Warmth, autumn, vitality, strength, energy, hope, happiness, decay, materialism, vigour, winter sun, action, cordiality, courage, modernity, excitement, activity, rest, earthiness, dullness (shade).

Green

Youth, dryads, jealousy, woodlands, rest, nature, tranquillity, healing, relaxation, envy, selfishness, coolness, freshness, rejuvenation, immortality, hope, neutrality, passivity, faith, contemplation, immaturity.

Violet

Melancholy, primness, negation, retirement, solemnity, resignation, affliction, penitence, Victorian, Royalty, dignity, modesty, age, mystery, refinement, martyrdom, elevation, aestheticism, richness, luxury, solidity, gentleness, reflection, philosophy, splendour, sadness, fantasy, sentiment.

Black

Depression, formality, death, gloom, sorrow, darkness, evil, secrecy, terror, the devil, piracy, smartness, neutrality, profundity, drama, contrast, severity, harshness, sophistication, mystery, solemnity.

Grey

Old age, passivity, humility, sobriety, neutrality, melancholy, twilight, frugality, subtlety, serenity, adaptability, dignity, resignation, restraint.

White

Luminosity, innocence, chastity, truth, serenity, cleanliness, airiness, delicacy, coldness, lightness, brides, surrender, uplift, purity, crispness, honesty, neutrality.

Space

The amount of space used in the design can be symbolic—a design using a lot of space can give a feeling of sparseness, tranquillity, modernity, restraint, and reflection, whereas a mass of plant material with little space is symbolic of abundance, exuberance, business, and heaviness.

Opposite: 'A Wild Surmise'—broom with an anthurium leaf, interpret the subject in an objective abstract design by Stella Coe.

Plant Materials

These have great symbolic possibilities but are usually associated with the particular arranger's environment. For example, in the British Isles, orchids are synonymous with luxury, wealth, elegance and sophistication whereas in Florida, where they can be seen growing in the trees, they are associated with informality, often being arranged with driftwood. In Alabama camellias are abundant and are arranged as 'simplicity' whereas roses are in short supply and are more symbolic of luxury and wealth. Grapes may be sophistication in Britain but could be symbolic of earthiness in France.

The most important use of plant material in symbolism is in its form, texture and colour more than its habitat and associations. 'Double the vision my eyes do see and a double vision is always with me. To the inward eye, an old man grey, to the outward a thistle across the way'—*William Blake*.

Containers and Bases

These can be expressive and symbolic. Pottery, basketry and wood suggest simplicity, strength, ruggedness and usually informality whereas fine china and silver are associated with elegance, sophistication and wealth; glass is symbolic of delicacy and fragility. Association plays a strong part in this symbolism.

Although these associations are symbolic, helpful in conveying a message and useful for communication between arranger and viewer, they can be limiting and can narrow the field. Sometimes an arranger uses something unexpected and not usually in association with the subject and as a result conveys unexpected sensitivity and a new slant on a subject.

When arranging an interpretative design, every component —plant material, container, base, accessory, drape and background should contribute to the theme through its associations and become part of the total expression. The conformance to the theme should also be apparent in the movement and rhythm, the style, scale and proportions, the amount of space used within the design, the use of contrast and the dominant feature. Every component used and the manner in which they are assembled should contribute to the one idea interpreted.

An interpretative arrangement may use any style including abstract, in which case the term often used to describe it is either 'Objective Abstract' or 'Interpretative Abstract'. Unlike non-objective abstract there is subject matter, but the outward appearance is not shown and the representation is not literal. The design reflects the designer's own feelings with regard to the subject matter interpreted. This may be a simple impression showing the essence or it may go deeper into the inner meaning of the subject matter. The latter is more abstract.

For example, when interpreting 'Storm':

A traditional interpretative design at its most realistic might show a landscape scene with 'a tree' bent over by the wind and a realistic figure taking shelter. This would show the outward appearance of a storm.

An impressionistic interpretation might use dark plant material with a single flash of brilliant colour giving the impression of lightning amongst dark clouds. It may be said that this is half-way between the landscape and the abstract interpretations.

An objective-abstract design, giving the arranger's feelings, might create an ominous, dark design expressing frozen terror of storm. Another arranger might feel that excitement is the essence and in consequence the colour could be vivid and the movement active. Yet another might reflect the aftermath of destruction.

Characteristics
1. There is subject matter
2. The appearance of the design is not realistic
3. Non-essential details are eliminated
4. The arranger's feelings about the inner meaning of the subject are reflected, alternatively a less abstract interpretation gives a simplified impression of the subject
5. There is an absence of realistic accessories to assist the interpretation. Replacing these is the use of symbolism in plant material, such as a sharp pointed yucca leaf to represent anger.

Left: Traditional interpretation of 'Frugality' by Jean Mawdsley, with a well chosen figurine and sparse plant material.
Right: Abstract interpretation of 'Frugality' by Bett Wareing, expressing it as an emptiness, enclosed and self-absorbed.

SUMMARY

Interpretative designs concentrate on conveying a message and not necessarily on being decorative.

They use a type of symbolism.

Interpretative designs form a major part of flower arrangement shows.

They are stimulating because of their different approach.

They may require research.

There are many subjects which can be interpreted but abstract ideas are usually more suitable for plant material than factual things.

In flower arrangement competitive shows it is necessary for the 'message' to be conveyed to the judge and the viewer.

First hand experience of the subject matter is the safest guide.

The message is best conveyed with the minimum of materials so that viewers can use their imagination. Suggestion is superior to detailed illustration.

Listing associated words can be helpful in setting the manner and selecting the components of the design.

Accessories can be invaluable if they are suitable.

Poor accessories are better omitted and plant material can suggest the subject.

Accessories must be integrated into the design.

Flowers have been symbolic in history for various subjects in different civilisations.

The symbolism of form, texture, colour is used more today than traditional meanings for plant materials.

Forms (including lines), textures and colours give strong effects which influence the viewer and suggest ideas.

Every component in the design should contribute to the total expressiveness of the design.

Interpretative designers in the abstract style express the inner meaning of the subject as seen by the designer.

CREATIVE STUDY

Observe:

The way artists and sculptors interpret a subject.

How composers, writers and poets describe a subject.

Many scenes and experience them fully, so that impressions can be stored for future use.

The use of accessories in Flemish and Dutch flower paintings.

Interpretative designs at flower arrangement shows.

Plants—(a) as horticultural specimens.

      (b) for form, texture and colour in design.

      (c) for association of habitat and use.

      (d) to represent abstract ideas.

Collect:

Postcards of paintings and sculpture with interesting interpretations of subjects.

Cuttings of interpretative flower arrangements.

Show schedules and imagine your choice of components.

Make:

Lists of associated words for different subjects.

A preparation list for a subject as suggested in the chapter on interpretative work.

Rough sketches of any useful associations.

Drawings to express in a simple way, an idea or emotion.

A list of interesting subjects to interpret.

Flower Arrangement:

Make an arrangement and add the accessory afterwards—remove to see if it is missed. Then place in position *first* and do the arrangement afterwards.

Interpret a subject using plant material and no accessory.

Use a pair of accessories.

Make an arrangement with or without accessories interpreting any of the following:

youth	dignity	drama
age	aspiration	day-dream
austerity	winter	femininity
elegance	wind	simplicity
gaiety	abundance	another country

Make a design with accessories interpreting a subject.

An arrangement to express your own personality.

Make an arrangement and then name it.

Using the same subject matter, create an arrangement in three different styles.

6

Settings

A flower arrangement cannot be separated from its surroundings, and although beautiful in itself it can look even more beautiful if it is well displayed. A viewer's awareness is always heightened by the controlled and conscious presentation of beauty—sculpture looks more dramatic against an open sky; a painting is enhanced when well illuminated and exhibited on a plain wall; a diamond looks more brilliant when cut and placed in the setting of a ring of gold and so on. By placing an object in a setting fashioned for it or by relating the object to an existing setting, the surroundings and the design are seen as one—in perfect harmony.

This is applicable whatever the setting, elaborate or simple —the home, stately house, church, hall, hospital, library, restaurant, school, office—wherever flowers are placed the setting of the design should be regarded.

HOMES

Placement

Flowers are highly decorative and by drawing attention to themselves provide an important accent, perhaps 'a centre of interest' in a room. They can also give a necessary colour link between various furnishings or take the place of a lamp or painting yet to be purchased. Consequently their position is important.

Good features in a room should not normally be hidden, but an arrangement can be useful placed to draw attention away from an awkward architectural feature or ungainly furnishings. Flowers are not clearly seen when placed in front of a window with the light behind them. A plain wall, a niche or alcove, or the corner of a room usually display an arrangement to best advantage. The flowers will not last long on a mantelpiece over a hot fire or placed directly in sunshine and for long life need to be in a cooler and shadier position. One or two arrangements well placed look better than several designs, which can unbalance the furnishings and make a room seem too dressed up.

Size

The chosen position for a flower arrangement will give the three dimensional space available for the placement. The existing walls, furniture and furnishings providing the boundaries. For example, a mantelpiece with a picture above it and ornaments on either end will give an oblong space bounded by the picture, the ornaments, the edge of the mantel and the wall behind it. This space should be filled with a design of pleasing proportions. Tables are often placed in a room for definite needs such as a lamp, magazine or books, glasses or coffee cups and in this case the flower arrangement should be of a size which leaves room for these things.

Shape

The space available will also suggest the shape of the design, wide but not high for the mantelpiece, tall and narrow for a slim niche, low and round for a circular coffee table. A wide expanse of bare wall may need a massed triangle and a bare corner may need a flowing pedestal.

Colour

This is suggested by the colours already present in the room. In a highly decorative room with many colours, a monochromatic colour scheme could be the most suitable and this could also apply to a design placed against a highly patterned wallpaper. A room that in itself is monochromatic or toned down in colouring, could take a colour scheme with more

Above: A wall arrangement by Sheila Macqueen.
Below left: A traditional foliage design by Peggy Crooks.
Below right: A well-composed grouping and a semi-permanent arrangement of glycerined plant material with fresh flowers by Helen Edwards. (By courtesy of *Lancashire Life*.)

variety, or the colour of a cushion or a lamp may be repeated in the flowers to give a repetition and a link. Often a complementary colour is striking such as a red flower arrangement in a green and white room. Warm sunny rooms may look better with cool colours, cool rooms with warm colours. An illusion of greater space can be created with receding colours in a small room, whereas a large room will look a little smaller if advancing colours are used. Rooms with transient use as kitchens, halls and corridors can take more brilliant colours than rooms for relaxing, working or sleeping. Several adjoining rooms without co-ordinated colour can be linked together by the use of the same colour scheme in the flower arrangements.

Style

This is an important consideration as an arrangement of contrasting style to the room can look incongruous. The furniture and furnishings, being more permanent fixtures, dictate the style. A traditionally furnished room looks better with traditional or period flower arrangements; one with Chinese furniture needs a Chinese type of design; a very modern room can take free-form and abstract designs and a sun-room may have an informal landscape design.

Lighting

Most objects are enhanced with good lighting—certainly with light falling on them—but a spotlight, although very effective, can be too warm for flowers and they wilt. A softly lit niche makes a beautiful setting. When a room is dark, colours which show up in poor light are advisable. The effect of different types of lighting on flower colours is given in Chapter 10.

STATELY HOMES

The same principles apply as for normal homes, but because they usually contain more decorative features and precious objects, the placement of flower arrangements must be even more carefully considered, so that they are not hidden. Larger designs are suitable and the style should be appropriate. Advice should always be taken from the custodian with regard to placement because of the valuable furniture and with regard to the movement of the public. A request should always be formally made before moving furniture.

CHURCHES

Arranging church flowers is a most enjoyable and peaceful occupation, but there are important considerations:
(1) The church probably has beautiful fabric and furnishings in carvings, memorials, paintings, stained glass, murals, statues, and pillars which should not be obscured. Flower arrangements should complement these, harmonising with the wood, stone, marble, glass and so on. The designs may also be appropriate for the inscriptions on memorials. It is often wise to use the spaces beside the furnishings, or the spaces between pillars, for flowers.
(2) Flower arrangements should never interfere with the movements of the clergy, choir or congregation and the clergy should always be consulted about placement and their wishes respected. For example, some incumbents do not like flowers to be placed in the font.
(3) The designs should be in scale whenever possible with the size of the church and suit its style.
(4) Nails and similar devices for support should not be knocked into walls or pillars.

Placement
This is governed by the existing furnishings, but as a general guide, flower arrangements have more value when placed high where they can be seen by everyone. They can be placed on pedestals, lifted on bases or in pedestal containers, placed on window sills, on top of screens and hung from pillars. Swags and garlands are particularly effective on walls and pillars. Usually a few larger designs are more striking than many small ones.

The Communion Table
The flowers placed here are in an important position and they should be treated with the 'reverence' given to flowers

Above left: An elegant cone of flowers, fruit and foliage in the Red Drawing Room of Syon House. Arranged by Julia Clements.
Above right: Flowers in Dartmouth House by Mrs. Dora Buckingham.
Below: For the church at Easter by Mrs. Dorothy Cooke.

by people in medieval times. The narrow-necked brass altar vases of the present day have developed from the simple pewter pots used for a single lily stem, which signified purity in medieval times. Following this example, a few beautiful specimens are often more appropriate than many fussy flowers and the cross should always dominate, with the flowers complementing the background, altar cloth and candlesticks. Stability and neatness are essential so that the vases are not knocked over. Small communion tables may look better with flower arrangements placed on pedestals at the side. The shape of the designs can be symmetrical or a pair of crescents or Hogarth curves can be effective.

Shape

Mass arrangements are usually more effective in churches because of the dim lighting and the size of the church. The outline or silhouette is important as this is seen rather than details, and most effective are light flowers against a dark wall or dark foliage or flowers against a light wall. When arranging, it is advisable sometimes to stand back, as far away as possible from the design, to look at the effect from a distance.
Static balance is the most suitable for a dignified and reverent atmosphere and for this reason also, stability is essential in the flower arrangements which should not be easy to knock over. Arrangements can usually be seen from all angles and care should be taken to hide mechanics.

Colour

Colours which show up in poor lighting are usually necessary and the existing furnishings should be considered.

Containers

These should be in keeping with the size and style of the church. Stone urns and garden vases, pedestals of wood, iron, stone and fibreglass, troughs and baskets of all descriptions, china tureens, bowls and tubs can all be used.

Weddings

On these occasions, the flower arrangements should also suit

the people concerned and the bride's choice is of first importance. The colour of the flowers should blend with the bridal
dresses as well as with the existing colours in the church.
Several large designs are usually more effective than many
small ones. Guests often have a long time to sit and look at
the flowers and so care should be taken over the designs.

HALLS

Style is not usually of importance as long as the designs are
large, but shape and colouring are most important. Advancing
colours are usually necessary for the flowers to be seen. More
value is obtained from designs placed high. It can be effective
to combine them with plants.

HOSPITALS

Flowers are of great importance to most people who are ill.
They help them to feel less cut off from the world outside,
give something beautiful to look at through a long day and
are often of therapeutic value.
They should never interfere with the work of the medical staff.
It is also a great help to nurses if flowers are arranged before
reaching the hospital, in containers such as plastic dishes with
plastic foam, or inexpensive baskets which need not be
returned. Designs intended for the top of lockers should be
clean, neat and small, as a locker has to hold many things and
flower arrangements can too easily be knocked over, to the
distress of the patient. Arrangements to be displayed in the
wards can be larger. Care should be taken over colour as
advancing and brilliant colours can be tiring to look at con-
tinuously. Long-lasting flowers are appropriate and a half teaspoonful of chlorhexidine to a pint of water will keep the
flower water fresh. The high temperature maintained in
hospitals should be remembered and small pot-et-fleur can
be very suitable for they can be taken home later.
Drapes, bases and accessories are not appropriate and get in
the way. Strong perfume is not always appreciated.

Opposite: An arrangement in a Scottish church by Mrs. Doris Scott.

LIBRARIES, RESTAURANTS, SCHOOLS, OFFICES

Flowers soften the lines of these rooms, but the function of the building is of first importance and flower arrangements should not interfere with it. Long-lasting flowers are important and neatness is essential.

TABLE ARRANGEMENTS

This term refers to flower arrangements placed on tables used for eating purposes. As this is their main function and not the display of flowers, the arrangement should leave room for the food and its serving. The flowers are to make the table more inviting.

SEATED MEALS

Size
A reasonable, general guide is that the flower arrangement should be from $\frac{1}{5}$ to $\frac{1}{3}$ the size of the table.

Shape
This can follow the shape of the table—oval, round, long and narrow. Since talking is an important part of a meal in company, the arrangement should not interfere with conversation, and it should be possible to talk over the flower arrangement, to avoid frustration. It is a good idea to be seated while arranging so that the design is seen at the right angle. It is normally necessary for the designs to be attractive from all angles.

Placement
A central arrangement with candles sometimes added on either side, or grouped, is popular. However, dependent on the number of guests and the type of meal, the placements can be varied:

Opposite: The Dining Room, Howroyd. A table arrangement, well scaled to the size of the table, and in harmony with the arrangements on the sideboard, by George Smith.

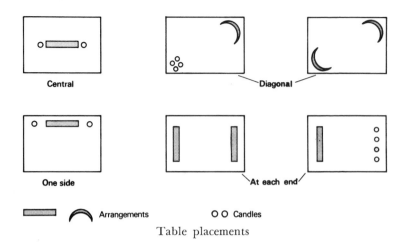

Table placements

Grooming
A flower arrangement used as a decoration for a luncheon or dinner party can be closely observed by those seated at the table. Grooming is essential for this reason and because the plant material is close to food. All foliage should be washed, damaged and mildewed leaves removed and green-fly avoided.

Colour
Table arrangements should suit the colours in the china, tablecloth, glasses and napkins as well as the room as a whole, so the choice is more exacting. As the china is the most permanent possession, this usually gives the key to the colour scheme. One or more of the colours on the plates can be picked up. If the china is fairly plain the colour scheme of the plant material can be more varied.

The Setting
The cloth is the background for the flower arrangement just as a niche in a show or a wall in a room provides a background. For this reason it is best to use a colour which enhances and does not vie with the flowers (as with all backgrounds). Beautiful wood is always an asset and mats can be used in place of a cloth. The traditional white cloths do not usually show flowers to advantage, and it can be a simple

matter to dye them in delicate tints or tones. Voile, lace, organdie and organza can be lovely over a coloured cloth. Plain glasses may be used or coloured glasses can be exciting and suit the colour scheme. Napkins are easy to buy in harmonising colours. Suggestions for colour schemes are:

Deep blue china, pale amethyst cloth, dark amethyst glasses and napkins and old silver with bright pink, violet and blue flowers and black grapes. Lime green is also effective with violet.

A wine red cloth with gold and white china, lime green and gold plant material.

A pale pink cloth with silver and white china, deeper pink flowers and grey foliage.

A navy blue cloth with white china, flowers and lime green foliage.

A modern setting could use a dull orange cloth, brown pottery with brilliant orange, pink and scarlet plant material.

Lighting

Candles may be used in the evening singly, paired or in groups, either in the container with the flowers or in candlesticks or candelabra. Colouring should be chosen to suit candlelight. Candles should not vie with the flowers in colour; cream, green and some of the darker colours, are the simplest to harmonise successfully.

BUFFET TABLE ARRANGEMENTS

These should have the same considerations as table arrangements with the exception of height. They are normally seen from a standing position and should be arranged at eye-level. Arrangements in pedestal containers take up less of the valuable space which may be needed for food and china.

SPECIAL OCCASIONS

On special occasions such as a golden wedding celebration, a christening party, farewell party or birthdays, the purpose of the party and the people being honoured should be considered, so that the style, colour and plant material are suitable for the special event. Accessories are often appropriate and make conversation pieces while they can also helpfully 'stretch' the flowers.

FLOWER ARRANGEMENT SHOWS

In competitive work, the setting for the designs is usually a niche of wood or corrugated cardboard or a space marked out on a table, with a straight background behind it. These are provided by the show committee. These niches and spaces should be regarded as the framework for the flower arrangement just as a painting is framed. The size and colour of the framework and the requirements of the schedule are the only considerations for the designer with regard to setting but she may like to provide her own background within the niche or space allowed if the schedule permits this.

Colour

The colour is often neutral or a neutralised colour and if other colours are used, a small sample is normally sent to the exhibitor. Colours and sizes are described in the show schedule.

Size

Most niches are higher than they are wide (pleasing proportions for these are given in Chapter 14). This means that designs to look pleasing in the framework have a dominant vertical movement or are lifted in some way by the container or with bases. Arrangements going beyond the framework in any direction are not usually allowed by the schedule and anyway they do not look attractive. A margin between the plant material and the walls of the niche is more pleasing, and there is a greater sense of unity when the composition is reasonably compact.

A general guide is to have a margin of not less than $1/_{12}$ the height or width of the niche. This means that with a niche of 36″ high and 24″ wide, a margin of 3″ at the top and 2″ at the sides should be the minimum. But there are no rules. The choice of container may present a problem—if the container is tall for the niche, it is difficult to obtain sufficient height in the plant material and to avoid carrying it above the top of the niche, which is not attractive. A general guide

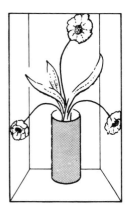 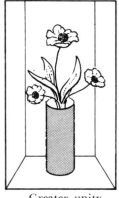

Greater unity

is for the container and base combined to be no more than $\frac{1}{3}$ the height of the back of the niche. A 36″ high niche would then have a container of approximately 12″ high. Overcrowding or under-filling the framework is not attractive and is not in accordance with the principle of proportion. A diagonal placement can give more three dimensional interest. As the arrangements are viewed from a standing position, they should also be arranged in this position and, if placed towards the back of the niche, they are not too close to the viewer.

Exhibitors' Backgrounds

Lighting
Exciting effects may be created by the use of spotlights (white and coloured), moving lights (also moving arrangements), silhouetting, creation of shadows, rheostat control giving gradual dim to bright lighting, on-off lights, black light and fluorescent paint, lighting behind opaque screens such as textured glass.
If the schedule allows exhibitors to provide their own backgrounds, there can be exciting results. These can be designed to provide the perfect setting for a particular arrangement (see Part 4), using appropriate colours, patterns and textures. This gives a finished appearance to the complete presentation.

7

Assessment

WHAT IS BEAUTY?

This question has been asked for centuries. Someone said 'Beauty in things exists in the mind that contemplates them' and a Chinese philosopher remarked 'Everything has beauty but not everyone sees it', in other words when someone says 'this is beautiful', they really mean 'To ME, this is beautiful'. Plato said 'Beauty of style and harmony and grace and good rhythm depend on simplicity' and Kahlil Gibran, the prophet, 'Beauty is eternity gazing at itself in a mirror'. Perhaps George Santayana should have the final word, 'beauty as we feel it is something indescribable, what it is or what it means can never be said'.

WHAT IS A WORK OF ART?

If beauty cannot accurately be described, what then can decide the quality of a work of art and how can it be assessed? Reg Butler wrote 'Great art is to be defined as art which provides the highest level of emotional experience for the greatest number of people over the longest period of time.'

There are certainly a few superb works of art over which there is little or no disagreement. There are many others that have aroused intense controversy at one time or another before eventually being elevated to the level of 'good', beyond doubt. It is these divergent views over what is good and not good that make art so fascinating and it would be very dull if everyone thought alike and anyway the act of controversy often helps to strengthen convictions.

There are some who feel that great art must always have beauty not merely cleverness, others that it should have a message of some kind, some like the purity of abstract work. There are people who value technical skill and technique above everything else and others who feel that the length of time involved in producing the object has a bearing on its quality. Many feel that being suitable for its function is a vital necessity. It seems there is no absolute criterion or final clear-cut test by which one may determine a work of art. It is dependent upon so many things—the mind of the beholder and the age in which he lives, the mind of the artist, his materials and techniques, the sympathy, if any, between the beholder and the artist. In the case of famous classical works of art, the fact that they are still admired and have stood the test of time is a sound reason for them being labelled 'great'. Perhaps here lies the key to assessment of all art. From the study of these classical paintings, sculpture and so on, have evolved standards which can generally be agreed by a number of people. These can enable us to say that this is bad, this is good by comparison. The same standards can be used in relation to all arts, and form a useful basis for assessment. It seems that they refer to:

Technical Skill
Few works of art have lasted which have little technical skill. This is physical and practical but a good artist is in sympathy with his materials and able to master their use.

Suitability
If there is a setting or purpose for the design, then the design should be suitable for that setting or purpose. But this is not always necessary for some works of art have appeared because of the designer's creative desires and for no other reason.

The Principles of Design
Values in aesthetic beauty have been evolved from the study of classical works of art which have used well the basic principles of design, based on nature's laws. Informed people differ about emphasis but generally they remain the same—balance, contrast, dominance, proportion, rhythm, and scale.

Expression
It is generally thought that a work of art should communicate something. This may involve an idea, concept, vision or observation on life, developed from personal experience and association, or it can mean simply that beauty of colour, form or texture is expressed.

Harmony
When there is technical skill and suitability for purpose, when the design principles are well used and the design expresses something, then there is usually a harmonious statement which communicates to the beholder a sense of unity. It has been said that 'Fine art is that in which the hand, the head and the heart of man go together.'

Through carefully considered assessment, perhaps based on the above, accepted standards are evolved which can be applied to all art whether it is sculpture, ballet or flower arrangement. A sense of values is reached by applying these standards. Some people have a strong, innate aesthetic sense and can quickly make assessments but normally it is acquired by training the eye. Once having learnt to assess flower arrangement it is fascinating to find that other art can be similarly assessed.

FLOWER ARRANGEMENT

It is necessary to learn to assess flower arrangements, both one's own and those of others, so that standards can be striven for and reached. There should be no sense of guilt or injustice in the practice of assessing other people's flower arrangements, as this is a vital part of the learning process (and of course it need not be said aloud). Also by studying design in all fields and attempting assessment of its quality and in listening to and in reading the assessments of others, perception is sharpened and a standard of values is appreciated. In any act of judgement, as when listening to a piece of music, looking at a painting and so on, there are normally four processes:

1. Reception of an impression or feeling at the first impact.
2. Closer examination of the content.
3. The formation of unspoken words in the mind which describe the impression felt.
4. The final judgement.

THE BASIS FOR ASSESSMENT

1. *Technical Skill*

This is easy to assess when one knows the medium and materials of flower arrangement and the skills necessary to keep plant material alive, support it in a container, preserve it and so on. Good and bad workmanship is easier to assess than anything else because it is so obvious.

2. *Suitability*

The purpose of a flower arrangement is often decorative and the design needs to suit its setting, its purpose and the event and people concerned, in style, quality, size, colour, texture and so on. There may be differences of opinion about what is appropriate because of personal feelings but this assessment is not difficult. If the design is for a show then it should be suitable for the show's schedule. Sometimes arrangements are made just to express the creative urge of the flower arranger in which case suitability is not a concern.

3. *The Principles of Design*

To go through each of the principles of design is a reliable method of assessment. This may take time at first but it eventually becomes intuitive. The good use of them is soon accepted and if a principle is not well used then it stands out and is noticeable, for example, a comment might be 'There is no contrast of form' or 'It lacks rhythm' or 'The container is out of scale' or 'The design is not balanced'. Faults in the use of the design principles are soon recognised, but if they are not and the design is dislikable for some reason the fault is soon found when the use of design principles is analysed. This is a good method when making an assessment of a new style or an original design.

4. Expression

Flower arrangement, as any other art, should express something which may be a mood, a story, an observation of life, an interpretation, or it may be simply beautiful colour, fascinating form, or lovely texture. Inspiration is the spark that often produces an expressive design and originality may or may not be a part of the expression.

5. Harmony

When the design is technically well executed and displayed, is suitable for its purposes, uses well the principles of design, expresses a quality, and the final form is well composed and integrated, then there is harmony and a work of art.

ASSESSING YOUR OWN WORK

It is necessary to be able to judge your own work. At first the assessment of another person, such as a teacher or advanced flower arranger, may be available and reliable, but sooner or later it becomes necessary to self-evaluate. This is much more difficult than evaluating other people's flower arrangements. It is difficult to see one's own work objectively for the difficulties met with in composing the design, the problem of finding the right components, the pre-occupation with one quality (such as a new flower), may cloud the judgement; in other words one can be too conscious of the separate parts of the design and not see the whole. A list of questions to go through can be helpful and two sets follow, one for new flower arrangers and the other for advanced students.

PROCEDURE

It is wise to complete the arrangement first and to enjoy doing it, to work quickly and not to attempt assessment too earnestly whilst actually arranging. Most plant material is short-lived and a bad design will not be around for long. Having found any faults, it is probable that they will quite naturally be corrected the next time flowers are arranged. It is sometimes difficult to assess a design immediately after it is completed for one is too involved with the details and it is better to return to the arrangement to assess it later.

QUESTIONS FOR ASSESSMENT

NEW FLOWER ARRANGERS

1. Is the plant material fresh and not limp in appearance? Is there any damaged plant material?
2. Are the mechanics stable and hidden?
3. Is the container suitable for the plant material? In shape, colour, texture, style?
4. Are some flowers turned or do they all face the front?
5. Is a base needed? Will the accessory be missed if it is removed?
6. Can everything be clearly seen? Is there enough space in the design?
7. Is everything related in size?
8. Do all the separate parts of the design belong to each other? Including the setting?
9. Do the colours seem related?
10. Is the design top-heavy, bottom-heavy or lop-sided?
11. Is one part of the design emphasised?
12. Is it suitable for its purpose?
13. Have I tried something new for me?
14. Have I enjoyed arranging it?

ADVANCED FLOWER ARRANGERS

1. Is the design technically perfect? Plant material in good condition, mechanics hidden, grooming perfect? Is it well displayed?
2. Is it suitable for its purpose?
3. Are the principles of design well-used? Is the design balanced? Is there some contrast or variety in forms, textures, colours? Is there something dominant? Is everything in scale? Has it pleasing proportions? Does rhythm take the eye through the design? Is there a feeling of three dimensions?
4. Has the design expressed something? An idea, observation, something of beauty? Have I kept to my original inspiration?
5. Is there complete harmony of all parts in the design?
6. Have I been original for me?

7. Have I enjoyed creating the design?

> 'One may do whate'er one likes in Art
> The only thing is to make sure
> That one does like it.'   *Robert Browning*

SUMMARY

Beauty cannot be defined clearly.

It is dependent on the mind that contemplates an object.

A work of art is usually assessed subjectively.

There are standards agreed by a number of people.

These have evolved from the study of past art.

They include good technical skill, suitability for the purpose, expressive communication, good use of the principles of design, harmony of all components and the setting.

The same standards of assessment can be applied to all the arts including flower arrangement.

Assessment of one's own work is a necessity for improvement.

CREATIVE STUDY

Use the questions listed for your own arrangements.

Analyse and assess other people's arrangements in class, at demonstrations, in flower shows, in homes, churches and elsewhere.

Study pictures of flower arrangements in magazines, newspapers and books and analyse.

Visit design centres.

Analyse and assess design in other fields.

PART 2

The Elements of Design
Texture, Form, Colour, Space

THE ELEMENTS OF DESIGN

Michelangelo took a rough piece of marble and worked with it to create an object of infinite beauty which he called 'David'. To be able to do this he had to know about marble, its possibilities, its limitations, and its qualities. In the same way other designers need to know their medium, woodworkers the qualities of wood, potters the possibilities of clay and so on. The medium in which he works gives the designer the materials of his expression and by understanding it he learns to control and fashion it as he wishes.

'You discover the spirit of your material and the properties peculiar to it. Your hand thinks and follows the thoughts of the material.'   *Brancusi*

Objects can be natural or man-made and they may or may not be beautiful to look at, but every one has its own physical characteristics of texture, form and colour. The designer uses his skill and the knowledge of these qualities in his own material to create a design.

The medium of flower arrangement is plant material which is particularly rich in beautiful textures, shapes and colours and is not often altered by the designer but is selected and composed. However by the study of these qualities in plant material perception is increased and designs can be created to enhance them.

'A good flower arranger is one who sees, who discovers nature and places her discovery in such a light that others may see it too.'   *Dorothy Riester*

138

Left: A block of rough marble; *Right:* Michelangelo's 'David'.

These physical characteristics of texture, shape and colour seen in all objects are often called the elements of design or the working qualities. Space must be added to them as although this is not a tangible feature it is necessary to all designs.

8

Texture

DEFINITION

Texture is the quality of the physical, tangible surface of an object. It is the touch quality which is sensuous and evocative. It denotes surface quality in its widest sense as it can also refer to the illusion created by a surface. All objects possess a definite textural quality whether they are natural or man-made and regardless of their beauty or lack of it. For example, a rose petal is silky in texture, a dustbin is rough and despite the fact that one has beauty and the other has none, both display textural quality.

IN DESIGN

Designers in all the visual arts regard texture as one of their basic working qualities, or elements, to be used to create effects in designing. It makes a unique contribution and is quite different from any other quality such as colour, although it can modify colour.

In recent years texture has been given prominence by interior designers, needlewomen, painters, potters, architects and weavers who are using it to give new interest to their work. Although texture is present in all objects, its presence alone is not enough and it needs to be selected and controlled

Above left: The fascinating texture of coral.
Above right: The soft, fluffy texture of a feather.
Below left: A container with texture similar to hard-baked earth.
Below right: Pebbles appear rough when grouped.

'Swan Upping' by Stanley Spencer. This painting gives a strong sense of textural qualities.

by the designer to produce a desired effect and an object of beauty.

IN FLOWER ARRANGEMENT

Actual and visual texture
In many objects the feel and the look are the same in

textural effect and we do not need to touch to know the texture. Young children need to touch everything to experience the feel of things but as we grow older, knowledge and imagination transfer the sensation into visual touching. We can 'feel' without actually touching. Texture therefore applies to both the sense of sight and the sense of touch, whereas colour, for example, only applies to the sense of sight. Most people have a keen sense of touch and respond quickly to any surface that is unusual or has unexpected qualities, and a textile, or tactile sense, latent in everyone, can be developed very successfully.

In some objects the feel and the textural appearance are *not* the same. For example, a carnation petal feels silky but when seen as part of the whole flower the textural appearance, or illusion, is of roughness. This is called *visual* texture. It is with visual texture that flower arrangers are mostly concerned: the textural *appearance,* not the textural *feel.* Few people can resist stroking a silky petal, a downy peach, a smooth piece of waxed driftwood or a rough pottery container, but flower *arrangements* are not usually made to be handled as are fabrics where the actual feel is as important as the appearance. In fact, in plant material, there are some textures which are much more pleasant to look at than to feel, such as a prickly thistle or a thorny rose stem.

TYPES OF TEXTURE IN PLANT MATERIAL

The tissue structure of plant material determines the actual texture or 'feel' and the way the surface is formed determines the visual texture. The surface of plant material cannot often be altered by the flower arranger as can the media of other designers. For example, a potter can create a rough or smooth surface on his clay, but a flower arranger is concerned with *selecting* textures already present in plant material and harmonising and contrasting them. There is a wealth from which to choose and the great variety offered by plant material is one of its most valuable assets. There are remarkable differences between the surface qualities—both actual and visual—of, for example, camellias, carnations, artichokes, chestnuts, pine-cones, teasels, dock seed-heads and old-man's beard. Some plant material shows more than one texture: the horse chest-

Above left: A carnation has a silky feel but a visually rough appearance.
Above right: Thorn, which both feels and appears prickly.

Below left: A horse-chestnut bud. This tree has many contrasting textures.
Below right: Houseleek (*Sempervivum*), smooth to the touch but visually rough.

nut is a single example of many contrasting textures in one tree with its rough bark, matt leaf, sticky bud, glossy chestnut in a prickly outer covering and silky flowers.

There are many descriptive words which can be applied to plant material, such as:

bristly	delicate	fluffy	leathery
sticky	coarse	downy	furry
polished	shiny	thorny	corky
dull	fuzzy	prickly	scratchy
tough	crepey	feathery	glossy
rough	silky	velvety	crinkly
fine	hairy	rubbery	slimy
waxy	crisp	firm	hard
satiny	smooth	woody	woolly

It is an interesting idea that plant material may well have been the source of inspiration for fabrics in the past, for example, the rich surface of a pansy may have given the idea of velvet.

THE USE OF TEXTURE

To be aware of the varying textures in plant material is not enough. It is necessary to understand how to group them for variety and balance in the arrangement of surfaces. The most usual faults are too little contrast and too many different textures. Texture is not nearly such a dominant quality to work with as colour which makes it easier but also necessitates using really strong contrasts to make an impact. The human eye finds variety more interesting than sameness and monotony results when only one texture is used in a design.

Contrasting textures have the effect of enhancing each other. For example, a shiny texture next to a matt surface gives an increased awareness of each, as when glossy red poppies are used in a matt surfaced container, or when rough textured dried plant material such as pine cones and achillea with preserved beech are used in a shi. "copper or brass container. Two similar textures together do little for each other and the effect blurs into one.

Sometimes a good contrasting texture cannot be found in available plant material but the contrast can be provided by

Left: Associated materials with strong textural contrast, arranged by Jean Taylor.
Right: A pedestal with great textural interest, arranged by Mrs. Elsie Lamb.

any of the components in the design, such as the base, accessory or container.

Although for good harmony the component parts of a design need to have some sort of association with each other, for instance an association of habitat, the textures of the individual components can be in contrast with one another. As an example, a design interpreting a tropical island using associated objects might use rough coral, polished shells, smooth foliage, silky flower petals to give textural interest in the contrast and variety of surfaces present.

Some designs require greater contrasts in texture than others:

1. Monochromatic (one-coloured) and subtle colour schemes without really strong colour impact need greater textural contrast for interest.

146

2. Dried arrangements are often monotonous because of the sameness of the textures and may need contrast in the container and base to give vitality.
3. Modern designs with their greater use of space and restraint in plant material need interest in contrasting textures.
4. Fruit and vegetables may have a continual repetition of form which can be dull so textural changes are helpful and there are many beautiful variations in fruit.

Using contrasting textures in a design does not mean using as many different kinds as can be found or spotting various textures about in a design where they become lost in a mass of detail. Three or four contrasting textures placed in groups are often far more effective.

THE EFFECT OF TEXTURE

The texture of an object can make a great difference to its power for drawing the human eye. A shiny texture has great eye-pull as it reflects the light so strongly. This means that a shiny container will need a design of plant material which is large or bold in comparison to attract the eye away from the container. Coloured glass containers very easily dominate a design by their light reflection so that the eye finds it difficult to travel to the plant material.

A shiny object of any kind is more dominant than a dull one and can easily affect the visual balance of a design unless placed correctly. A small amount of shiny texture balances a much larger duller surface.

Texture greatly influences colour. A carnation of the same red as a shiny poppy may appear darker because of the light being broken up in the carnation.

Lighting makes a considerable difference. In very poor lighting little textural difference can be seen. Half-light often gives a more interesting sense of texture as the shadows are deeper and full light is not as enhancing. Exciting effects can be obtained by varying lighting so that it is stronger from one angle. If the plant material is turned to different angles it will catch different lighting and give more interest.

The visual texture is often changed when objects are grouped. For example, a pebble worn down in the water will look and feel smooth by itself, but when it is part of a beach of many pebbles, the visual appearance is rough.

Textures have certain associations for people which can be used in interpretative designs to suggest ideas. Roughness is often associated with masculinity, fineness with femininity, shininess with gaiety, dullness with sadness and so on.

SUMMARY

Texture is the physical tangible surface of an object.
It establishes the boundaries of a surface.
There is actual and visual texture.
These are not always the same in one object.
Flower arrangers work with visual texture.
There are many varieties in plant material.
It is not as dominant as colour.
It modifies colour and form.
Contrasting textures enhance each other.
All design components contribute to the textural effect.
Designs which need strong textural interest are monochromatic, dried, fruit and vegetables and modern.
Shiny textures have greater eye-pull than dull.
Lighting affects textural appearance.
Grouping objects changes the visual textural appearance.
Textures can have associations useful in interpretative designs.

CREATIVE STUDY

Observe

glass	leather	satin
rock	oil and water	coral fan
pebbles grouped	skin	shells
larva	flaking paint	feathers
metal	old brick	angora
plastic	velvet	rubber
sandpaper	foil	coral
fur	tweed	net

In fruit:

gourds	eggplant	grapes
broccoli	bulrushes	lemons
cauliflowers	avocado pears	water melons
pineapples	lychees	onions
pine cones	cacti	peaches
strawberries		

Foliage in many plants, undersides also.

Bark of trees.

Different textures in a room.

The use of texture by sculptors, weavers, painters, embroiderers.

The flowers, foliage and fruit of one plant to see how nature uses contrasts.

The effect of a spotlight or torch on texture.

The feel and look of plant material textures for differences in the two.

The textural effect created by windows on skyscrapers.

The difference when objects are grouped.

Collect:

A group of dried plant materials and assemble in like groups and give a collective name such as 'rough'.

Scraps of fabric and group in similar textures.

A group of textured objects from one habitat, e.g. seashore.

Pairs of contrasting fabrics, e.g. rough and smooth, hard and soft.

Pairs of contrasting plant materials.

Words which describe texture.

Plant materials to correspond with pieces of fabric, e.g. poppy and silk.

Seed-heads, skeletonised leaves.

Make:

Changes in the texture of driftwood by stripping, sanding and polishing.

A plaque of preserved plant materials or seeds such as lentils, coffee beans, dried peas, grasses, corn, sunflower and bird seed.

149

A pressed flower picture.

A collage of materials of any kind with interesting texture.

A collage of pasted newsprint, poster or magazine paper.

Rubbings with a wax crayon and thin paper of any objects, e.g. a brick, ribbed glass, canework.

A collage of materials in the same colour but with different texture, e.g. white card, lace, buttons.

A design with a felt tip pen on paper creating texture with markings, e.g. stippling.

Designs on cardboard with lace, paper d'oylies, net, tissue paper, scrim, voile.

Pairs of contrasting materials in texture and mount on board.

Home-made containers with interesting textures.

Flower arrangement

Make designs featuring fruit, vegetables, driftwood, foliage, basketry, fabric, lace, stitchery, rope, string, shells, coral, **rock, coral fan, metal.**

(a) Using a container of glass, metal or shiny plastic.

(b) Using only two contrasting textures.

(c) In dried plant materials.

(d) Mixed with dried fresh plant material.

(e) With a similar background in texture.

(f) With a contrasting background in texture.

(g) With plant material and associated objects from the beach, woodland, lakeside, roadside, stream, or mountain.

(h) Interpreting malice, femininity, hardship, masculinity, or elegance.

(i) A design for a highly textured setting.

9
Form

DEFINITION

The term 'form' refers to the shape of something and also to the arrangement of its parts. It is the total effect produced by an object's outline or contour. Although colour and texture affect form, it is quite a different quality and should be considered separately. Sometimes the word 'shape' is used instead of 'form' but shape is often thought to be two-dimensional whereas form is regarded as having depth as well as height and breadth.

Form is strongly related to space since only against space (or against a strong colour contrast) can it be clearly seen. When many forms are cluttered together such as in a rubbish heap, few individual forms are obvious. The outline of the rubbish heap against surrounding space is all that can be seen. If the individual forms are to be noticed they too need space around them or a plain background.

IN DESIGN

TYPES OF FORM

Form can be regular or irregular, symmetrical or asymmetrical, geometric or free of geometric form, angular or curved. Forms can be solid as an orange or volumetric (with space inside) such as the flower of an arum lily. They may look a different shape when viewed from another angle or from a

Above: Driftwood with intricate and interesting form.
Below left: Solid form seen in *Echinops* (Globe thistle).
Below right: 'Pelagos', Barbara Hepworth, 1946.

distance, e.g. a bird looks like a round dot when in the sky but not at close range. When objects overlap each other a different form results, and overlapping hosta leaves can give quite a different shape from a single leaf.

Overlapping hostas

Form repeated but with variety and unity

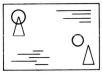

Several types of form – variety but less unity

FORM AND DESIGN

When grouping forms in a design, a single type of form continually repeated may be used throughout the design such as a circle or parts of a circle. Alternatively several different forms may be combined with irregular shapes or with lines and triangles. Most people find a sense of repetition necessary but a variety is enjoyable also and the eyes are best satisfied when there is repetition combined with variety for interest.

FORM IN FLOWER ARRANGEMENT

Both the individual pieces of plant material and the completed flower arrangement are usually three dimensional. Both have form, as a lemon has an oval form. If it is used in a design of fruit and flowers, it is also part of the total form of the completed arrangement, which will include many individual forms like those of the plant material, base, container and perhaps accessory, all of which contribute to the total effect. Designs are made up of forms within a form.

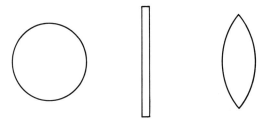

Round, line and transitional shape

Volumetric form in *Lilium longiflorum*.

DESIGN ANALYSIS OF FORMS

It is possible to simplify forms in plant material into three basic shapes and it is helpful to analyse these and to understand their use in design. These three basic shapes can be very much simplified and classified into rounds (or points in design terms), lines and in-between shapes. No adequate word seems available for these, which can be named transitional shapes, or stepping-stones.

154

POINT

Many meanings of 'point' are listed in dictionaries but in the language of design point refers to a form which attracts and holds the eye because its directional movement is inward to a central focal spot.

in contrast to a line

which moves the eye differently.

A point can be the simplest unit but at the same time it can be the most compelling form seen in a design. In other words the strongest visual symbol.

It exerts this great force because it holds the eye and stops all other movement except for the inward pull which it attracts to itself. To test this force, look at an open dahlia or a narcissus full face and see how your eye is held in one place.

TYPES OF POINT

A point can vary from a regular shape, such as a round or square, to an irregular shape

'A Girl with a Kitten', Perronneau. The little girl's eyes are the dominant feature of this lovely painting.

but squares and irregular shapes do not attract and hold the eye as strongly as circles, although all move the eye inward to a certain extent. A point can be solid ●
or an enclosed space ○
Both have the same effect.

Things appear as 'point' according to the distance from which they are viewed, because distances can blur outlines. For example, a bird appears as a point in the far distant sky and a leaf in a maple tree is a point at the top of a tree. The stars at night, traffic lights, eyes in people's faces, the sun, are examples of point and think of the 'drawing power' of each of these.

Enclosed spaces seen as points. Arranged by Jean Taylor.

Because of its strength a point must be used with discretion. A point of any kind has more attraction and holding power than any other form and so it is important to use a point where you want the eye to be held and where you want emphasis and attraction.

Large points will obviously have greater powers of attraction and hold the eye longer than smaller ones. A point can stabilise a design when well used and upset the balance completely if wrongly placed. The following diagram shows how much stronger a force it is than other shapes.

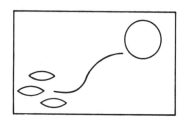

The eye is continually attracted to the top right-hand corner and away from the other shapes.

A design of nothing but points can be monotonous

Variety in size is helpful

If the spaces or intervals between the points are also varied, still further interest can result.

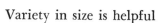

If points are placed very close together there is an increase in the sense of unity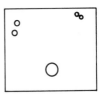

When placed further apart space becomes a more important quality and there is greater eye movement

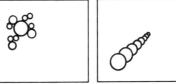

When points actually touch there can be a sense of over-crowding.

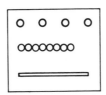

If points are overlapped
a different form results which may no longer be a point.
If points are placed in a row they become a 'line'

as together they contribute to movement *along* instead of inwards.
Placed closer together they become an even more visible line.

159

Left: The flower of the narcissus when seen full-face is a very dominant point. *(Syndication International.)*
Right: The centre of a daisy flower is made up of many smaller points, carrying the eye to the centre.

IN FLOWER ARRANGEMENT

Examples of plant material which can be regarded as point when seen full-face are round gourds, oranges, all open circular flowers such as daisies, water lilies, chrysanthemums, roses, dahlias and, in foliage, rosettes of echeveria. Any plant material which is round or near round can be regarded as point. As so many flowers fall into this classification, this type of form is of special importance to flower arrangers.

Because of the strong attraction of a point, flowers seen 'full-face' should be used sparingly and carefully in an arrangement. For example, a design of all points, say narcissus all facing forwards, can be static and unattractive. The eye travels to one point (or narcissus) and then to another and each time is held. There is no easy rhythm or movement in the design.

This does not mean that an arrangement cannot be made of all points—no other plant material might be available—but a more fluid and interesting design can be made by turning most of the flowers so that they do not appear as points.

If points are turned in a flower arrangement so that a side view is seen, there is less force as a flower seen thus

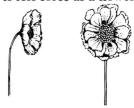

is no longer a point, as is a flower seen full-face.

As stabilisers, points are excellent and without any in a design, there can be too much movement so that the eye is never rested. Instead of weightiness resulting from using all points, there is restlessness from using none. The eye tends to travel to the container for resting.

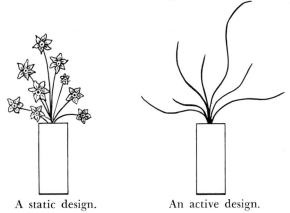

A static design.   An active design.

CONTAINERS AND BASES USED AS POINTS

A round container such as a goldfish bowl can be regarded as a point and easily becomes dominant in a design. In this case it is necessary to have very tall or bold plant material to offset the attraction of this type of container. A round base can be similarly eye-catching but the shape is often broken by the foot of the container which lessens the impact.

161

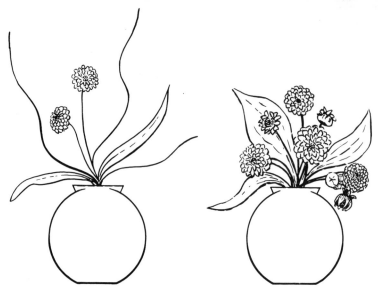

A round container needs taller or bolder plant material.

IN TRADITIONAL DESIGN

In traditional design, points are often used at the centre to give stability and a resting place for the eye, a pivot to which the eye can continually return from its wanderings around the design. This pivot is sometimes called the focal point or centre of interest. Many rounded flowers are used in traditional designs but they are gradually turned away from the centre and few are seen full-face.

MODERN DESIGN

Modern and abstract designs differ from traditional design in that points are not necessarily used in the centre, but are placed where emphasis is needed and where they help in visual balance. Hence the term 'emphasis points' meaning eye-attractions placed wherever needed in the design (and this might be at the top). This is further explained in the chapter on balance.

LINE

Line can be classified as a type of form but often because of its importance in design, is classified separately.

There are many definitions in the dictionary including 'long narrow mark, direction, row, series, a threadlike formation, something distinct and marked as if drawn by a pencil'. In the language of design and flower arrangement it refers to a form which moves the eyes strongly *along* instead of holding them in one place as a point. A line causes eye movement more strongly than other shapes.

'Man Pointing', Alberto Giacometti, 1947, Bronze. Line seen in sculpture.

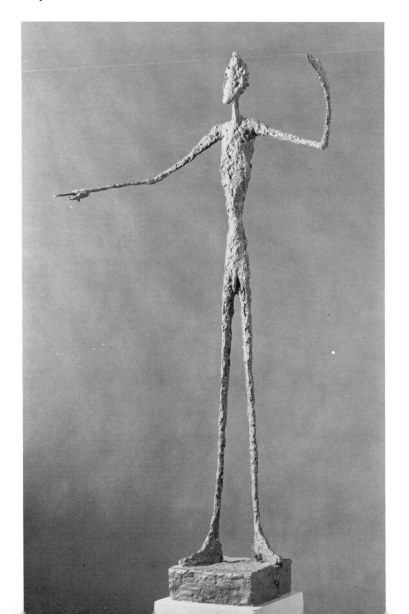

TYPES OF LINE

Lines can be thick, thin, straight, broken, curved, complicated, simple, crossing, bent, wavering, firm, delicate, bold, strong, weak, stiff, fluent. Their common essential quality is movement which can be fast or slow.

A design can be made up entirely of lines or lines may be combined with other shapes. Designs made entirely of lines can have lightness and delicacy. They can be very active

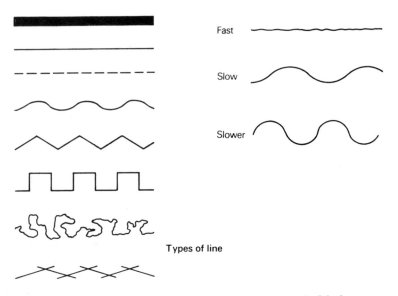

Types of line

and full of movement as there are no points to hold the eye.

In any design lines are used wherever movement, slow or fast, is desired, the whole effect being altered by the type of line used because lines are very expressive. For example, straight lines are rigid, strongly curved ones can be graceful, slightly wobbly ones are fast, thick ones are slow and so on.

Direct line
When the line is solid and visible it is called a direct line. An example is the branch of a deciduous tree in winter. Such lines are tangible.

164

Above: Mahonia leaf with repetition of shapes giving vertical movement.
Top right: 'Linear Construction' by Naum Gabo.
Centre: Stepping stones forming an indirect line.
Below: A row of trees giving horizontal movement.

Indirect line
There are indirect lines as well as direct lines. A point holds the eye.

But when a second is added a new movement is created as the eye travels from one to the other.

The eye can move along without following direct and visible lines. The line between those two points is invisible and is an imaginary line formed by the eye's movement. If a series of points is added the line is more visible.

The 'Plough' of stars in the sky is an example of points and invisible 'lines' making a shape. When points actually merge as in a string of beads they once more become a direct and visible line.

An indirect line does not have to be made up of points. Sometimes the line is formed by a repetition of shapes which if alone would move the eye differently. A row of trees is an example. Each tree growing alone would move the eye vertically, but in a row with others the movement becomes horizontal.

Lines of Continuance
There are also invisible 'lines' made by the eyes being attracted to various things in a design. In this case they are not of necessity in a row or series. The eye is attracted to bright colours, shiny textures, rounded shapes. These attractions move the eye through any design along certain definite paths giving a pleasant rhythmical movement if the design is good. When eye attractions are not equated through the design the rhythm is static and the eye held in one or two places.

Lines of continuance are visual paths that the observer feels within a design even though nothing tangible may mark the line. They are very important as they constitute the rhythm of the design.

Outline
This refers to the line which can be drawn around the silhouette of, for example, a sculpture or flower arrangement. It is the contour or boundary of an object.

IN FLOWER ARRANGEMENT

PLANT MATERIAL

There are many examples of line in plant material. Direct line is seen in bulrushes, bare branches, iris leaves, delphiniums and many more. These are normally termed 'line plant material'. Indirect line can be formed from a series of rounded forms such as carnations placed in a row.

'Bacchante and Cupids', Joseph Marin, Terracotta, 1793. Lines of continuance can be traced from the girl's face, along her arm to the child, to the child's face on the left, down to the girl's left foot and then back to her face.

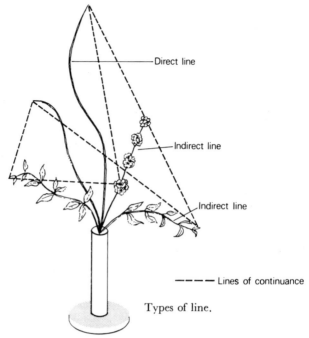

Direct line

Indirect line

Indirect line

- - - - - Lines of continuance

Types of line.

Lines of Continuance

These are formed in flower arrangement with eye-catching elements such as rounded flowers, brilliant colours, shiny textures and tips of branches. In a traditional arrangement these lines usually follow a path which starts in the centre of the design at the focal point and then travels to the tips or extremities of the design and back to the centre. In a modern design the eyes travel with less regularity to eye-catching elements placed *throughout* the design.

Outline

This is usually relevant to mass designs where there is little space within the design itself and the outline is clear and simple. The outline of a pedestal arrangement, or any arrangement designed to be seen from a distance, is important as the detail within is not clear and the outline shape is a dominant feature. The term outline is hardly applicable to line arrangements where there is little solid mass and a very indented contour.

A line arrangement with dominant line plant material, restraint and a great use of space. Arranged by Jean Tayor.

Line Arrangements

This term refers to a design in which the line plant material is dominant. Space must also be a necessary feature as lines cannot otherwise be seen and will not be dominant. Restraint in the remaining plant material is also important as lines cannot be seen when muddled with solids. In the past, geometrically shaped flower arrangements have sometimes been called line arrangements. This is correct when the design shows dominant line plant material (in direct or indirect lines) but not when a *mass* of plant material is used, as in this case *line* is not a dominant feature. Arrangements based on geometric forms such as triangles, crescents, and Hogarth curves can be either line or mass designs depending on the amount of plant material present. The characteristic quality is a matter of quantity not shape. There can be mass triangular arrangements or line triangular arrangements. A bouquet of flowers is a mass, a branch of apple blossom a line—to illustrate the difference. Whether they possess a recognisable geometric shape is not of concern to their classification as a line arrangement.

There are some designs which do not fit clearly into either category and in America these designs are called 'massed-line'.

Line as Movement

The word 'line' has so many definitions that it can also be used in reference to the general direction of a design, and the general style of a composition with respect to the sequence or arrangement of the contours.

Arrangements are spoken of as having vertical, horizontal or diagonal lines, meaning movement or dominant direction.

The term 'vertical' has come to refer to a narrow design with extremely dominant upward movement. Often it is a very thin triangle. Most designs move more strongly in one direction than another, and this is less confusing if referred to as 'movement' rather than line. Both line and mass arrangements, whether geometric or free form can be vertical, horizontal or diagonal in movement. For example, a Hogarth curve can be arranged upright (vertically) or horizontally as in a table arrangement.

Left: A skeletonized magnolia leaf, which is transitional in shape.
Right: Aspidistra leaves provide a gradual change between the lines and points. Arranged by Jean Taylor. (By courtesy of *Popular Gardening.*)

TRANSITIONAL SHAPES

IN DESIGN

There are many shapes in between a line and a point. They cannot be said either to move the eye along or to hold it in one place. These shapes may be termed the peacemakers or harmonisers in a design. They draw the strong contrasts of line and point together.

There is a big jump or contrast between the first two shapes. When the in-between shape is added the change is more gradual. There is a stepping-stone for the eye and the eye movement is not strong or sudden.

This transitional shape has both the holding power of a point and the movement along of a line but in neither case is it as strong.

Transitional shapes, such as these, are not always desired in a design. It depends upon whether a gentle rhythmic movement is needed or a faster more definite one.

IN FLOWER ARRANGEMENT

Plant Material

Many leaves can be classified in this group such as hostas, beech, bergenia and many others. It also includes half open flowers and oval fruits, and flowers turned on one side so that they are not seen as a point but as an oval.

In flower arrangements the type of design decides whether these transitional shapes are used. Traditional arrangements tend to use many of them and very few strong lines, giving a soft and easy rhythm and a sense of fullness. Line designs often use them to lessen the strong contrast between line and point.

Abstract designs with strong contrasts often leave transitional shapes out altogether.

When planning a design it is helpful and a good guide line for selection of plant material, to think in terms of these three forms—line, point and transitional material— whether each should be used in the design and in what quantities. When faced with a garden or shop, full of plant material of many kinds, this simplification can help selection.

SUMMARY

FORM

Form relates to the shape of something and also to the arrangement of its parts.
Form and space are closely related as form can only clearly be seen in space.
There are many types of form.
When used in a design a single form can be repeated or varying forms can be combined.
Forms can be simply classified as points, lines and transitional forms.

POINT

This is a strong visual force because its directional pull is inward.
Point is a stabiliser in design as it modifies the restlessness of lines.
It gives variety and interest when used sparingly.
It must be carefully placed as it strongly affects the balance.
Distance alters the shape.
The position and size of points in a design alters the effect.
Points placed in a row become a line.
Traditional arrangements use points at the centre of a design.
Modern designs use points anywhere to give good balance.

LINE

Line is movement.
There are many types of line.
The speed and activity of line varies.
Lines can compose the design or be combined with other shapes.
Lines can be expressive.
Direct line is visible and tangible.

Indirect lines are formed by a series of regular shapes.

Lines of continuance are invisible lines or movements of the eye, impelled by various attractions.

Rhythm results from the use of lines.

There are many line plant materials.

Outline refers to the contour of a shape.

Line designs have dominant line plant material, restraint and space within the design.

Geometrically shaped arrangements can be in line or mass style.

Line can refer to the movement of a design whether horizontal, vertical or diagonal.

TRANSITIONAL SHAPES

The harmonisers in a design.

They reduce contrast.

They both move and hold the eye but not strongly.

Transitional shapes are used for easy gentle rhythm.

Foliage, half-opened flowers, turned flowers and oval fruit are examples in plant material.

In traditional arrangements, many are used.

In line designs they are used as stepping-stones.

In abstract they are not often used.

Analysing the shape of plant material in the garden or shops aids selection.

CREATIVE STUDY

FORM

Observe:

The shapes of fruit, vegetables, shells, driftwood, musical instruments, buildings, sculpture, summer trees, crystal formations, fungi, cloud formations, hedges, changes of form in one plant—flowers, leaves, seed-heads.

The way form follows function in nature.

Flower arrangements against a window or silhouetted.

How forms change when turned in different directions.

Collect:
Seedheads with varying forms.
Shells, driftwood, stones.
A list of plants to fit each of the three basic forms.
Groups of plants and name the 'form' group.
Volumetric forms.

Make:
Drawings of geometrical shapes, free-form shapes, symmetrical
   and asymmetrical shapes.
Drawings of plant forms simplifying the shape to the essential.
Cut out paper shapes in the three basic forms and create
   patterns on paper, black on white and white on black.
Prints of plants. Ink plant material with a roller drawn in
   one direction. Print on to absorbent paper by rubbing.
   Use leaves, stems, tendrils, rootlets.
Imaginary flowers in cut paper.
Patterns with tissue paper. Overlap for colour changes.
Plaster sculpture. Cast plaster in a cardboard box. Use plaster
   tools, a 1″ wood-working chisel or straight bladed knife for
   carving. Smooth with glass-paper. If slabs are needed,
   cast in tins. Cut when set by drawing sharp point across
   and snapping. (Liquid paste joints.)

Flower Arrangements
Designs against a plain background. Silhouette them with a
   lamp.
A design using one type of form, then two, then three.
A design emphasising the form of a container.
Geometric, freeform, symmetrical and asymmetrical designs.
A cone.
A volumetric design.

POINT

Observe:
Berries, the crosscut of a tree, grapes, a mushroom, the base
   of a pine cone, a gourd, onion, orange, nut, narcissus, pansy,
   daisy, auricula, any round flowers.
Swiss cheese, a giraffe, spots, stars, a pudding bowl, a plate,
   a mirror, faces, butterfly markings, Christmas baubles,

shells, bulbs, a flock of birds, small pictures on a wall, knots in wood, a ball, a globe, raindrops, ripples on a pond, a peacock's feathers, a cabbage centre, a cauliflower, a beetle, Miro's paintings.

A point in a picture—cover and watch the effect.

Faces in a photograph of many people.

Collect:

Flowers and leaves which are points.

Advertisements using points.

Seedheads.

Round stones.

Plant material, cane, rushes, broom such as willow to loop into points.

Make:

A collage of points in plant material.

Cut out paper circles placed inside each other in a pattern.

Drawings of interlacing circles.

Patterns, using point and line as motifs in paper and with a felt-tip pen.

Cut out paper circles in black and white on grey in a pattern.

A pattern of white poster paint spots on black paper.

A collage of buttons and coins.

Flower Arrangements:

An arrangement of points. Try not turning flowers, then try turning them.

An arrangement in a goldfish bowl.

A design using a round container and a round base, then try a square base.

A design incorporating fabric with a pattern of spots.

A circular arrangement.

A design with circular motifs and a background decorated with a pattern to match.

LINE

Observe:

Branches of deciduous trees in winter, espaliered trees, forest tree trunks, trees at sunset.

176

Giacometti's sculpture.
Japanese line drawings.
Silhouettes.
Fencing of direct and indirect line, balustrades and banisters, long hedges.
Italian garden design, the horizon at night.
Church spires, telegraph poles, railway shunting yards, cranes at the docks.
Ivy and wisteria on walls.
Rock strata, stepping-stones.
Long feathers, long shadows.
Deer leaping.
Lines on the beach left by the tide.
Leaf skeletons.
The back of an achillea flower.

Collect:
Bare winter branches and prune.
Line materials—beads, string, knitting wool, a metal rod.
A list of line plant material from a nursery catalogue, book or magazine. Plant some in the garden.
Line plant material to suggest peace, growth, speed, anger, fatigue.
Pictures of lines—any materials.
A list of plant materials under the headings—straight, curved, twisted, angular.
Containers for line arrangements.

Make:
Drawings of expressive lines.
A collage on a board using string, different widths. Alternatively use pipe cleaners, spills, knitting wool, matches.
Take a line 'for a walk' with a felt-tip pen on paper. Fill in some spaces.
A pattern of line strokes with a pen or felt tip or brush.
A three dimensional design with strong copper wire bent with pliers.
A 'sculpture' of pieces of straw strung together on heavy wire or a mobile on light wire.
A pattern using drawing pins in a row on board.

Drawings of lines touching each other, then one of lines not
touching, and then of crossing lines.
Three dimensional designs with cane and thread combined,
to hang.
A design of wool or thread held in place with pins on a board.

Flower Arrangements:
Turn a line arrangement into a mass arrangement.
Use one type of leaf, one type of line plant material, one type
of flower to create a design.
Only straight line plant material.
Only curved line plant material.
Interpret wind, lightning, fire, speed, a whirlpool, a maze, in
line plant material.
A design using crossing lines.
A line design, first one of curved, then one of angular, then
one of straight lines.
A design following the movement of an accessory, e.g. a plate,
ornament, sculpture.
A design using cane.
Designs interpreting frugality, aspiration, rigidity, elegance
and playfulness.

10

Colour

Colour is a sensation evoked as a response to the stimulation of the eye and its attached nervous mechanisms by radiant energy of certain wavelengths and intensities. It is an infinitely variable phenomenon for it has no existence at all as an objective fact, which is difficult to realize. It is neither absolute nor constant and no surface actually possesses a colour entirely on its own, independent of lighting and surroundings. What we experience as colour is the effect upon a certain part of the brain when rays of light are transmitted through the optic lenses. These colours can be seen when white light is decomposed by passing it through a prism and it breaks into a number of clearly differing colours. The same effect is seen in a rainbow.

The colour rays fall on to objects which have the ability to absorb or reflect them. An object which reflects all the colours of the spectrum appears as white; one which absorbs them all appears black. Other objects appear yellow, green and so on according to the colour rays absorbed.

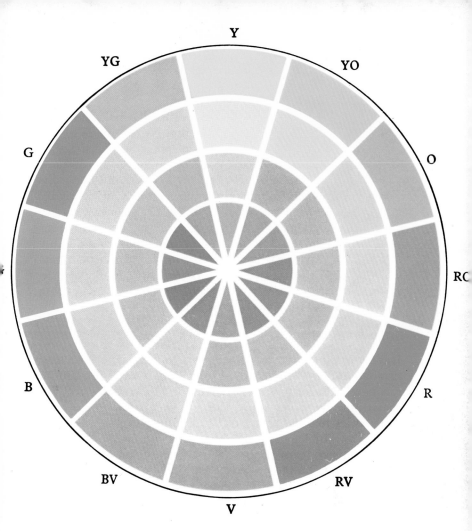

The circle is labelled, clockwise from top: Y, YO, O, RO, R, RV, V, BV, B, G, YG.

Above: A COLOUR CIRCLE
Key to colours: Y—yellow; YO—yellow-orange; O—orange; RO—red-orange R—red; RV—red-violet; V-violet; BV—blue-violet B—blue; BG—blue-green; G—green; YG—yellow-green.
Outer band—pure hues.
Band 2—tints, hues with white added.
Band 3—tones, hues with grey added.
Inner band—shades, hues with black added.

There are many tints, tones, and shades of hues but only one of each is shown on the above colour circle.
Opposite: 'A poem portrayed—Where the bee sucks . . .' A summer design using garden plant material including campanulas, lilies, peonies, poppies, rue, ferns and moss in tints.

COLOUR IN DESIGN AND FLOWER ARRANGEMENT

The study of colour is a wide and confusing field and it is wise for the flower arranger to distinguish the limits of her concern. For example, the mixing of paint and accuracy of colour matching are unnecessary except to increase awareness. The flower arranger works in prepared colour and her main concern is to select colours from those already in existence. Other considerations are the functioning of colour in a variety of different relationships such as with other colours in different lighting and in settings (because colour alters considerably in different situations), and the expressive quality of colour which is useful in interpretative designs as it has emotional and associative qualities. Even so, a basic knowledge of existing colour theory in all aspects is useful.

COLOUR SENSE

It is not possible to learn 'colour sense', but it can be developed through awareness. Even someone who is a natural colourist can have her colour sense strengthened by training and her visual judgement developed through experience.

Theories tend to be scientific and often highly academic. Colour terminology is inconsistent and confusing. All that is necessary is to learn enough of a theory to help the natural 'eye for colour' and to provide a working basis for understanding family relationships in colour. Enjoyment of colour is the most important aspect—if you enjoy it you will work well with it.

THE PIGMENT THEORY OF COLOUR

A universal basis for colour theory has not yet been agreed upon and physicists, psychologists, physiologists and artists have each adopted theories to suit their needs. The artist uses a pigment theory and this one has been adopted by flower arrangers as being the most workable for them.

THE DIMENSIONS OF COLOUR

The essential measurements of colour (or characteristics) are:

182

1. *Hue*

The quality which distinguishes one colour from another, e.g. red from orange.

2. *Value*

The quality of lightness or darkness, the modification shown in tints, shades and tones when black and white are added (in pigment) to hue.

Tints are hues with white added.

Shades are hues with black added.

Tones are hues with grey added and these can be light or dark according to the amounts of black and white added. In pigment tones can also be made from mixing colours together which lie opposite on the colour circle. These are the muted colours which are often so fascinating.

The term 'tone' is universally used for any colour deviating from a pure hue. The term 'tonal value' refers to any modification of a colour with regard to lightness and darkness.

'The Basket of Fruit' by Mark Gertler. Varying values give interest to this painting. The jug is the lightest value and the table the darkest.

3. Chroma

The quality of saturation of pure colour, the measurement of the colour content, its strength or weakness. Pure hues are of maximum saturation. Chroma is weakened by the presence of grey, black or white.

Spectrum colours as seen in the rainbow are clear, bright and unmodified but colour is not always this way and the modifications made by varying value and chroma, in addition to the hue, give an infinite number of colour variations, including clear tints, rich shades, subtle, greyed colours, strong and weak colours. As a result there is much confusion in nomenclature and difficulty in selection. Individuals tend to name a colour from its association, like 'salmon pink'. This is unreliable and does not mean the same to everyone although the language is decorative. It would technically be better to say 'a tint of red-orange with medium chroma'.

THE COLOUR CIRCLE

To show colour relationships and to encourage the eye to discriminate subtleties, colours are placed in a circle, although there is no scientific basis for this. Any number of colours may be used in the circle but for simplification twelve hues are often separated. The Colour Circle illustrated shows twelve hues with a tint a shade and a tone for each hue. Only one of each can be shown for practical reasons but there is of course an infinite range.

The colours must be logically graded, e.g. orange appears between yellow-orange and red-orange. It is easy to make a circle like this if three primary colours are placed equidistant. Most practising artists are agreed upon basing the circle on three primary colours, although other numbers may be used. The primary colours are red, blue and yellow, so called because they are 'first' colours in paint, and cannot be produced by mixing.

Opposite: 'Simplicity'. A design for early spring using neutralized colours. The plant material includes hellebores, pine cones, preserved fern and ivy with a tree root.

If the primaries are mixed in twos together, i.e., red + yellow = orange; yellow + blue = green; blue + red = violet, secondary colours result and are placed between the appropriate primaries. Tertiary colours are obtained by mixing the primary and secondary colours together, thus orange mixed with yellow gives yellow-orange and so on, giving six inter-mediate colours as shown. The three primaries, three secon-daries and six tertiaries make up the twelve segment circle, which can be used for reference to colour relationships. It is very helpful, at least once in a lifetime, to make a colour circle, as the actual painting of it is very revealing of the nature of colour. It will be found that whereas in theory the three primaries should produce all the other colours, different blues are needed for mixing green and violet.

NEUTRALS

Black, white and grey are neutral in colour effect. Theoreti-cally, they neither help nor hinder a colour scheme. In practice they often lose their neutrality as they are influenced by surrounding colours and can appear tinged with them and they can also intensify or subdue other colours. Neutrals are also called achromatic colours. The spectrum hues are chromatic colours including their derivatives by intermixture; (there is no black, white or grey in the rainbow). True neutrals are rarely found in nature, particularly plant material. If a collection of white flowers is made, it will be seen that there are many whites, as the cream-white of a rose, pink-white of prunus, and green-white of the arum. If these are held against white fabric they look anything but pure white and all are really very pale tints of a colour.

NEUTRALISED COLOUR

This is a useful term referring to colours with weak chroma, but not to neutrals. 'Beige' driftwood, for example, possesses a neutralised colour. There is only a tinge of colour present and this is not always definable as a hue. Because of this tinge neutralised colours have more character than neutrals and are easier to blend with other colours. Colours so neutralised are most useful for containers, bases, accessories and back-grounds as they offer no competition to the colours of

186

plant material which most flower arrangers agree should predominate in a design. A brightly coloured drape can quickly detract from the flowers which are the 'star performers' needing only support and not competition from the other players.

Basic colour schemes have names and are the combinations of colours which have been found pleasing to many people because of an obvious relationship existing between the colours.

There is, however, no absolute right or wrong in terms of colour harmony. If rules are hatched, some great colourist goes against the rules and explodes them. Flower arrangers should always feel free to experiment with different combinations and proportions in colour. Often the lighting, surroundings and amounts of each colour have more relevance to the total effect than the actual colours used.

The basic colour schemes are given for reference but students are advised to evolve their own schemes or relationships, appropriate for their purpose and satisfying to their own eyes.

BASIC COLOUR SCHEMES

Monochromatic
The use of tints, tones and shades of one colour. This can be a monotonous harmony as it has such close relationships in colour. Strong textural contrasts and extremes of value and chroma are helpful in giving interest, for example, pale pink, dark brown-red and a little brilliant red are more effective than three reds which are similar. This type of colour scheme, though often moving and beautiful in effect, is difficult in plant material which is rarely one-coloured.

Adjacent
The use of two, three or four colours lying next to each other on a twelve-colour circle (or one-third of the colour circle on any other). This is an easy and pleasing harmony as the colours are closely related but not monotonously similar, e.g. in an adjacent scheme of orange, red-orange and red all three

colours have a lot of red in them, a common blood, so to speak. It is not usual to use more than four hues as the 'family feeling' is not so apparent with colours lying further apart, for example, there is a trace of red in blue-violet but little obvious relationship—'a second cousin, twice removed'. It is not necessary for a primary colour in itself to be included in an adjacent colour scheme.

Complementary

The use of colours which lie opposite or approximately opposite each other on the colour circle. This is a satisfying scheme because each pair of complementaries gives a balance of cool and warm colours. It also provides the full primary colour complement.

    Red with green (mixed from yellow and blue)
    Yellow with violet (mixed from blue and red)
    Blue with orange (mixed from red and yellow).
Complementary colour schemes are not limited to primary and secondary colours. Every colour has its complement and when used together these colours always give maximum vividness to each other.

Triadic

The use of three colours equidistant on the circle. Childhood training leads one to think in terms of three primary colours at full spectrum value: 'daffodil' yellow, 'cornflower' blue, 'pillar-box' red, and the image is jarring. But a triad of a blue tint, a tone of yellow, and an accent of a dark tone of red is most unusual and satisfying.

Polychromatic

The use of many colours together. This multi-coloured scheme is difficult to blend well. It is helpful to use soft colours with little or no strong chroma or dark value, as a number of brilliant colours cancel each other's effect.

Opposite: 'The Rich Earth'. A design using a complementary colour scheme of reds and greens.

Nature is abundant with wonderful colour harmonies. They can be seen in plants, birds, animals, shells, jewels, rocks, skies, seasons, weather, mountains, woodland, moorland, and seashore. Inspiration can also be found in the work of artists who themselves have been inspired by nature—painters, weavers, embroiderers, stage, film and television designers. Inspiration comes unexpectedly as just before a storm, on a snowy day, on a misty morning, looking at oil in a puddle of rain. Although the theoretical knowledge of colour and basic colour schemes is a useful help in understanding its make-up, natural objects provide an endless supply of colour ideas and interest.

In following a natural colour scheme, allowance can be made for the ever-changing colouring of plant material. This is not always possible with schemes based strictly on the colour circle. A flower can change colour as it ages, a normally green leaf may develop an interesting streak of yellow, a red rose can become violet-red, stamens are yellow but can turn brown with age. All these, and many more variations give interest and vitality to flower arrangement and it is tragic to miss this beauty because of restrictive colour schemes.

COLOUR TEMPERATURE

Orange and red are warm colours, blue and green are cool. Violet and yellow appear warm or cool according to their surroundings. A warm colour appears hotter when placed against a cool colour, than it does if placed against other warm colours or a neutral, for example, orange against blue. This also applies to cool colours.

There is a cooler and a warmer version of every colour, for example, a red with a lot of blue in it is a cooler version of red than an orange-red.

WEIGHT QUALITY

Colours appear light or heavy according to their tonal value. Tints have less weight than shades. Pure hues in pigment vary in weight, violet being much heavier than yellow. In the spectrum all the colours are weightless. Colours of equal weight do not normally enhance each other in a design.

Some colours give the illusion of being relatively closer to the viewer. These colours are orange, red and yellow. Violet and blue recede and green is neutral in movement. This, however, is only a generalisation as it is dependent entirely on the chroma, value, area, texture and surrounding colours. Some blues and greens can be so brilliant that they do not recede.

If two identical flower arrangements could be made, one in orange and one in blue, the orange one would appear both nearer and bigger. This is useful knowledge in relation to the size of rooms. A large hall needs 'advancing' colours. Small rooms can be claustrophobic with advancing colours and receding colours are more effective. In abstract designs advancing and receding colour blocks are used deliberately to give energy to the design.

Movement also occurs when colours are seen against other colours, for example, if a blue square is placed on a white background and another on a black background, the blue on the white seems to contract and the blue on the black seems to expand. Conversely, yellow seen on white expands and on black contracts.

LUMINOSITY

This is the quality that makes some colours more visible than others in poor light. White and hues mixed with white have a high luminosity. For this reason white needs to be handled with care, as it tends to 'separate' from other colours and from a distance may stand out as 'blobs' in an arrangement. White is often better combined with tints. A white container tends to dominate an arrangement unless some white plant material is used to tie it in.

Generally speaking, yellow is the most luminous chromatic colour, followed by orange and yellow-green. Violet is the least luminous and will disappear in poor lighting. However, the *value* of the colour always alters the luminosity, any tint being more luminous because it has white in it. Dark rooms need arrangements with high luminosity.

COLOUR AREAS

Small areas of pure colour are more acceptable to most people than large areas because pure colour is more exciting to the eye and therefore more tiring. We are also accustomed to seeing smaller areas of brilliant colour compared with larger areas of duller colour in the world around us. For example, we see a few brilliantly coloured flowers in a garden against a background of duller greens and browns. The amount of colour to use in a design is a matter of trial, error and experience as no definite guide can be given with so many computations of colour and lighting.

LIGHTING

Lighting alters colours considerably. A green carpet may appear black at night and each wall of a room looks a different colour because of the varying light. Curtains with little light directly upon them often look much darker when hung in position.

Many colours disappear in candlelight which is so weak that only colours with high luminosity remain 'in orbit'. White fluorescent lighting is disastrous with reds which appear like muddy browns without variation, but blue is enhanced with this lighting. Reds, oranges and yellows are attractive in tungsten lighting but blue dulls and recedes. Blues and violets are at their best in good daylight.

When choosing colour for the home it should always be observed in the lighting in which it will be seen, and at all times of the day. Any painting with pigment should be done in good daylight for accuracy of colour.

Opposite: 'In the manner of a Flemish flower painting.' This design uses a polychromatic colour scheme.

In the small area occupied by most flower arrangements it can be helpful to keep to a colour 'key' which can be subtle or brilliant, delicate, rich, dark, strong and so on. Observe how many of the great painters tend to keep to a colour key like Constable's subtle earth colours, and Gauguin's strong colours.

REPETITION AND VARIETY

Harmony is often helped by colour repetition. Colours which seem to have little relationship with each other can be used together successfully if each is repeated so that a sense of continuity is given.

Variety in value and chroma can give a lively and more interesting colour scheme. For example, plain green holly with carnations in one red can be flat in appearance; the addition of yellow-green ivy or variegated holly gives the colour scheme more vitality.

THE EXPRESSIVENESS OF COLOUR

This is one of its most fascinating assets. It is capable of being dramatic, soothing, gay, restful, harsh, rich, brittle, voluptuous, frugal, gentle, depressing, poetic or fantastic. This is partly a matter of association on the part of the viewer as colours are often linked with seasons or moods, weather, events, people and so on. Colours also have personality which varies with the tonal value of the colour. Pink (a light value of red) seems feminine, bright red aggressive and dark red, rich. This ability of colour to give atmosphere is one of its loveliest and most fascinating qualities and of inestimable use in creating interpretative flower arrangements.

COLOUR JUXTAPOSITION

It is almost impossible to isolate colour from its surroundings as it changes when it is under the influence of other colours. Colour next to mid-grey is probably seen at its truest.

Each different environment causes a colour change which alters the effect and colours can either enhance each other or cancel each other out. It is the infinite variety provided by this continual change which gives colour its excitement and energy.

'. . . Colour, which vibrates just like music, is able to attain what is most general and yet most elusive in nature, namely, its inner force.'

Gauguin

Colour then has an ever-changing, moving, kaleidoscopic quality which is both frustrating and exciting.

What are the causes of this 'vibration'?

1. *Light and dark*

When placed together the dark appears even darker and the light lighter. There is a change in value. Strong contrasts of value give a sense of space and the two different colours tend to split apart. This applies to both achromatic and chromatic colours.

2. *Warm and cool*

Each makes the other look warmer or cooler. Surrounding blue makes orange look hotter than when it is next to warm colours, and vice versa.

3. *Vividness*

Vividness or brilliance is changed by relationship with other colours, which appear at maximum vividness against the complement of each. A colour also appears moderately bright against weaker chroma but dull against stronger chroma.

4. *Hues*

Hues actually change and appear quite different. For example, if orange is placed against mid-grey, it appears a normal orange, but placed against a still lighter orange it may look more red and against red it looks yellowish.

5. *Simultaneous contrast*

If you stare at a red square for some time and then close your eyes, a green square appears. The eye, tiring of red, seeks relief in its complement. This is called 'successive contrast'. The same kind of physiological reaction occurs when colours are placed next to each other—red appears tinged with green. This can be illustrated if grey squares are placed against red and on green. In each case the grey is tinged with the complement of the colour on which it is placed. This is simultaneous contrast and happens with all complementary colours

FLOWERS AND BACKGROUND COLOURS

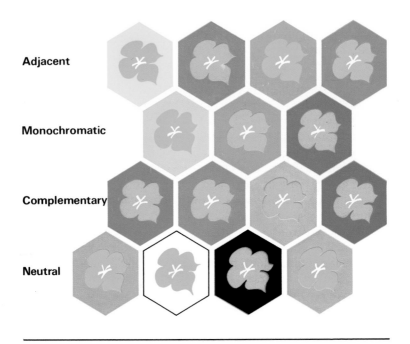

Adjacent

Monochromatic

Complementary

Neutral

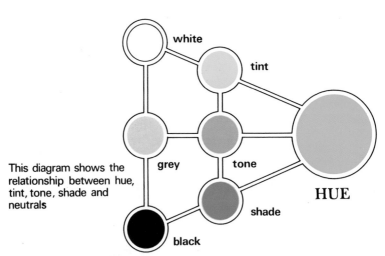

white

tint

This diagram shows the relationship between hue, tint, tone, shade and neutrals

grey   tone

HUE

shade

black

Opposite: 'The Simple Life.' The painted background gives the atmosphere of a summer day on a hill top.

although more strongly with red and green. An equal strength of two complementary colours will cause the eye to twitch uncomfortably and to fluctuate between the two.

6. *Colour areas*

Different amounts of the same colour will give quite different effects and two colours may not sit happily together unless the area of one is altered.

7. *Shape and texture*

Both these affect colour, for example, a point of red will appear more static than another shape in the same colour and a thick texture next to a delicate one will alter the colour effect.

Colours, then, can lie happily together, can vibrate next to each other, may blend imperceptibly or cancel each other out. Only general guidance can be given and it is necessary for everyone to experiment with the juxtaposition and sequence of colour, an enjoyable occupation in itself.

SUMMARY

Colour comes from white light.
The pigment theory of colour:
> The dimensions of colour are hue, value, chroma.
> The colour circle is used to explain colour relationship.
> Neutrals are black, white and grey.
> Neutralised colour has weak chroma.
> Colour schemes which are basic are monochromatic, adjacent, complementary, triadic, polychromatic.

Nature's colour schemes are inspiring.
Colour can appear warm or cool.
Colour appears light or heavy according to tonal value.
Some colours give the illusion of being closer to the viewer.
Luminosity is the quality that makes some colours more visible in poor light.
Small areas of pure colour are more acceptable to most people.
Lighting alters colours.
A colour key can be expressive.
Repetition helps harmony, variety gives interest.

The expressiveness of colour is useful for interpretative designs.

Colour changes according to its environment.

CREATIVE STUDY

Observe:

The number of 'whites' on a snowy day.

The impact of colour in advertisements and on hoardings.

Turner's paintings of light.

Tapestry colours.

The strength of Gauguin's colours.

Constable's use of subtle earth colours.

The use of polychromatic schemes in Flemish flower paintings.

The names of colours in fashion.

Stained glass windows.

Pebbles under water.

Rocks, shells, old bricks, flaking paint, crinkled foil, oil on water.

The colour of the garden at twilight.

Flowerbeds in parks.

Colours before a storm.

The blending of colours in tweeds, silks, soft furnishings.

The effect of candlelight, fluorescent, tungsten and daylight on colours.

The proportion of colour in flowers such as pansy, strelitzia, rose, hydrangea and foxglove.

Contrast in colouring of flower and foliage in one plant.

Colour schemes in rooms.

Paintings in any art gallery.

People in an arena.

A gang of workmen in overalls.

Experiment with a spotlight and acetate sheets to watch colour changes.

Nature's colour harmonies.

Collect:

Foliage in as many greens as possible.

Foliage in as many colours as possible.

All the names given to blues, and write them down, e.g. powder blue, navy blue. Then the names given to groups of other colours.

Words associated with each colour, e.g.
Yellow—spring, youth, sunshine, vitality.
Blue—tranquillity, depth, space.

Plant material with coloured stems.

Colour sensations on a walk.

A list of colours seen in a sunset, fire, jewel, shell, rock.

One colour in swatches of different fabrics, noting the textural effect.

A list of colours for each emotion, e.g. red for anger.

A tint, tone, shade of each colour in paper, fabric, plant material.

Shade cards for paint, artists' colours, wool, embroidery thread.

Make:

Paint a simple pattern with colours seen in natural forms, e.g. a cross-section of tomato, a rock, a flower. Do not try to reproduce the exact structure. Carefully match the colours and use the same proportions of colour. Paint quickly and do not labour.

Paint at random any colour then select the combinations that are the most satisfactory to you and paint another paper with them.

Set down colours that express emotions.

Paint as you listen to music, matching the colouring to the mood.

Paint the worst combination of colours you can imagine and then make it 'work' by changing values, areas, positions..

Choose paper of one colour. Place small amounts of paint on it to find the most pleasing complement, e.g. green paper—find the best red.

Opposite: 'Eternity.' A single rose with a branch expresses the title with the help of the setting.

Combine squares of fabric or paper and find the most pleasing combination.

Start with two pools of complementary colours, gradually mix, in different amounts, and at each mix paint squares to form a strip of graduated colour with the complementary colours at each end.

A background of one colour. Try different flowers against it.

A collage of coloured paper from magazines using the basic colour schemes.

Three blobs of paint (different colours) in the centre of a piece of paper. Fold over, press with the palm, open and observe the colour blending.

Paint colours on paper for lightness, gaiety, drama, weight, fire, cold, woodland. Do not make shapes but only fill the paper with suitable colours for the subject.

Paint strips of red, red-orange, violet-red in as many values of each as possible. Cut out and arrange together overlapping in different directions. Notice relationships and spatial qualities.

Paint two colours on a piece of paper next to each other in blocks, e.g. red and green. Work a little green into the red and a little red into the green.

Flower Arrangements:

To harmonise with fabric.

To harmonise with wallpaper and curtains for a room.

Analyse colours in a painting and produce in an arrangement.

Make any arrangement. Try different backgrounds, including black, white, grey and the complementary colour.

A design mixing cool and warm colours.

Make an arrangement inspired by the colours of any of these:

richness	delicacy	drama	anger
frugality	subtlety	fantasy	jealousy
gaiety	sadness	harshness	passion

Make an arrangement inspired by the colours of any of these:

dawn	storm	animal	seashore
sunset	heatwave	bird	desert
evening	mist	butterfly	woodland
night	rain	moth	moorland
dusk	snow	insect	mountain

twilight	rainbow	fish	jungle
sunlight			
candlelight	brick	fruit	shell
shadow	china	bark	coral
lamplight	wallpaper	leaf	jewel
moonlight	fabric	flower	metal
high noon	a painting	fungus	rock

A design with strong contrasts of light and shade.

Use colours to give movement in the design.

Use colour popular in certain periods of civilisation, e.g. Victorian, Regency, Egyptian, Phoenician, Aztec.

Use colour as seen in a Flemish flower painting.

Use colours favoured by certain peoples, e.g. Mexicans, Africans, gypsies, bullfighters.

11

Space

DEFINITION

Space is defined in the dictionary as 'extension in all directions'. Sometimes it is boundless as in outer space but usually it is limited and 'an interval between points or objects viewed as having one, two or three dimensions'. Space defines and enhances form; because of space we know objects which would not otherwise be recognisable, just as because of night we know day, because of sadness, joy. The one is unknown without the other. Anne Morrow Lindbergh wrote in *Gift from the Sea:*

'For it is only framed in space that beauty blooms. Only in space are events and objects and people unique and significant ... and therefore more beautiful. A tree has significance if one sees it against the empty face of the sky. A note of music gains significance from the silence on either side. A candle flowers in the space of night. Even small casual things take on significance if they are washed in space, like a few Autumn grasses in one corner of an Oriental painting, the rest of the page bare.'

Opposite: Lappet, Brussels. Eighteenth century. The forms of the flowers are clearly seen.

Embroidery, 1899. The flowers are clearly seen with surrounding space in this lovely piece of work.

IN DESIGN

Appreciation of space in design has long been present in the East, it is part of the way of life, originating with Buddhism, and related to a disregard of personal possessions and a regard for the virtue of giving away and not possessing. The Western world, on the other hand, has concentrated more on material objects and their prestige. Homes have been somewhat cluttered—think of the Victorian parlour—cities ill-planned, decoration ornate, but during this century the use of space has become a dominant characteristic of the arts of the Western world. This is probably caused by our crowded cities and shrinking countryside. Space has developed as a necessary feature of modern design. It can be seen in the large glass windows and walls of new buildings, the protection of green belts and national parks and the 'open' plan of some new homes. In front of the Rockefeller building in New York is a large open space of incalculable building value on the congested island of Manhattan. Despite its value this space has been preserved as a treasured area of trees and sky where people can gain tranquillity amidst the tall heavy buildings of the city.

In modern design, space is no longer just a gap, a void, a left-over part, a background or a nothingness. It is now an essential, considered part of life and environment, and many people have come to understand its necessity and its power. Space gives a great sense of order and tends to eliminate untidiness and clutter. It can also give grace and meaning to an object which would otherwise be unnoticed. For instance, a weed by the roadside when separated from other weeds and shown in space may become an object of art to be experienced and enjoyed.

IN FLOWER ARRANGEMENTS

All arts tend to show the same general trends as an expression of our inner needs and flower arrangement is no exception.

By tradition, designs in the West are glorious masses of flowers, solid in silhouette and using little space within the design. Although the flowers may not actually touch each other in a traditional arrangement, there is so little space between them that the general effect is of closely packed flowers, their shapes only revealed by a contrast of colour in neighbouring plant material and not by means of much space around each shape.

The interest in following known geometric shapes such as crescents and Hogarth curves brought some awareness of space into flower arrangement because the silhouette of the geometric form needs to be seen against space for clarity. However, both traditional and these massed geometric

'A tree has significance if one sees it against the empty face of the sky'
—*Anne Morrow Lindbergh.*

designs are solid, stressing the overall shape or silhouette and not the individual form of each flower. The arrangements are placed within a block of surrounding space but the space is not carried into the design itself.

In contrast, modern designs use space within the design revealing the distinctive beauty of each individual flower form, its shape surrounded by space. In modern design space is a quality, controlled and used as carefully as the solids of flowers and leaves.

WORKING WITH SPACE

Auguste Rodin described sculpture as 'the art of the hole and the lump'. To a certain extent this is also true of flower arrangement, which is related to painting in its use of colour

208

but more closely related to sculpture in its use of three dimensional form. Both are three dimensional in concept and are placed within three dimensional space, using space within the arrangement of solids.

SURROUNDING SPACE

The first consideration is the area for which the design is created. The boundaries of the space are normally the surrounding furniture, walls, windows, curtains. In a flower show it is the size of the niche or the space allotted to each exhibit. Unlimited space is often more difficult to work in than bounded space. Certain boundaries give a more manageable area in which to work and give an indication of suitable size for the design.

It is helpful to think of the specified space as a block or cube to be filled pleasingly. This does not mean that it should be completely filled. There needs to be a pleasing relationship between solids and space. The arranger's own judgement is a better guide than mathematical measurement or rules, as the proportions depend on the type of arrangement desired, its function and the style of the room.

The important considerations are that the flower arranger is working *within* a given space and that underfilling and overcrowding the space are both unattractive. Underfilling tends to make the arrangement look insignificant. Overcrowding makes it look large and ungainly.

Underfilling   Overcrowding

The amount of space within the design depends on the style of the arrangement but it is as important as the surrounding space. In traditional designs of massed flowers there should be a small amount around each form. When flowers are squashed together much of their value is lost as from a distance all shapes blur together and no beauty of form is seen. In modern designs stressing the beauty of individual flowers, leaves, branches and so on, space should be considered as one of the working qualities or elements of the design. The eye moves around the arrangement enjoying the relationship between space and solid and the clearly seen qualities of the individual plant material. There is vitality in designs using more space as the eye moves around more actively, whereas when little space and many solids are used, designs tend to become static. This is no fault. Sometimes quiet, static designs are needed, such as in church.

Good design greatly depends on the clever balancing of the elements of solid and space and both should be part of a well-planned whole. Some areas in a design require greater density of solid plant material so that emphasis is given. These are called variously, focal points, emphasis points, centres of interest. Forms are often given much greater emphasis by being seen against space.

ENCLOSED SPACE

This is a feature of modern design. An enclosed space can be as dominant as a solid area as it attracts and holds the eye (see chapter on form). It has strong 'eye-pull' and can be used for emphasis and to balance solids. It can be found naturally in driftwood or formed by plant material being bent, curved or twisted, such as cane. It can also be formed by the placement of several pieces of plant material.

Opposite: Top left: This traditional arrangement by Judy Pownall fits the space of the lighted alcove pleasingly. *Top right:* Space around each flower in a mass arrangement by Jean Taylor. *Bottom left:* Free-form design using enclosed space for balance. Arranged by Jean Taylor. *Bottom right:* Free-form design with enclosed spaces balancing the anthurium flowers, by George Smith.

211

This can be attractive as it 'lifts' the arrangement and gives it buoyancy. Some designs appear to be very heavy and to sink into the table on which they stand because of the visual weight at the bottom and next to the table. The value of many flowers can be lost. This can happen when the mechanics are difficult to hide or because the container is low and heavy in appearance. To gain valuable space below the plant material, and to give the design a sense of lightness, many designers use stemmed containers, legged or footed bases and pedestals. Another technique which originated in Japan is to keep the stems very close together in a column as they rise from the container, the flower heads, of greatest attraction, being placed high above the container. Low containers look effective arranged in this way especially with spring flowers such as iris and daffodils (see balance). This method of creating space between the container and the plant material is particularly useful when using a heavy container and visually light-weight plant material as it lessens and balances the visual weight of the container in comparison with the plant material.

SUMMARY

Space is the opposite of solid.
It can be bounded or limitless.
It defines and enhances form.
It can give a sense of order.
Traditional designs use little space within the design.
Modern arrangements use space as consciously as solids within the design.
Flower arrangement is similar to sculpture in its use of solid and space.

Opposite: Top left: 'Play on a Circle'—a decorative abstract design with enclosed spaces, by Jean Taylor. *Top right:* 'Curved Form' (Travalgan), Bronze, 1956, Barbara Hepworth.
Bottom left: 'Upright Form,' Rosa aurora marble, Henry Moore, 1966.
Bottom right: The visual weight of the bowl is balanced by lifting the plant material and using space below it. Arranged by Jean Taylor.

Space surrounding the design shows the silhouette clearly.
Flower arrangements are placed into a cube of space.
Underfilling or overcrowding a given space is unattractive.
Space used within the design can give activity.
Little space in a design makes it more static.
Enclosed space has greater eye-pull than open space.
Enclosed space can be a point.
Space below the arrangement of plant material gives lightness.

CREATIVE STUDY

Observe:

The work of architects in modern buildings to create a sense of space, and archways, bridges, piers.
The roofs of traditional cathedrals.
How the artist achieves a sense of space in two dimensions with colour and form.
Space-solid relationship in black and white photography.
Birds in flight.
A design silhouetted against a light to study the shapes of the spaces.
The handling of space by sculptors such as Henry Moore and Barbara Hepworth.
The volumetric space in some flowers.
The sensation of walking from a cave or passage into open air.
The amount of space used in Oriental paintings.
Magazine pictures of rooms and the effect of windows, doors, furnishings, colours.
Deciduous trees in winter, the spaces between the bare branches, their silhouettes.
The use of space in shop window displays.
The use of space in cities, parks, shopping precincts.

Collect:

Pictures of flower arrangements in settings to study the proportions of space and solid.
Postcards of sculpture which use space within the design.

Postcards of paintings featuring the sky.
Magazine cuttings of rooms, modern and traditional.
Advertisements using space well.
Plant material with which to enclose space, e.g. cane, broom.
Bare branches and prune.
Leafed branches and prune.

Make:
A mobile.
A pressed flower picture concentrating on space.
A plaque in the same way.
A design of wire.
Drawings of flower arrangements in a square, a rectangle, a circle, and oval of pleasing proportions.
Drawings of the *spaces* between a group of objects, or a single object such as a chair.

Flower Arrangements:
Using a pedestal: A stemmed container, a footed base, candle-stick, glass bottle.
A design in a given space or niche.
Think of space and not solids for once when arranging.
Using enclosed space.
A design using two solid points and then substitute two points of enclosed spaces.
Incorporate many accessories and then see how many can be removed.
A design within a picture frame.
Make a packed design and then remove plant material.
Make a line design then turn it into a mass.
A design for a large hall using large scale plant material.
A miniature.
An arrangement with regular spaces, e.g. fan-shaped.
Balance a visually heavy container with fine plant material.
Make an arrangement which 'frames' one flower, e.g. with driftwood, cane, foliage.
A design using illusionary space, i.e. a landscape to scale.
A 'water' arrangement.

PART 3

The Principles of Design

THE PRINCIPLES OF DESIGN

DEFINITION

A principle is a basic law, an essential or characteristic constituent, a basis for reasoning, a general law as a guide to action.

IN DESIGN

This term refers to the *ways* in which an artist, whatever his medium, uses his working qualities—those of texture, form, colour and space. They are laws of relationship giving a plan of organisation which determines the way in which the elements must be combined. The principles of design are a universal language common to all the different forms of creative expression that can be called 'the arts', they effect similar results in all art forms, both visual art and music, poetry, literature, ballet. They are both timeless and without personal, national or cultural barriers. This is because they are based on the laws of nature and have evolved from our knowledge of gravity, light, movement, growth and so on. They are the essence of design and creative work and are a sounder basis than many trivial man-made rules which change with time and fashion. Principles of design are not so much limitations but guides in creativity, giving more orderly concepts of aesthetic design. The general acceptance of these principles by artists throughout history has helped to create our great works of art as they establish the basis for universal criteria.

'To those who have and hold a sense of the significance of form what does it matter whether the forms that move them were created in Paris the day before yesterday or in Babylon fifty centuries ago?'

and

'What quality is shared by all objects that provoke our aesthetic emotions? What quality is common to Sta. Sophia and the windows at Chartres, Mexican sculpture, a Persian bowl, Chinese carpets, Giotto's frescoes at Padua and the masterpieces of Poussin, Piero della Francesca and Cezanne? Only one answer seems possible—significant form. In each, lines and colours combined in a particular way, certain forms and relations of forms stir our aesthetic emotions. These . . . I call significant form . . . the one quality common to all works of visual art.'

Clive Bell

If 'significant form' is universally appreciated, it is reasonable to assume that the design relationships or principles of design used in each work of art are similar. The human eye is basically the same everywhere and similar things are generally appreciated, making the design relationships or principles of design universal and constant, the essence of creative work. Whatever the medium, flowers, paint, or stone the same basic principles or methods of organisation when well-used have produced works of art. Although in the early days, principles of design were not put into words, many artists worked instinctively with them, and still do. Nowadays, the common qualities in great works of art have been recognised and fully discussed for several centuries by experts in aesthetics and the qualities determining a great work of art have been analysed and put into words. From these observations it is generally agreed that the principles of balance, rhythm, scale, proportion, dominance and contrast must be well used before a man-made object can be regarded as a work of art.

The images of design vary with each civilisation and style changes from generation to generation, nation to nation, culture to culture, but these basic principles of design are 'the rocks below the changing styles and fashions'—Dorothy Riester. When a completely new style of work emerges, they are the only basis upon which it can be assessed.

The final form may be different according to the artist, his medium, his technique, his own particular style and interests, but the same basic principles of organisation must be used. It is sometimes difficult to isolate one from another as they are all deeply interrelated but the presence of visual balance, a sense of scale, pleasing proportions, rhythmic movement, and a degree of contrast for interest are all necessary, or the creation is not appreciated.

When, as sometimes happens, these principles are solidified into laws or rules they become stifling. All the arts have at times used rules and they are certainly a quick method of producing certain limited results, but their basis is rarely understood by the student. This means that truly creative artists who need freedom to experiment have not the right atmosphere for their work. Besides, few rules are safe in the hands of true artists, and the principles of design are a much better basis for learning design than man-made rules of the moment.

At first, rules may seem easier but principles eventually become intuitive and to many artistic people they are instinctive. The artist is then free to concentrate on other aspects of design.

'By the intense study of examples in Nature, one can discover underlying principles which can be used to produce a new and unique work owing its unity to the artist's instinctive comprehension of the laws of Nature.'

Graham Sutherland

12

Balance

DEFINITION

A state of equipoise between weights, different elements or opposing forces; equilibrium; a state of stability; equal weight.

Life is unpleasant when our natural sense of balance is disturbed. Most people have a fair sense of balance and can also feel unbalance. Through observation and practice they become sensitive to fine adjustments.

There is seldom unbalance in the world around us and when there is, we feel uncomfortable, such as when looking at the Leaning Tower of Pisa, being tossed around on a rough sea or walking upstairs in a subsiding building. Few people can resist straightening a crooked picture on a wall because our normal sense of balance is based on a vertical line and a horizontal line set at right angles. When we walk up a hill our body adjusts to the slope. This sense of stability in the environment we live in is an in-born necessity and we cannot ourselves move comfortably around unless it is stable.

'The first quality that we demand in our sensations will be order without which our sensations will be troubled and perplexed and the other quality will be variety without which they will not be fully stimulated.'   *Roger Fry*

IN DESIGN

ACTUAL BALANCE

This simply means that an object stays up and does not fall over and this is not difficult when a certain amount of technical skill has been mastered.

VISUAL BALANCE

The *look* of stability is as necessary to viewers as actual stability. It is necessary for an object to *appear* balanced and not top-heavy, bottom-heavy or lop-sided. This is sometimes more difficult to see than actual balance, the lack of which soon reveals itself when the object falls over. What is it that attracts the eye to one part of a design more than to another to cause a sense of unbalance? Certain 'forces' must be more attracting than others and exert more 'eye-pull' to draw our eyes so strongly to one part of the design.

ALL THINGS BEING EQUAL:

1. Larger forms attract more quickly than smaller.
2. Shinier textures are more eye-catching (because of the light reflection) than duller.
3. Colours that have strong chroma, are warmer in colour or more luminous, have more emphasis than those with weaker chroma, cooler colour or a lack of luminosity.
4. A point has more drawing power than any other form.
5. Enclosed space attracts more than open space.
6. Compact forms have more force than airy forms.
7. An object further away from the central axis has more eye-pull than one near to it.

It is repeated that in each case all other qualities must be equal.

ACHIEVING BALANCE

If objects are assembled haphazardly around the centre of a design without regard to visual balance, the design is uncomfortable and the viewer's sense of equilibrium is disturbed. To achieve pleasing balance, objects must be assembled at either side of an imaginary vertical axis and horizontal axis in a design so that the eye is equally attracted to both sides.

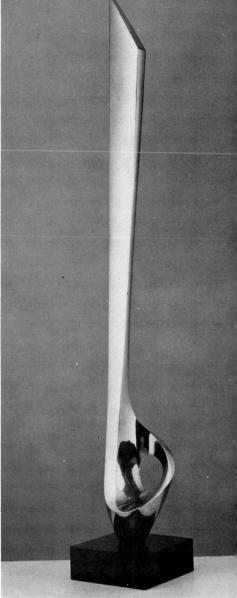

Left: The Leaning Tower of Pisa. The design could have been inspired by the ancient plant of equisetum (horsetail). The tower is not about to fall over, but lacks visual stability.
Right: 'Praze', Denis Mitchell, 1964, bronze. A beautifully balanced sculpture.

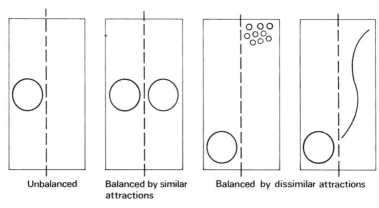

| Unbalanced | Balanced by similar attractions | Balanced by dissimilar attractions |

This does *not* mean that the objects should be exactly similar but it does mean that they should add up to having equal powers of attraction. They can be strikingly dissimilar but still have as much force or visual weight.

Two similar objects can be so monotonous that they cancel each other out and more vitality and interest can be obtained with dissimilar objects. Equilibrium is still reached but with the variety that Roger Fry suggests we need.

STATIC AND DYNAMIC BALANCE

Balance can be described as either static, that is without motion, quite still and in perfect equilibrium; or dynamic, that is active and moving (the eye is not held still) but still in balance. Similar objects either side of the vertical axis give static balance. Dissimilar objects move and interest the eye more and this active type of equilibrium is called 'dynamic balance'.

SYMMETRY

This term refers to reverse repetition on opposite sides of a centre or an axis. It can be seen in animals, insects, fish, flowers. Objects can be assembled within a symmetrical framework or outline and this helps the sense of balance more than an asymmetrical framework. Each outline either side of the vertical axis (and sometimes the horizontal axis) is the same and a mirror-image of the other. This gives a strong feeling of stability.

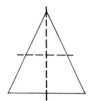

It is not necessary however for objects contained *within* the outline or framework to be similar either side of the axis. This gives a very static balance. Greater interest is achieved if they are not similar. There can be subtle rhythms of movement giving dynamic balance *within* the outside symmetrical outline.

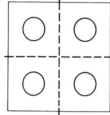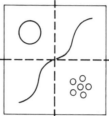

ASYMMETRY

Here the framework is dissimilar either side of the axis and in addition, the objects inside the framework are dissimilar. It is not as easy to achieve balance with an asymmetrical framework as with a symmetrical one.

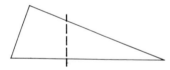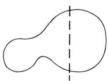

NO FRAMEWORK

Where there is no definite framework, that is when objects are assembled in open space, balance can be achieved with similar or dissimilar objects.

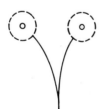

Above left: Bronze ritual vessel (Tsun). Chinese, Shang-Yin Dynasty (traditionally 1766-1122 BC). A symmetrical design in every way.
Above right: Shiva Nataraja. Bronze from S. India (Chola Dynasty) c. 10th century AD. A symmetrical framework containing an asymmetrical figure.
Below left: East Greek Amphora 550-525 BC. A running man. Found at Fikellura, Rhodes. A symmetrical amphora with an asymmetrical decoration.
Below right: 'Acrobats', Mark Gertler, 1917, bronze. Perfect balance without a symmetrical framework.

It is necessary only for the 'forces' to have equal attraction. Balance between dissimilar or uneven parts concerns all designing either within a symmetrical or asymmetrical framework or in open space.

IN FLOWER ARRANGEMENT

VISUAL WEIGHT

By comparison it is easy to see that larger and shinier plant material, warm, luminous and saturated colours, points, enclosed spaces, compact forms and those placed far from the central axis attract the eye more than their opposites. Look at:

1. A larger flower with one of similar variety but smaller.
2. A shiny camellia leaf and a beech leaf of the same size and colour.
3. A bright red zinnia and a dull green one of the same size, a white carnation and a dark red one, a pale beige leaf and a bright yellow-green one.
4. A leaf in a point shape and a leaf in an oval shape, for example a water-lily leaf and a laurel leaf.
5. A bare branch which has an enclosed space and one which has not.
6. A white chrysanthemum bloom and a white iris of the same size.
7. A flower with a long stem in a container and a similar flower in a similar container with a short stem and placed near the centre.

ACHIEVING BALANCE

In the past small flowers were always placed at the top and extremities of the arrangement and this is still suitable for traditional triangles and most geometric designs. But this 'rule' is not necessary for all work. In modern arrangements, balance is achieved if desired, with the largest flowers at the top of the design, deliberately placed to draw the eye to the top and give a different visual effect.

227

Left: An autumn pedestal by Mrs. Joyce Wright in St. Nicholas' Church, Great Yarmouth, in reds and greens. A symmetrical framework with variety of plant material and composition within; *Right:* Altar flowers at St. Michael and All Angels Church, Headingly. Symmetry of framework and of the plant material within it, well-suited to the dignified symmetrical surroundings. Arranged by George Smith.

There are no rules for assembling plant material and associated objects around the axis, other than following the simple and very general guides as to what constitutes greater visual weight. Each material exerts a different force in different circumstances. After building up a design the balance can be evaluated and adjustments made if necessary.

SYMMETRICAL SHAPE

The outline of a triangular, oval, circular, or fan-shaped design gives a symmetrical framework but within this, dissimilar plant material can be placed to give interest. One side of the arrangement does not need to be a mirror image of the other except in the outline shape. Interesting movements can be created within it.

ASYMMETRICAL SHAPE

An asymmetrical triangle, crescent, or Hogarth curve need not have the same plant material on either side of the vertical and horizontal axis, although the visual attraction must be the same.

MODERN DESIGNS

These do not depend on any definite framework which must be filled in. Balance is achieved through equal attractions either side of the axis without the help of an outline. It is better for the method of construction to be different to that used for arrangements with a solid outline. The following is suggested:

1. Choose a container and mechanics with plant material selected to suit the container in colour and size.
2. Select a variety of plant material so that there is some contrast in texture and form.
3. Place a piece of the plant material on one side of the container, off-centre. This unbalances the design, which started when the container was placed in position. To balance this first piece of plant material add another of a different type on the other side. The first placement will probably suggest the second.
4. The second piece of plant material may not be sufficient to balance the first and if the design still looks lop-sided, add further placements to the side with less 'eye-pull'. The plant material can be of the same variety or it can be a different variety, and it should be added until the sides look of even attraction of 'eye-pull'.
5. Unbalance the design again by once more placing something on one side, then balance it again. Continue balancing and unbalancing until there is enough plant material in the container or until you are at a loss to know where to put the next placement, not forgetting that space is an essential material!

At any time placements can be made in the centre, these do not affect the balance either side of the imaginary central

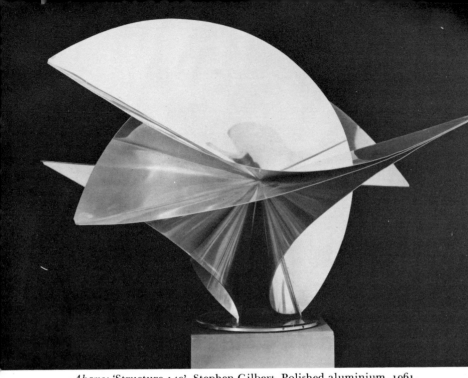

Above: 'Structure 14c', Stephen Gilbert. Polished aluminium, 1961. Cover the right side of the sculpture and see how it then appears to tip to the left. *Below:* Modern design of the Ichiyo School by Joan Lutwyche. There is tensional pull between the two outside daffodils which gives the feeling of balance. Cover one up and see the effect.

vertical axis although they may upset it either side of the horizontal axis as explained later.

CONTAINERS

The container is very important in the achievement of equilibrium. The visual force of each alters with form, size, colour, texture and the pattern on its surface. Containers which are similar in every way but one, can still differ in eye-pull. For example, a container of the same size, shape and colour will attract the eye more if it is shiny in texture than if it is dull. Brightly coloured and patterned containers will attract more than dull coloured or plain ones. The same general guides are applicable, as for plant material, in judging visual weight.

When plant material is small in scale for the container, equilibrium can be achieved by the use of greater height. Similarly, if the plant material is large in scale for the container, much less height is needed.

Containers add visual weight to the part of the design below the horizontal axis.

Material used at a greater height than normal but container is balanced and needs no base

Plant material visually heavy for the container needs less height. A base adds more visual weight to the container

BASES

So often a base is used unnecessarily. When the container seems too small for the plant and material, then a base adds needed visual weight to the part of the design below the horizontal axis. If the container seems big then a base should not be added.

ACCESSORIES

When one accessory (or more) is used in a design, confusion in balance often results. But an accessory is just one more object with visual weight and eye-pull, and should be assessed in the same way as all the other components. If it is placed in the design after the flower arrangement is complete and 'self-balanced' then it is very likely to make the design appear lop-sided.

It should take the place of plant material which would have been needed had the accessory not been used. For this reason it is easier to place the accessory in position *before* arranging the plant material as it is then taken into account while creating the arrangement. Otherwise it is likely to look like an afterthought.

ASSESSMENT OF BALANCE

The Vertical Axis
When the design is complete, assess it by holding a stick or pencil (forming a solid not imaginary axis) up and through the centre of the container, and looking to see if the eye is pulled equally to either side of it, or if there is a lop-sided appearance. The sides do *not* have to be measured for equal size and shape. It must be a visual judgement. There is no rule to employ because each piece of plant material is different in its force when placed in a different situation, that is with varying objects and relationships. It is necessary to feel and observe any unbalance, and then to achieve balance by moving plant material around until you are satisfied with the equilibrium.

Opposite: 'Ancient Treasure' by Mrs. Dorothy Woolley. The figurine is beautifully integrated into the design and would be missed if removed.

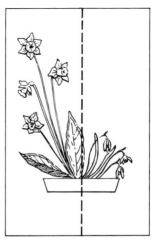

Lop-sided—too much visual
weight on the left

Bottom-heavy

Better visual balance

Top-heavy

Better visual balance

The Horizontal Axis

It is possible for the arrangement to appear bottom heavy or top-heavy as well as lop-sided. To test this, place a pencil or stick across the middle of the complete design. If the eye is attracted more to the bottom than the top then there is unbalance. Either a greater quantity of plant material, taller plant material or something more striking must be added to the design. Alternatively something can be removed from the bottom half of the design.

Top-heaviness is caused by too much eye-attracting material at the top of the design. In this case the container can be enlarged or a base added or some plant material can be removed or lowered.

No set rules can be given as each situation is different and colour, size, texture, form and position must all be taken into account. Judgement soon becomes second nature.

BALANCE BY PLACEMENT

Most plant material is arranged in a container with the centre of the container being taken as the position for the imaginary central vertical axis. In other words plant material is placed in such a way that the container remains in the centre point of the design.

This is not always necessary and it is interesting to place everything on one side of the container in a 'wind-swept

Balance by placement. Arranged by Jean Taylor.

effect'. The plant material seems unbalanced in relation to the container, but it can be balanced by the position in which it is placed on a table or in a niche. Taking the plant material and container as the complete design, judge the position of the centre of the design by holding a pencil (vertical axis) in such a way that the eye finds equal attractions either side of it. Place this centre and *not* the centre of the container to correspond with the centre of the table or niche. The design will then appear balanced by its position or placement.

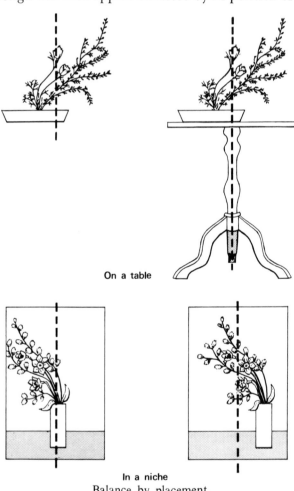

On a table

In a niche

Balance by placement.

Sometimes a quiet design with a sense of formality and repose is needed in flowers. Such arrangements are used in churches and cathedrals to give tranquillity and peace, and dynamic balance is not required. Triangular designs with rather static balance are more suitable. These quieter designs with less internal movement can also be more suitable for hospital arrangements where patients may not be able to take restless designs and brilliant colours.

There are other occasions when active arrangements with dynamic balance are needed for excitement and interest, occasions such as parties and receptions. Modern buildings often need this type of arrangement where the elements are distributed to create an equilibrium of visual forces in such a way that an active, stimulating result is achieved.

SUMMARY

Balance is a state of equipoise between opposing forces.

There is actual balance and visual balance.

Some objects exert more eye-pull than others.

Larger forms, shinier textures, colours that have strong chroma, are warmer or more luminous have more eye-pull than smaller forms, duller textures, colours that are weaker, cooler, less luminous.

Points have more eye-pull than other forms, enclosed space than open space, compact forms than airy forms.

Objects placed further from the central axis than objects placed close to it also attract more attention.

The above apply only when all other things are equal.

Balance is achieved in a design when objects of equal eye-pull are assembled either side of an imaginary vertical axis and an imaginary horizontal axis.

Similar objects achieve balance but can be monotonous.

More interest is achieved when dissimilar objects are used but with equal eye-pull.

Similar objects give static balance.

Dissimilar objects give a more dynamic balance.

A symmetrical framework can be used for a design.

This means outline either side of the vertical axis is the same. Objects within the framework can be dissimilar.

An asymmetrical framework means a different outline either side of the axis.

Objects within the framework can be dissimilar.

If no framework is used, balance can be achieved with similar or dissimilar objects with equal attraction.

Traditional flower arrangements use a framework which may be symmetrical or asymmetrical. Small flowers are placed at the extremities of the design.

Modern designs use flowers of any size anywhere as long as balance is achieved.

They can be built up by unbalancing and then balancing the container alternately until the design is complete.

Containers, bases and accessories have visual weight as well as the plant material and are part of the whole design.

The scale of plant material used, in relation to the container, affects its height in the design.

Bases should be used when more visual weight is needed at the bottom of the design.

Accessories are better incorporated into the design at the start.

Assessment of balance is made by creating vertical and horizontal axes and judging, not measuring, the relative eye-pull on either side.

Arrangements can be lop-sided, top heavy or bottom heavy.

Balance can be achieved by placement on a table or in a niche, if the centre of the container does not coincide with the centre of the design.

Static balance is suitable for some designs and dynamic balance for others.

CREATIVE STUDY

Observe:

Paintings, holding a pencil to create an axis and judge balance.

The balance of trees.

Windows on houses.

Sculpture and buildings.

238

Dominoes with equal numbers.

Several small children on one end of a see-saw and one child on the other (the one child needs to be bigger).

If a picture is altered by anyone if hung crookedly.

Collect:

Pictures of well and poorly balanced flower arrangements.

Postcards of paintings with interesting balance.

Make:

Vertical and horizontal lines with a pen across a newspaper picture of a flower arrangement and assess the balance.

A chart comparing visual weight of different forces e.g. warm and cool colour. Draw and paint or cut the objects from magazines.

A mobile.

Draw a rectangle with a line through the centre. Draw different articles each side but balance them.

Cut a piece of paper with 'windows' giving vertical and horizontal axes. Place over newspaper photographs of flower arrangements to assess balance.

Tie two sticks together at right angles for assessing balance.

Draw a leaf and then draw a similar leaf with a different direction. Draw many pairs of the same leaf and assess which has most tension.

Draw a leaf form and balance with a line.

Draw a leaf form and balance with a point.

Draw a leaf form and balance with a different shape.

Flower Arrangement:

An arrangement with an accessory.

A symmetrical design.

An asymmetrical design.

A modern design without a clear outline.

A top-heavy design and correct it.

A lop-sided design and correct it.

A design balanced by placement.

A design in a very shiny or highly patterned container.

A design called 'Poise'.

Interpret 'Acrobat', 'Tension', 'Fall'.

13
Rhythm

DEFINITION

A harmonious correlation of parts as a result of a series of accents and pauses, or motion and rest. It is movement marked by regular features, elements, phenomena, and has repetition so that there is unity and co-ordinated movement.

Rhythm is basic to existence and all nature moves to it. It is fundamental to organic growth. There are lapping waves, rolling clouds, waterfalls, waving cornfields, seagulls gliding on the wind, fish swimming, people walking or dancing. Less actively, rhythm is also seen in the branching of trees, the petal formation of flowers, strata in rocks, cobwebs, and sand dunes. Rhythm occurs in the seasons, tide changes, bird migration, the ebb and flow of sap, night and day, the life cycle of man and of plants. All these things have rhythm in that they have a recurring sequence of some kind although there are differences in their type of rhythm.

Nature shows that rhythm is the moving together of many small counter-movements into a large rhythmic pattern. Smaller rhythms run through the main one creating a rich interplay of movement and giving contrast and vitality. The tides ebb and flow but they are made up of large waves contributing to the overall movement, each wave again having many smaller waves contributing to its own larger rhythm.

Above left: Radiation, repetition and transition giving rhythm in a dahlia.
Above right: Parallel rhythm seen in lines left on the beach by the tide.

Below left: Rhythm, with more variety, seen in the strata of rocks.
Below right: Rhythm with variety in a spider's web.

Rhythm is also basic to art. To sustain interest and hold the eye of the viewer, a design must have motion and rest.

'Areas of heightened interest or tensional pull are necessary to the life of the design.'

Dorothy Riester

The rhythm is built up as the composition evolves. It cannot be added later. The designer adds accents to hold the eye and carry it through the design. There is a feeling of motion and then rest in a good design, the eye pausing at each accent or force and then moving on. If the force is too strong, such as a very dominant focal point, the rhythm is lost and the design is static. Good rhythm is an easy, deliberate movement around a design, either fast or slow. Poor rhythm is lack of movement or an aimless wandering movement. Some say rhythm is the binding quality of a design.

Creating rhythm in a design has no firm formula for it is a matter of individual feeling which some people have naturally more than others.

REPETITION

A sense of rhythmical pattern is essential to all forms of art and this stems from a certain amount of repetition. A straight line has no rhythm by itself but a number of straight lines can be rhythmically related.

A curved line has a certain sense of rhythm because of its repeated curves, but is even more rhythmic when it is combined with other lesser curves.

Lines and other forms, colours and textures need to be repeated so that the eyes find a link as they travel around the design. These echoes give a relationship between one part of the composition and another.

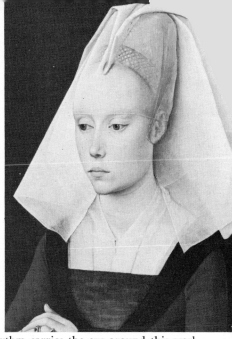

Above left: 'The Kiss', A. Rodin. Rhythm carries the eye around this work.
Above right: 'Portrait of a Lady', R. Van der Weyden. Early Netherlands School. The shape of the chin is repeated in the neck of the dress and in the shape of the hat, giving a sense of unity.
Below: 'Three Ladies adorning a Term of Hymen', Sir Joshua Reynolds, 1773. The garland of flowers gives rhythm.

ince your ambition prompts you to Excellency in the making of curious Knots & Flourishes, I here present you with a Method for the exact performing of those belonging to Text Capitals.

Above: Engraved plate showing the formation of the letter S from *Magnum in Parvo* or *The Pen's Perfection*, Edward Cocker, 1672.

Opposite: 'The Promising Future' by Jean Taylor. A sense of unity given by repetition of shape in the pink anthurium flowers, the green and white caladium leaf and the white stone.

An architect tries to unite windows into rhythmical groups. Poems, paintings, symphonies are built up from patterns of repeated shapes or sounds and this kind of repetition is rhythm. In any complete work of art individual units are grouped together rhythmically—sounds, shape or colour—and then the groups themselves are arranged in such a way that they form the rhythm of the whole work.

TRANSITION

Transition or gradation is a sequence in which the two extremes are bridged by a series of harmonious, but changing steps. It is seen in twilight between day and night, the waxing and waning moon, the ebbing and flowing tide, the seasons.

Transition gives a very easy gentle rhythm as it is regular and orderly change and it can be used in form, colour and space. In form, transitional shape acts as a stepping stone between a point and a line giving a sense of easy change and no sudden jumping. In colour, orange is between red and yellow (in pigment it is mixed from them) and its use with red and yellow gives a gentle, easy change and so a sense of rhythm.

245

Top: Radiation shown on a *Begonia rex* leaf with a gradual transition from thick to thin.
Bottom: King's College Chapel, Cambridge showing the fan-vaulting. Beautiful radiation created by craftsmen.

Gradual change in the size of spaces, from the density of solids to the openness of complete space also gives easy rhythm. Although transition is an easy, graded change, this is often not desired in a design and sometimes a stronger more exciting rhythm is needed with little or no transition.

LINES OF CONTINUANCE

Certain forces in the design attract the eye—they have energy or tensional pull—colours, forms, textures. The eye, as it is attracted from one to another, follows a path or 'line of continuance'. If these forces are equated through the design the eye moves rhythmically through it, not necessarily following direct, visible lines but moved by these stimuli through the design.

RADIATION

This means lines starting from one given point which can give a satisfying sense of order and is a way of arriving at rhythm. It is seen in many plants, snow crystals, and starfish and has often been used in art. The fan windows of the Renaissance and the interior roofs of cathedrals are famous examples. Radiation has been used so often that many regard it as a minor art principle although it is not a necessary characteristic of good design.

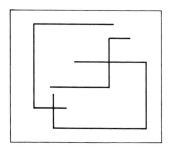

Repetition, little variation

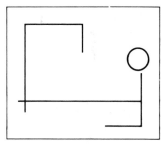

Variation but not enough repetition of the circle

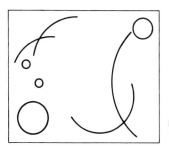

Repetition but with variation

VARIATION

This is also often called a minor design principle. It has been included as a minor form of contrast in that chapter. It contributes to rhythm as the minor movements in the sea contribute to the tides. It gives counter-movement which help to emphasise the main movement in a design.

TYPES OF RHYTHM

Generally speaking there are two types of rhythm:
1. Regular repeated rhythm which is stylised and recognisable. Sometimes it becomes monotonous as in the ticking of a clock.

2. Free variable rhythm, when the eye or ear is led through a composition but not evenly. This is a more subtle freely balanced rhythm.

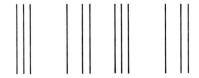

RHYTHM AS EXPRESSION

Though pleasing for its own sake, rhythm can also be used for a purpose, that is to express a feeling through its activity or motion. This can be gentle and peaceful or disturbing, even stabbing. Both suit their purpose and are pleasing for different reasons. For example, the lively rhythm of a Spanish dance or the strong beat of 'pop' tunes are sometimes needed, at other times the regular rhythm of Bach's music or the quiet tones of Sibelius.

Opposite: Free, variable rhythm. Arranged by Margaret Punshon.

Rhythm can be seen in the way a plant grows—in its 'habit' of growth. Some have curves, others straight, repeated lines; a piece of plant material may suggest to an arranger the type of rhythm to use.

REPETITION

In flower arrangement rhythm can be created by repetition of colour so that one colour is not seen in isolation unless for deliberate effect.

It is also rhythmic to repeat forms and include more than one point and transitional shape. This does not necessarily mean several varieties of flowers with the point shape. It might mean two points of the *same* variety, perhaps slightly different in size. One of a kind, especially point, often stops all eye movement.

There should also be repetition of lines so that the main line is supported by lesser ones to give easy movement.

Both direct and indirect lines give rhythm. With direct line, the eye follows visible paths of movement and with indirect line the rhythm comes from the eye being moved from one attracting force to another.

Repetition of any distinctive feature is always helpful. For example, if the plant material is curved, then a curved container and base give a repetition of the curve and a sense of rhythm. Straight plant material can similarly be used with an angular container and base. There are many examples of repetition in nature. The shape of a holly bush is repeated in its leaf. The outer shape of a daisy is repeated in the centre. *Macleaya* (*Bocconia*) and many other plants have repeats in their branching habits.

TRANSITION

Grading of sizes gives an easy rhythm to follow. This is

natural in plants and can be seen in a gladiolus stem, a holly-hock and in the thick trunks of trees which gradually, through the branches, taper to slender twigs.

Grading is a characteristic of traditional designs which use large flowers in the centre of the design. Gradually the sizes are reduced until the outer edges of the design have the smallest sizes and perhaps just slender, tapering tips. In traditional design also the spaces are graded from having no space at the centre—a density of solid plant material at the centre of interest—to a gradual increase of space until the space around the whole design is reached.

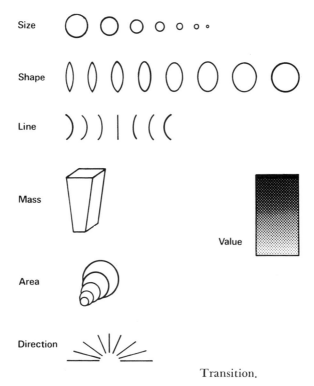

Transition.

LINES OF CONTINUANCE

Modern flower arrangements without necessarily a central point of interest, equate the eye attractions around and any-where in the design. This is particularly characteristic of abstract work. The eyes move between these forces and rhythm is achieved without necessarily using transition. This rhythm is often more staccato and exciting than the type used in traditional designs as the strong contrasts of motion and rest cause more abrupt eye movements.

SIMPLIFICATION

A flower arrangement containing a lot of plant material, many different varieties and many overlapping forms will have less rhythm than a simpler design.

Pruning lines gives clarity. The main movement is then obvious and the side lines, used to give variation, do not carry the eye away on another path.

Too much foliage and many small flower buds can give confusion and some of these also need removing.

Rhythm is sometimes helped by reducing the number of varieties of plant material. In modern designs it can be helpful to use only one type of plant material for lines and only one for points. This gives clarity and repetition. In a modern design using restraint in plant material, too many varieties stop easy eye movement as each new type of plant material is arrived at and examined; if there is only one of each type, there is no linking repetition to make the eye travel. Traditional designs can take more varieties because transition is used so much in size, colour and form.

RADIATION

This has so many examples in nature. Most flower petals and sepals radiate from a centre. Leaves like echeveria radiate in a rosette form, palm fans out from a tight centre, and yucca is an example of three dimensional radiation. The majority of plants arise from roots in a tightly packed mass and then radiate in different directions so that the plant receives maximum light, air, sunshine and moisture. A seed produces radiation in two directions—the roots and the stems.

In flower arrangement radiation can give poise and grace. Keeping the stems tightly together at the point where they are impaled on the pinholder, with the stems arching in different directions, gives great elegance. It is a particular characteristic of pedestal and traditional triangle arrangements. Ikebana designs show it beautifully when the stems arise tightly from the container and then radiate above it. It is a happy form of rhythm for flower arrangers, who have to keep the cut ends of plant material in water as it means that these stems can be centred in one place in water and the holding receptacle may be kept quite small.

Abstract designs tend to avoid radiation as being too traditional in appearance, but to avoid radiation in flower arrangement can be a problem, often only solved by using containers with more than one hole or dried plant material.

VARIATION

This has been discussed under contrast, as it contributes to this principle. It gives interest while also staying within the unity of the design.

A fan-shaped flower arrangement has strong repetitive rhythm but it tends to be monotonous. More interest is aroused when the lines are varied.

Repetition

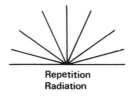

**Repetition
Radiation**

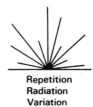

**Repetition
Radiation
Variation**

CURVED PLANT MATERIAL

Curvilinear plant material is often considered to have greater rhythm than straight probably because the curves are repeated. It certainly adds grace and elegance. Really strong curves give a very strong sense of movement and rhythm.

253

Repetition
Radiation
Variation

THE EXPRESSIVE QUALITY OF RHYTHM

In flower arrangement, as in art, rhythm should be used to express a feeling through its activity. In traditional triangular arrangements soft gentle rhythm gives a sense of tranquillity and elegance. Modern designs often use a more active, even sharp rhythm. Either is pleasing and should be suitable for the purpose. Either type needs variation and repetition to help the rhythm. Transition and radiation are used according to the style of the design.

SUMMARY

Rhythm is movement marked by regular features.

It is basic to all existence and there are many examples in nature.

It is also basic to art, as a design needs motion and rest.

Rhythm is built up as the composition evolves.

It can be fast or slow.

Repetition is necessary.

In design repetition relates to colour, form, space. It is less necessary in texture.

Transition is grading of size, form, colour and space to give gentle rhythm.

Lines of continuance are unseen lines, but a sense of rhythm develops from the eyes' movements from one stimulus to another.

Radiation is lines starting from one point giving a type of rhythm and there are many examples in nature and art.

Opposite: The cut palm leaves give a strong sense of repeated rhythm. The baubles give contrast. Radiation, repetition, transition and variation are all present. Arrangement by Sandra Rawcliffe.

Variation, a minor form of contrast, is needed to contribute
   to the many counter-movements of rhythm.
Rhythm can be regular, repeated. It can be freer and more
   variable.
Rhythm is a means of expression.
Flower arrangements need repetition of forms, and colour.
Transition in flower arrangement gives easy movement and
   is used in gentle traditional designs.
Lines of continuance give rhythm in modern designs, particu-
   larly abstract.
Simplification by pruning and reducing the number of varie-
   ties of plant material helps rhythm.
Radiation is useful to follow so that plant material can be
   in water in one container.
It is used in particular in traditional triangles, pedestals
   and Ikebana arrangements. It gives grace and elegance.
Abstract designs do not use radiation as often.
Curved plant material is more rhythmic than straight.

CREATIVE STUDY

Observe:
Waves, cornfields, clouds, smoke, flames, bubbles, waterfalls,
   a snowstorm, the sun's rays, a river running.
Seagulls, fish, deer leaping, elephants walking.
Cobwebs, rock strata, sand dunes.
People dancing, walking, running, jumping, rowing.
Flowers, plants, vine tendrils and stems.
Car driving.
Calder's mobiles.
Rembrandt's drawings.
The paintings of Miro, Jackson Pollock, Turner, Degas.
Palm leaves, fans, flower centres, veins on leaves.
Garments flowing in sculpture, on figures dancing.
Listen to different types of music, the wind, feet marching,
   train wheels, birds' wings beating in flight, clocks, machines,
   typing, other languages, people talking.
Railway lines at a junction, telegraph poles in a line.

Collect:
Flowers with radiating rhythm in petals, sepals.
Leaves with radiation either in form or veins.
A list of words associated with rhythm.
Pictures of rhythmic designs.

Make:
Simple drawings of lines for elegance, waves, wind, flames,
    flight, gaiety.
A pattern of threads or wool held by nails or pins on a board.
A pattern with one shape—black circles on white paper.
A pattern of curved lines.
With tracing paper, trace the main movement lines on a print
    of a picture, a picture of a flower arrangement. See if it
    is with direct lines or lines of continuance that the eye
    moves.
A pattern with many colours but one repeated throughout.
A pattern with lines starting from one point in pen or pencil.
A pattern with spills glued on coloured paper.
A spiral of cut paper.
A string design on paper.

Flower Arrangement:
A design interpreting wind, hurricane, tornado, tempest.
A design interpreting elegance, grace.
A static arrangement.
Interpreting rhythm, a dance, a piece of music, flight, fire,
    a wave, a march.
A spiral design.
A fan-shaped design.

14
Scale and Proportion

SCALE

DEFINITION

Scale concerns relative dimensions. It refers to size relationship. Good scale results when there is a pleasing relationship between the size of individual units in a design. Size is a relative term as a thing is only 'big' in relation to something else. A horse looks a normal size next to another horse, but next to a mouse will seem huge in comparison. Scale is an imaginary yardstick used to bring all elements into harmonious relationship.

IN DESIGN

Within the boundaries of a design all the component parts need to be within a certain range of size otherwise they appear incongruous.

The small point here seems 'out of scale' in this group but in another group it would seem 'in scale'.

If items of disparate sizes are used together, they can be brought into scale with each other by the addition of many intermediate sizes.

The intermediate sizes act as stepping stones or harmonisers. When disparate sizes are used together one will seem unduly dwarfed and the other appears magnified. By keeping everything related in scale each object appears its normal size.

Sometimes scale can be dramatised and disparate sizes used together for a special effect, but it is normal for sizes to be closely related.

IN FLOWER ARRANGEMENT

Good scaling is important for the flower arranger to understand as there are so many separate components in flower arrangement. The objects used can be widely differing and the designer must ensure they are related in scale. The size of these individual components which include the container, base, drape, accessory and each piece of plant material, needs to have a consistent relationship to look pleasing. For example, a slender grass and a large hydrangea are uncomfortable partners, being very different in size. It is possible that they could be used together if there were many other pieces of plant material in graded sizes between them, acting as stepping-stones. However, in some cases too many stepping-stones may be required for a good design to result, and the two extreme sizes cannot be happily linked.

In flower arrangement scale needs to be considered in relation to the size of the plant materials one to another, the accessory to the whole design, the container to the plant material, the base to the design, the design to its setting.

Plant Material

Nature usually scales the flower with its own leaf, although there are some exceptions. *Crambe cordifolia* has a tiny gypsophila-like flower and huge leaves, but the height of the stem and proportion of flowers helps to restore it to normality. With a little practice in observation, good scaling soon results and seems obvious.

Accessory

This is often too small for the design and appears as an afterthought instead of as part of the design. A good test is to remove the accessory and see if it is missed. An accessory that appears too large can be made to look smaller by pushing it back in the design.

Small accessories in relation to the design may be pulled forward or lifted up to give the illusion of being larger.

Container

The container usually falls over if it is too small for the plant material, or it can appear insignificant and lost. If the container is too big, it tends to attract the eye more quickly than the plant material, which should be dominant. No firm rules can be given as much depends on the colour, form and texture of the container.

Base

Here most mistakes occur. Bases tend to be too big for designs and to dominate them. It may be that the arranger is thinking in terms of a table top, but the base is an integral part of the whole design, and can easily overwhelm the container and plant material if it is too big in scale.

Setting

Scale becomes of great importance when decorating halls,

Opposite: Above: The flowers are not in scale with the container in either arrangement.
Below: The containers have been changed over and the flowers are now in scale with their container.

churches and cathedrals. A cathedral needs flower arrangements, almost bigger than can be created if they are to show up in the vast space. A small hospital locker needs a tiny arrangement in scale with the locker top. A dining table filled with big flowers to the exclusion of food shows a poor use of scale.

Landscape designs
Scale is important in a realistic landscape style in which nature is being exactly repeated and a scene copied. Every component should be scaled as the natural scale in life. For example, a tiny white china lamb is not in scale with a daffodil and appears unnatural, not only because it is man-made, but because in reality a lamb is very much bigger than a daffodil. Natural objects, such as pine cones, rocks, toadstools are easier to use in a landscape design as they are correctly scaled to other natural things, such as leaves and flowers.

If a twig is used to represent a tree in a design then a figure of a man should have the same scale relationship to the twig, as a real man to a real tree.

The necessity for such careful scaling only applies to designs which are meant to look exactly like natural scenes. A white china lamb could be used with a container and plant material if the design is to be more formal and not intended to be lifelike and realistic. In this case the size relationship concerns the size of the actual ornament to the size of the container and plant material.

Miniature arrangements
These are reproductions in effect of an artistic exhibit of larger size, the only difference being that they are smaller than normal. They need very small flowers in scale with the small container. The base should also be related in size, but often it is too big and dwarfs the arrangement. A good test is to photograph the design so that the actual size is not realized as surrounding objects are not seen. The design then appears as an average sized arrangement with every component in scale. Containers are often thimbles, doll's house vases, perfume bottles, or tiny lids. Tweezers and embroidery scissors make good tools and mechanics can be plastic foam or fine sand.

Above: Two miniature arrangements by Renée Mottershead. *Left:* A miniature 3½ inches high; *Right:* Dried plant materials arranged in an old brooch. *(Both by courtesy of H. Leadbetter.)*
Below left: 'A Primatial Pedestal' well suited to the size of The State Drawing Room, Bishopthorpe Palace, York—home of His Grace The Lord Archbishop of York, arranged by George Smith.
Below right: In Manchester Cathedral. A greater proportion of flowers used because no flowers are large enough for the huge setting. Arranged by the Nether Alderly Flower Club. (By courtesy of *Lancashire Life.*)

Above: Careful scaling can give an illusio
space in a design. Jean Taylor.
Left: 'Acrobat.' Disparate sizes used toge
for a special effect make the flower seem m
precariously balanced. Jean Taylor.
Below: 'Buttermere Lake with part of
Cromack Water, Cumberland, a shower',
J. M. W. Turner.
An illusion of space.

Pedestal arrangements

As miniature arrangements need smaller flowers, so pedestals with a larger container need larger flowers and foliage. Stuffing the container with many smaller flowers increases the proportions (or amounts) of flowers to the container but does not improve the scale.

Interpretative designs

Scale can be dramatised and sizes used which are not related, in order to induce special effects. For example, when interpreting 'captivity', a relatively small flower encircled with large thorny branches (a poor use of scale in the normal decorative arrangement) could be used in order to convey a feeling of the dominant captor, and the fragile captive. In this case the exaggeration is suitable.

Illusionary space

Artists working within the limits of two-dimensional canvas must create a sense of distance and of three dimensions, with forms and colours. A painter can give the impression of great distances—this is called illusionary space, and is achieved by careful attention to scale.

In three-dimensional designs, this illusionary space is less important, but it does have application when a special effect may be desired of greater size, space or distance, than actually exists. For example, if an impression of a lake is needed, groups of foliage can be arranged with larger ones in the front and receding groups which are very much smaller, towards the back of the container. This can give the impression of a large expanse of water, the feeling of a lake. An illusion of distance is created.

SUMMARY

Scale refers to the size relationship of individual units.
It is a relative term.
A small range of sizes is necessary in most designs.
Disparate sizes can be brought together with many 'stepping-stones'.

Using disparate sizes dwarfs one and magnifies the other and neither appears normal.

Scale can sometimes be dramatised for effect.

There are many components in flower arrangement so it is necessary to scale carefully.

In flower arrangement scale must be considered in relation to the container, accessory, each piece of plant material, the base and setting.

Landscape designs are naturalistic and need scaling which is accurate to nature.

Miniature designs need very accurate scaling with smaller plant materials.

Pedestals need accurate scaling with larger plant materials.

Interpretative designs can dramatise scaling for effect.

Illusionary space gives a sense of space greater than actually exists and uses careful scaling to achieve this.

CREATIVE STUDY

Observe:

The effect of a big tree in a small garden and a big tree in a big garden.

The size of a cup compared with a saucer, a pen with your hand, a spoon to your mouth, a chair to your body.

Compare a flower with a leaf of the same plant.

A small woman with a large hat and vice versa.

Bases in pictures of flower arrangements.

A child walking in her mother's shoes.

The size of a painting in a large stately home (and imagine it in your own).

A small painting on a large wall and a group of small paintings on a large wall.

Collect:

Pictures of rooms and study the size of the furniture.

Leaves and then group them in different sizes.

Do the same with flowers, fruit, seedheads.

A group of leaves and find the correct size of container for each one.

Example of poor scaling in pictures.

Make:

Cut out circles of black paper in different sizes, see how much contrast can comfortably be used in a design.

Cut out two black circles, one of 6″, the other of 1″, and see how many further circles are needed to draw the first two together in size.

Flower Arrangements:

A landscape, scaling the accessories to the natural scale.

Similarly, a water arrangement with water plant material.

An arrangement with small flowers and large leaves.

An arrangement with large flowers and small leaves.

A design using a natural looking figure and a twig for a tree.

An arrangement to a given size, e.g. 9″ in any dimension.

Interpret captivity, dare-devil, fear, dominance.

Interpret the atmosphere of a lake.

A miniature using small leaves and flowers.

A pedestal using large leaves and flowers.

A small arrangement with a large accessory.

A large arrangement with a small accessory.

PROPORTION

DEFINITION

The relation of one portion to another or the relation of one portion to the whole. It refers to quantity or amount, not to individual sizes which is scale. It implies the practice of using measurements and quantities in comparison with one another such as height and width or height, width and depth. In the visual arts it is a designed relationship and measurement.

Many people find it difficult to understand the difference between proportion and scale and they are closely allied. It is helpful to think of a plant—the size of a flower in relation to a leaf is a matter of scale but the area of the plant's flowers in relation to the area occupied by foliage is a matter of proportion. In a flower arrangement, each flower in relation to the container is scale, but the amount of plant material in relation to the container is proportion.

IN DESIGN

Proportion in design is largely a problem of adjustment and most people have an instinctive feeling about it, perhaps because there are so many examples of nature combining two units of one thing with three units of another or three with five, five with eight and so on. We therefore become accustomed to and enjoy such proportions or ratios.

Mathematicians have always been fascinated by finding a formula for perfect proportions—in other words pleasing to most people, although different cultures and ages have not always agreed on what is the most pleasing. A number of books have been written to demonstrate that these relationships can be obtained mathematically.

The Ancient Egyptians were the first to use proportions in art which were worked out by mathematics and this can be seen in their wall paintings. They discovered many interesting proportions including what is now known as The Golden Section. The pyramids, several of their huge statues and some tomb monuments were built using it as a basis.

Legend says that a Greek mathematician called Eudoxos who lived in 350 B.C. tried to find out why the golden section was so pleasing and conducted a simple 'poll' amongst his friends asking them to mark on a stick interesting points. To his amazement most of them agreed and it was at the golden section. He worked out a formula to express it and called it PHI after Phidias, an artist who used the golden proportion in his sculpture.

The following represents Eudoxos' stick:

The most pleasing position for C on the stick is found to be where

AC is to AB as CB is to AC

From this it can be calculated that if AB is 1,000 units long—AC is 618 units or about three-fifths of AB and AC and CB are in the ratio of three to two.

The golden section also applies to areas and volumes. The following is an area similarly divided:

268

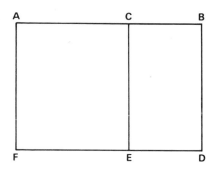

The most pleasing position for the line CE to divide the rectangle ABDF is found to be where

ACEF is to ABDF as CBDE is to ACEF. As before ACEF is about three-fifths of ABDF and ACEF and CBDE are in the ratio of three to two.

Pythagoras proved that the human body is based on this same proportion and the Greeks found that many good designs could be made based on it, as seen in some of their vases and paintings. However it was in architecture that it was used extensively and every part of the major buildings in Greece were constructed upon it, from the general shape down to the smallest detail of decoration.

Medieval builders of churches and cathedrals planned their designs in much the same way as the Greeks and their buildings were constructed on the golden proportion both inside and out. Not only did these designers think it was beautiful to look at but they believed it came from God, because so many things in nature are examples of it from the human body to many small plants. As a result they called it the 'mystic proportion' and Luca Paccioli, an Italian in the fifteenth century, wrote a book calling it 'the divine proportion'. Leonardo da Vinci worked out the human proportions in great detail just as Pythagoras had done.

Gustav Fechner (1801-1887), a psychologist, conducted experiments to find out the proportions pleasing to most people and tested them by asking for a choice of the most pleasing size from a number of envelopes and other groups of things. The results came remarkably close to the golden proportion.

269

Above: The Parthenon, Athens. *(Syndication International.)*
Below left: Pleasing proportions in the windows of a modern building.
Below right: A Passion flower. The proportions of 3 : 5 are seen at its centre.

So it seems that Nature, the Golden Section and people's polls all arrive at the same ratio for the most pleasing proportions.

Put simply, equal amounts lack interest and widely contrasting amounts are not satisfying, as one part seems to predominate too much over the other.

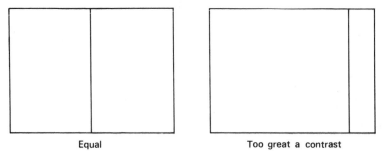

Equal   Too great a contrast

Proportion is not necessarily a cold mathematical thing. Mathematics gives intelligible order which does result in beauty but the designer's instinct and intuition in the development of pleasing proportions is most reliable.

IN FLOWER ARRANGEMENT

We certainly do not want to use rulers with plant material but as a general guide the proportions of 3 : 2 are safe. The larger proportion refers to the component that is to be dominant. In our generation the plant material is dominant, but in ancient Chinese and some Egyptian arrangements the container was dominant. Many Victorian arrangements used an equal proportion of container and plant material.

It is a mistake to use very definite measurements for the height of plant material in relation to the container in a flower arrangement, as people come to rely on measurement instead of using the eye to judge proportion—and so height. The height is dependent on so many variables including the colour, texture and form of the container and the plant material, the setting, and possibly in some designs, the interpretation. The judgement of the designer is the best guide and this develops with practice.

The above proportions are however a good basis for the construction of niches and spaces for exhibits at flower shows. It is also good for backgrounds. For example, if a background is 36″ high (3 × 12″), then a pleasing width is 24″ wide (2 × 12″). This has used the ratio of 3 : 2. This is aesthetically pleasing to most people and certainly more so than 24″ × 24″ (4 : 4) or 36″ × 12″ (6 : 2).

SUMMARY

Proportion relates to measurements or quantities in comparison with each other and the relation of one portion to another or to the whole.

Nature often combines things in a ratio of 2 : 3 or 3 : 5 or 5 : 8.

Proportion can be worked out by mathematics.

Ancient Egyptians first did this.

The Golden Section has been used often in architecture and other forms of art.

Greek buildings were based on it.

The Golden Section has been called the Mystic proportion and the Divine Proportion.

Experiments have proved it is pleasing to the majority of people.

Equal amounts lack interest.

Too much predominance is not satisfying.

Rulers and mathematics are not appropriate to flower arrangement.

The eye can usually be trusted to assess pleasing proportions.

Scale and proportion are closely allied but scale refers to individual units and proportion to amounts.

Proportion in flower arrangement is dependent on the colour, texture, form of the container and plant material, the setting and the interpretation.

The Golden proportion can be used for niches which are pleasing in size.

Opposite: Screen made by Fong Long Kon, 1690. Wood painted, lacquered and gilded. The container is dominant in this Chinese arrangement.
(The Metropolitan Museum of Art. Gift of J. Pierpoint Morgan, 1909).

CREATIVE STUDY

Observe:

Proportions of rooms found pleasing.

A gladiolus spike, how many flowers face each way.

A picture of the Parthenon.

The proportions of envelopes, pictures, frames, doors, windows, modern buildings, a book page, fields.

The proportions of the human body.

Medieval cathedrals. Ancient Greek buildings.

Landscape paintings—the amount of sky in relation to land, sea, the position of the horizon.

The discomfort of long narrow rooms or windows.

An artist's division of the canvas, the position of the centre of interest.

Leonardo da Vinci's analysis of the human figure.

Mondrian's paintings.

Collect:

Pictures of doors, windows.

Postcard prints of paintings with horizons and Renaissance paintings with good proportions.

Pictures of flower arrangements with good proportions.

Pictures of arrangements on dinner tables.

Make:

Mark on a stick a point pleasing to you.

Mark on a rectangle a division pleasing to you.

Draw a rectangle and divide it into smaller rectangles.

Colour the shapes to see if this alters the effect.

Draw a frame and put a simple drawing of a flower arrangement into it.

Draw a container, then draw plant material to give a pleasing proportion.

Make stripes of black and white paper and newsprint and arrange.

Cut out black and white rectangles and paste on grey paper in a pleasing design.

A background with pleasing proportion for use with flower arrangements.

Flower Arrangement:

A design in a given space or niche.

An arrangement in a heavy container of light plant material.

A tall narrow arrangement for a tall narrow space.

A square design for a square space.

An arrangement with the container dominant.

An arrangement against a background to a point half-way up, then to $\frac{3}{4}$ of the background, then to $\frac{2}{3}$ of it.

Try different heights of container against the same height.

Make arrangements expressing elegance, squatness, weightiness.

15

Dominance and Contrast

DEFINITION

Having command over something, possessing more importance or influence. By emphasising one part of a design it becomes dominant. Dominance also implies subordination as without a comparison, one part cannot have emphasis.

Dominance is closely allied to proportion in that equal proportions are not considered pleasing by most people.

IN DESIGN

Dominance provides a sense of order. Two equally important things compete with each other for attention and unity is destroyed. If two things are of unequal emphasis, then one is dominant. Cohesion is possible when interest is not divided and one thing is stressed.

Emphasis can be achieved by means of quantity, size, colour, density, form or position. Holding the viewer's attention in a design is essential but it is equally important to avoid monotony and therefore the attention must be released to something

Opposite: Head by A. Modigliani, c. 1914, Euville stone. A striking effect is given by the dominance of the vertical lines.

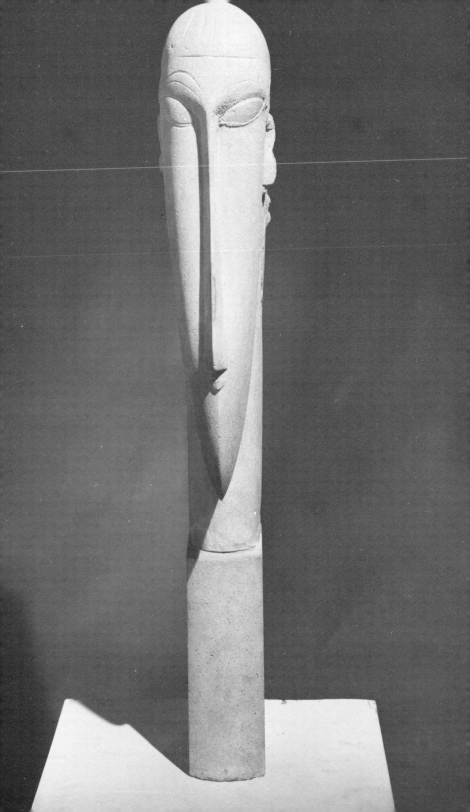

else to provide variety. This something else should have less impact. For example, a theatrical performance needs one or two star performers but the other actors in smaller parts are just as important. It is difficult to hold heightened interest continually. Relief and a little less concentration are necessary and as essential to a production as the stars (though not as dominant).

IN FLOWER ARRANGEMENT

Beautiful flowers always attract attention. It is easy for them to be the 'star performers' as they are examined and admired, but then interest wanes if there is nothing else to look at. The viewers' eyes need to wander over the container, base and foliage for a change, returning eventually to the beautiful and dominant flowers. Everything but the flowers in the design are in supporting, but very necessary roles.

Most flower arrangers are agreed that plant material in some form should be dominant over all other components in a design, but it is all too easy to let other things compete.

BASES, DRAPES AND ACCESSORIES

These should be subordinated. If brilliant colours, shiny textures and large areas of these are used, the plant material has a difficult job to appear dominant. This does not mean that shininess, brilliance and large size can never be used, but it does mean that the plant material must be particularly striking to predominate over these strong attractions. It is safer to use dull colours and textures and small areas for these 'small part players' who are there to provide variety and to enhance the plant material.

CONTAINERS

The application of this principle to containers is very dependent on the style and on the period, for example, in some abstract work the container is of equal importance to the plant material, being very much part of the complete design. In some periods, such as early Chinese or Egyptian, the container was considered to be the dominant element and

278

so arrangements in the manner of such periods should follow their style. In general the principles that apply to the choice of bases can also be applied when selecting containers.

PLANT MATERIAL

Within the plant material itself, emphasis can be achieved by various things. It may be large flowers, striking colouring, unusual texture or form, a larger quantity of one type of plant material, a concentration or density of one type or the position it holds in the design.

An arranger may arrange plant material because she has been struck by the beautiful colour or the shape and so on. This can be the key to selection of the dominant quality in the design. Often the initial inspiration becomes lost in a maze of other pieces of plant material, accessories and so on. For example, a piece of driftwood with an exciting shape—the initial inspiration—disappears under a mass of other plant material, such as foliage and there is no dominance.

Areas of heightened interest are necessary to design. In traditional designs such an area is called the focal point and a large flower is placed in this position for dominance. This area may also be called the centre of interest—implying more than one flower—perhaps a grouping of plant material for emphasis. Modern designs which do not always centralise emphasis also require areas of greater interest, usually in a well-placed 'point' as a single flower, a group of flowers or an enclosed space. Something is made dominant. In abstract, they have come to be called 'emphasis points' meaning areas of greater interest than the other parts of the design.

LACK OF DOMINANCE

This can be seen when there is—
1. Equal height and width in the design. This shows poor use of proportion. One dominant movement is better.
2. Equal height and attraction of design and accessory.
3. Equal weight of colour so that the attention is split between the two uncomfortably. A change of amount or value helps.
4. No centre of interest or points of emphasis.
5. The use of many plant materials of equal interest, such as the use of all points facing forward.

Half close the eyes and see which particular quality seems most important, which thing the eyes travel to when first looking at the design. If it vaguely wanders, then the design lacks any emphasis. If it goes to the base, drape or accessory, then the emphasis is mis-placed. Alternatively, to ask a new viewer what the design 'speaks' to them can be very revealing.

SUMMARY

Dominance is emphasis.

It also implies subordination.

It is closely allied to proportion.

It provides a sense of order and gives cohesion because it avoids equal attraction.

It avoids monotony.

Flower arrangers usually prefer plant material to predominate.

Accessories, drapes, bases should not predominate.

Brilliant colours, shiny textures, large areas in accessories, bases and drapes can easily make them predominate over plant material and should be used with care.

Containers usually are subordinated except in some period and abstract designs.

In plant material, emphasis can be achieved by size, quantity, type of form, colour, position in the arrangement, density.

The quality to emphasise in plant material is usually the one to which the arranger was first attracted.

Focal points, centres of interest, emphasis points are names for dominant areas in the design.

Lack of dominance is seen in equal height and width, equal attraction of accessory and design, equal weight of colour, equal interest in all plant material, no area of greater dominance.

CREATIVE STUDY

Observe:

In a flower show, the dominant quality in each arrangement.

Pictures of arrangements—check the dominant quality.

Paintings similarly.

The most dominant feature in a room and check the reason.

The outstanding player in a play—why?

A lawn without a feature.

The dominant idea in a discussion.

A double one domino.

A church spire, a skyscraper, windows, pictures of Greek buildings.

In music the dominant theme or instrument.

In a shop window, the dominant goods.

In a poster, or advertisement, the 'message'.

Collect:

Pictures of flower arrangements which show dominant qualities and those which show no dominance.

Postcards of paintings with a dominant quality.

A group of plant materials and choose the most dominant one.

A group of fabric swatches—choose the most dominant.

Look at the colour circle—does any colour dominate it?

A group of foliages, select the dominant one.

A group of objects and choose the most dominant one.

Make:

A pattern of different coloured squares. Which colour dominates?

A pattern of different black shapes on white. Which dominates and why?

Cut out several long strips of black paper all the same. Add one shape to dominate them.

Flower Arrangement:

Make the base dominant.

Make the accessory dominant.

Use enclosed space as the emphasis.

Make a design with dominant line plant material.

Use an interesting piece of driftwood.

Make an arrangement without a centre of interest and then add one.

Make a design of all line plant material, creating emphasis
also with the lines.
Interpret 'Power', 'Subservience'.

CONTRAST

DEFINITION

Opposition, conflict, unlikeness. To contrast means to observe
noticeable differences when placed side by side. To place or
arrange so as to set off or bring out differences. Diversity of
adjacent parts in colour, emotion, tone, and so on. A milder
form of contrast is variation.

'Life consists of things and the difference between things. By
contrast opposites are intensified and derive their meaning.
From the contrast or interval between things, is woven the
rhythm that is life. Contrasting long and short waves,
bombarding ears and eyes create sound and colour. Warm,
soft, rough, cold, hard, smooth: through fingertips' contrasting
sensations, life vibrates inward. Contrast, opposition, conflict
or variety is the dynamic essence of all existence—and of all
art forms that dramatise the life of man.'

Maitland Graves

Our environment is full of contrasts—one would be unknown
without the other, joy and sadness, night and day, hunger and
satisfaction, love and hate, heat and cold, summer and winter.
Nature is full of interesting contrasts in weather, scenery,
flora and fauna, all contributing to its unending fascination.
The principle of two contrasts is everywhere in life, strong
and weak, God and man, Heaven and earth, with usually
one predominant.

The Chinese believed that the harmonious balance of
opposites was the underlying principle of the universe and
a conformity to 'yang-yin' as it is called, runs through all
the Chinese arts. Yang is male, sturdy and strong and
included light, day, summer, sun, evergreens, trees, shrubs
and open flowers, while yin is female, dark, night, winter,
moon, grasses, tight buds, small flowers, overblown flowers!

'The Cholmondeley Sisters', British School c. 1600-10. At first sight the sisters appear identical, but on closer examination slight variations are seen which give greater interest.

Living in a country without seasons is very uninteresting for the warmth of summer seems more enjoyable after winter frosts and sunshine is a delightful contrast to rain. Contrast makes each of the opposites more intense and emphasises the differences between the two. It is closely related to dominance as contrasts which are equal in effect give disunity, and one should predominate.

IN DESIGN

Vitality is added when there is something that contradicts the main effect. If not a strong contradiction, at least a slight variation can add interest. The introduction of contrast or variation tends to emphasise the main effect. It also spices the composition and arouses excitement. A design lacking in contrast or variation is often monotonous and insipid.

In introducing contrast the designer must be careful that the principle of dominance is not forgotten and that the two contrasting things are not equal to each other. Dominance and contrast must be closely related, otherwise there is disunity. The clever use of contrast is within an overall unity. Something added for the sake of contrast alone may not be

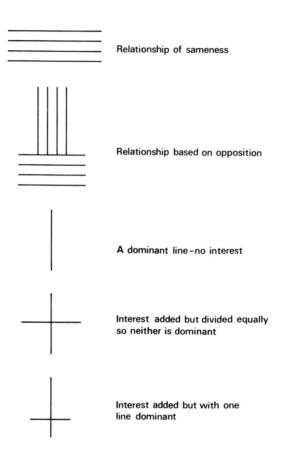

Relationship of sameness

Relationship based on opposition

A dominant line – no interest

Interest added but divided equally so neither is dominant

Interest added but with one line dominant

related to the rest of the design and may therefore cause dis-unity rather than the planned emphasis which is needed.

Horizontals and verticals working together in design are very satisfying—perhaps because together they symbolise perfect balance. That is, man standing vertically on horizontal ground by a gravitational pull, supported by a flat surface. There is contrast in the two opposite movements which is pleasing. In design it can be called the law of opposition. Confucius recognised this law when, after contemplating for a full day, he announced 'Trees grow upright!'

Right: 'The Golden Stairs', Edward
Burne-Jones, 1880. The girl leaning
down near the top of the stairs
gives a relief from the regularity
of the other figures.
Below: Head of the Buddha. Lime
composition from N.W. India 4th-
5th century. A symmetrical
design with a little variation
given by the tilt of the head.

DIRECTION

The necessity to have the stems of most living plant material in water makes it difficult to create opposing vertical and horizontal movement but the required contrast can be supplied by the rim of the container or by the base. In dried designs it can be provided by stems placed at right angles to each other.

TEXTURE

Contrast in texture is particularly effective and strong contrasts can be used because texture is not a dominant quality. Rough enhances smooth and each emphasises the quality of the other.

COLOUR

Variation is probably more often used than strong contrast and is always important in the use of colour. A design of one or two colours is flat and uninteresting. Vitality is added when one or both colours have variations. Contrast in value, temperature, complementary colours and areas is referred to in the chapter on colour.

FORM

A design can be made of only one form, but if this is of points, it is usually necessary to turn some of them to give variety. Designs of all line plant material may need the lines placed in such a way that spaces are enclosed to give contrast. Satisfying designs usually include points *and* lines which are a complete contrast to each other. One or the other is usually dominant. Often transitional shapes soften the strong, sharp contrast of points and lines.

STYLE

Traditional designs use variation rather than contrast, but modern designs with less plant material depend on strong contrasts for interest and to emphasise individual qualities in the plant material. The whole vitality of abstract designs depends on contrast and extremes are used for impact. This

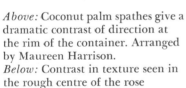

Above: Contrast of direction
seen in an anthurium flower.
Below: Contrast in texture
seen in the rough outside
and shiny inside of a shell.

Above: Coconut palm spathes give a
dramatic contrast of direction at
the rim of the container. Arranged
by Maureen Harrison.
Below: Contrast in texture seen in
the rough centre of the rose
compared with the smooth petals.

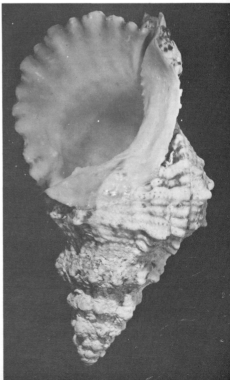

Contrast in the delicacy of the flower in comparison to the strength and bulk of driftwood and the stoneware container. Arranged by Jean Taylor.

may be why many abstract designs are disturbing as there can be a strong dose of excitement, whereas traditional designs are much more restful with just a little use of variation and no strong contrast.

SUMMARY

Contrast is opposition.
It emphasises differences.
A milder form of it is variation.
Our environment shows many contrasts.
Contrast adds vitality to a design, variation adds interest.
Designs lacking contrast or variation are monotonous.
The principle of dominance must be remembered to avoid disunity.
Contrast must be related to the remainder of the design.

In flower arrangement contrast of direction can be provided by base and container, and in dried designs by stems used at right angles.

Contrast in texture can be strong.

Contrast in colour may be used but variation is nearly always needed.

A design can be of one form. A change of form can give contrast or variation.

Traditional designs use variation rather than contrast.

Modern designs use stronger contrast than traditional ones.

CREATIVE STUDY

Observe:

Patterned curtains against plain walls and against patterned walls.

Male and female ducks.

A harbour with the masts of sailing boats.

A maple tree with horizontal branches and hanging seeds.

The angle of rose foliage to the stem.

Horizontal lines on modern buildings.

Trees on the horizon.

The many contrasts in one plant of shape, colour, texture.

A fence with cross posts.

Contrasts of form in paintings.

Contrast of vertical and horizontal lines in paintings.

Contrast of space and solid in sculpture.

Telegraph poles, lamp standards, bridge standards.

Nature's many contrasts in seasons, weather, times of day, scenery, emotions, behaviour and so on.

Collect:

A list of contrasting words, such as hot and cold.

Rough and smooth leaves.

Contrasting fabrics.

Simple leaves and fussy flowers.

A list of plants which have contrasts of form, texture, colour in a single plant.

A list of contrasts in nature.

Make:

A design in black paper on white in points and lines.

Then add transitional shapes to the points and lines.

A design of squares and circles using cut newspaper or black paper.

Draw a pattern of horizontal and vertical lines.

Flower Arrangement:

Designs interpreting 'Night and Day', 'Summer and Winter', 'Youth and Age', 'Dark and Light', 'Hot and Cold', 'Beauty and the Beast', 'Rough and Smooth'.

A foliage arrangement with strong contrast in colour, texture and form.

An arrangement using all line plant material.

An arrangement using all points.

A design of curved *and* straight lines.

16

Harmony

DEFINITION

In one word it is 'agreement'. It is said to be concord between the parts of a design or composition giving unity of effect and an aesthetically pleasing whole. Alvin Redman defines it as 'The arrangement of parts in pleasing relation to each other'. It has also been described as a work in which various components are brought together in such a way as to display their essential unity and agreement. It can be described simply as 'ordered relationship'.

Harmony is sometimes regarded as a design principle. Alternatively it can be regarded as the final achievement when the principles of design are used well.

There are innumerable examples in Nature of harmony but not as many in the environment man has made for himself. For instance there is little harmony in the centres of many big cities with a hodge-podge of buildings, hoardings of advertisements fighting each other for attention, traffic and people herded together, signs and lights of all descriptions. On the other hand where town planners have made a superb effort there are cities with pleasing, well-designed centres showing harmony and good taste.

Our National Parks are wonderful places for sensing great harmony. For example, the Borrowdale Valley has a misty

Ullswater from Glencoyne Park, looking north-eastwards. *(By courtesy of Geoffrey Berry.)*

lake, rocky falls, gushing streams and tumbling waterfalls, the soft tracery of ferns growing below the tall trees, a grey-blue sky. Each so different and to be separately enjoyed and yet these separate identities merge into an overall design of blended colours, textures and forms, just as the sounds and silences of music contribute to one total effect.

A rose has silky texture, beautiful form and colour, dainty leaves and a sturdy stem, all combined to make a thing of beauty—even the thorns contributing a contrast to the delicacy of the flowers and enhancing them. A tree has many parts—bark, leaves, roots, branches, trunk—all of individual beauty but normally seen as a harmonious whole.

IN DESIGN

It is easier to enjoy, feel and recognise harmony and to understand its meaning than to create it in a design.

292

A good design is one that is pleasing to the eye in its unity and when no part of it is unrelated to the other parts or to the whole, unless for the purpose of relationship, as in contrast.

Michael Benz says that 'design *is* the harmonious arrangement and balance of all principles and elements for the development of the single idea or theme'. It can certainly be said that it is interdependent with composition.

'Any general theory of art must begin with the supposition that man responds to the shape, colour, surface and mass of things and that certain arrangements of these will give him pleasure while others will cause revulsion. Certain shapes and colours will trigger off a series of deep and often uncomprehending emotions, others will leave him quite unmoved. Art could, therefore, be simply defined as an attempt to create pleasing or stimulating form; such forms satisfy our sense of beauty when we are able to appreciate a unity or harmony of formal relations.'

Bernat Klein in 'EYE FOR COLOUR'

Four random notes are not music but four notes with rhythm and pitch can turn into a song. Four apples in each corner of a page can never make a pleasing design as they are separate units. On a plate near the centre, they are a whole. The difference is the arrangement or way in which they have been composed.

'We hear music by virtue of the relationships in sounds between different notes and their relationships in time. We see art, which includes design, by virtue of the relationships in appearance between the different visible features of a thing, its formal elements and by virtue of their relationships in space. The point I wish to make is that design—the music of design—depends on the relationships between distinguishable and separable features of things which are to a certain extent analogous with the elements of music, its notes and chords.'

David Pye in 'THE NATURE AND ART OF WORKMANSHIP'

He also gives the example of a rubbish heap which contains forms, lines, textures and colour but since there is no ordered relationship in it there is no quality of art about it. Art is a result of arranging all these things in such a manner that they have a relationship one with another and to the whole.

Harmony lies between the two extremes of monotony and discord, one of which is boring and the other too violent. The design can be nearer one extreme or the other according to its style.

IN FLOWER ARRANGEMENT

'When a container is incorporated into the design as is usually the case, the arrangement may be likened to a symphony in which the flowers are the musicians, the container the conductor and the arranger the composer. All are individual artists in their own right but perform together to produce a work of surpassing merit. The work will stand or fall according to the quality and harmony of its component parts.'

Norman Sparnon

How then to achieve harmony in a flower arrangement which can be said to present more difficulties than any other art because the materials are changed so little by our own hands? For example, in painting a correction can be made with paint and brush whereas in flower arrangement replacement of a component may be involved. Selecting and assembling the component materials form the basis of flower arrangement and the right components are not always readily available such as a certain type of base or container or a desired colour in a flower. It presents a tremendous challenge to make a harmonious design when the perfect component is not available, but this is part of the excitement of flower arrangement, the never-ending collection of things that might 'come in' and be the missing part of the jigsaw puzzle, so that each component is related to the others.

ACHIEVING HARMONY

There are no rules because each situation is unique and must be solved by the designer herself but there are helpful guides:

1. *Relationship*
(a) Watch for relationships in appearance. There are often similarities between materials. It may be colour, it could be that the texture of a leaf is similar to the texture of a container, that an accessory has the same curve as the stem of a flower. The resemblance need not be exactly similar but a link however small helps harmony, and the different parts of a design are related through these 'echoes'.
(b) Look for relationships of association or of habitat between components, all of which could come from the countryside or seaside; they could be associated with a foreign country or a hot climate or they might all be greenhouse grown, of similar idea or from the same period in history.

2. *Simplicity*

'Simplicity is not an end in art, but one arrives at simplicity in spite of oneself in approaching the real sense of things.'
Constantin Brancusi

It is easier to integrate fewer materials in a design. Too many components muddle it. It can be compared with a sauce with many ingredients which can become so complicated and offer so many sensations that no clear flavour is received.

A good design is one to which no more can be added and at the same time, one from which nothing can be subtracted without causing an emptiness or feeling of incompletion.

3. *The Design Principles*
If these are well used there should be harmony. If something seems wrong assess that the balance is correct, contrast present, that there is a correct scale relationship, pleasing proportions and rhythm so that the eye may travel easily around the design. A centre of interest or emphasis points in a design (used for the principle of dominance), unify a design remarkably.

4. *The Style*
The style of each component should be similar. For example, a period arrangement is not in harmony with a modern black glass base, or an ancient Chinese base with a landscape design. The arrangement, container, base, accessory should be of the same style and also of the same age or period in time.

5. *Integrating Components*

Each component needs to be integrated into the contours of the design and not set apart. This does not mean it touches anything else but is so much part of the design that it is missed if removed.

Containers can easily split the design into two parts and colour is often at fault. A white container can, for instance, stand out alone if there is no white or very light tint in the design. Black containers harmonise better with flowers having black centres or dark values. Whenever a strongly coloured container is used a repetition of the colour in the plant material gives a link and harmony. The earth-coloured containers in browns, greys, greens are the easiest to integrate in colour with the plant material.

Bases can be difficult because of association. It is not always possible to find the right style of base for the rest of the design. Slate, stone or unpolished wood are suitable for a landscape but not a velvet-covered base. Many period arrangements should not have bases, to be in the true manner of the period, although the Chinese used them with nearly every container in their very early days of flower arrangement.

A lack of harmony results when bases vie with the plant material in colour instead of providing a background.

Accessories are more difficult than any other component to integrate. They often seem totally unrelated to the remainder of the design, but it is a mistake to think of them as separate objects. Unfortunately, they can be inharmonious in so many ways—style, association, habitat, size, shape, and colour. It is better to omit an accessory if it is not correct in every way, as nothing can destroy harmony more quickly. Integrating more than one accessory can be difficult and it is wise to group them as part of the design.

Drapes should often be omitted. They are a whim of fashion at present and are totally unsuitable for some designs—for example a landscape design. A woodland is never seen with a drape hanging up behind a tree! They can be very

Opposite: Arum lilies in differing stages of development and The Madonna of the Flowers, arranged in perfect harmony by Gregory Conway. *(By courtesy of Random House Inc.)*

elegant with traditional designs, when well draped and harmonious in colour, texture and fabric. The fabric should be suitable for the style and period of the flower arrangement.

In modern work a painted background can be effective as there are no muddled spaces and a cleaner appearance is given. A repeat of the main 'motif' can be echoed or the design continued on to the background.

Plant Material is the easiest component to handle. There is a natural affinity between most plant materials and as long as the design principles are followed there are few problems. It is the man-made components that need more care in integration.

6. *Repetition*
Repetition is one of the easiest ways of achieving harmony. It is important with regard to rhythm but repetition in all the components, of colours, forms and textures, is always unifying.

7. *Setting*
Setting should be considered before the design is composed. This does not often apply to a niche or space at a show but it does apply at home and for exhibition work in large country houses and for churches, hospitals, schools and so on. The design should belong to its setting in every way in colour, style, period, size, and formality.

'The artist is born to pick and choose and group with science, these elements, that the result may be beautiful—as the musician gathers his notes and forms, his chords, until he bring forth from chaos, glorious harmony.'

James A. McNeill Whistler

SUMMARY

Harmony is ordered relationship to give agreement.
It is the final achievement when everything works well together.
All components need to be related by the designer.
Some relationship in appearance between each component is helpful.

Relationships of association, habitat, environment can be used as a link.

The design principles should be well used.

The style should be similar throughout the design.

The components should be integrated and be missed if removed from the design.

The container's colour is of importance.

Care should be taken of the associative aspect of bases.

Accessories are the most difficult to integrate as so many factors can be out of harmony.

Drapes are not suitable for all designs and may easily dominate the design.

Plant materials associate easily with each other.

The setting must be considered as the design should harmonise with it.

CREATIVE STUDY

Observe:

A rose, a tree, a beautiful landscape—analyse the parts and then enjoy the whole.

The cast of a production in the settings made for it.

The planning of good city centres.

Pleasing advertisements.

The background of television productions.

Flower arrangements in exhibitions, for their settings.

Still life pictures.

Collect:

A list on holiday, of colours, shapes, plant varieties, accessories, seen in one place.

Prints of paintings with harmony you particularly admire.

Prints of paintings showing repetitive elements.

A list of colours seen in any one landscape.

Pictures of plants with flowers and foliage in natural harmony.

Collections of plants from one habitat or list them.

A list of words associated with various things such as *cold* . . . blue, white, stone, ice, water (these can be used for interpretative designs).

Make:

Cut out objects from a magazine and compose them into a group. Link them with paint if necessary.

Cut out felt shapes and arrange them on a piece of felt harmoniously.

A plaque of dried plant materials concentrating on repetition of elements in the design.

Flower Arrangement:

A design using all curved components.

A design using all straight components.

A design with one accessory and then with several accessories.

A design with an integrated background.

Using materials from only one habitat.

Using materials from one country, i.e. interpreting another country.

To complement a painting.

PART 4

Skills and Techniques

BASIC EQUIPMENT

Tools for cutting:
Flower scissors for soft stems, light wire.
Flower cutters for all but thick, woody stems, light and
    medium weight wire.
Secateurs for thick, woody, stems.
Wire cutters for all wire.
Knife for scraping and peeling, some cutting.

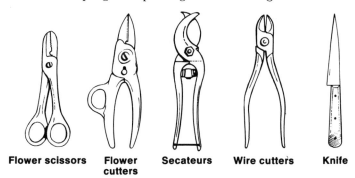

Flower scissors   **Flower**   **Secateurs**   **Wire cutters**   **Knife**
               cutters

Other Equipment:

Buckets for soaking plant material	Stubwire
Polythene sheeting and bags	Wire netting, $2''$, $1''$, $\frac{1}{2}''$ mesh
Containers	Plastic foam
Bases	Watering can (long spout)
Pinholders	Elastic bands
Wire on a reel	Plasticine, sealing strip, oasis-fix
	Hair-pins

Reel wire

Stub wire

Watering can   **Bucket**

Cocktail sticks
Dowel sticks
Candlecups
Candleholders
Tubes
Cones
Accessories

Pins
Florists' binding tape
Plaster of Paris or Polyfilla
Ball of wool
Plumbers' lead
Backgrounds

CONTAINERS

Receptacles for plant material, formerly called vases. These may or may not hold water. They can be part of the decorative visual appearance of the design or they may be hidden by a variety of materials. Containers hold the supports for plant material and can be bought, home-made, or devised. They can be made of any materials and fashioned into any shape, colour and size.

Containers

A container, seen or unseen may be placed on a base. This may be used to protect furniture, to give good balance visually, and to add to the decorative or expressive value of the design. If the base is seen it should be an integral part of the design. It may be any shape, material, size or colour.

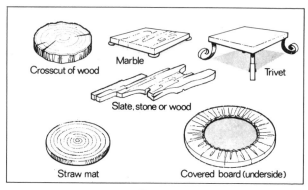

Bases.

Suggestions:

Slate	Crosscuts of tree trunks
Stone	Wood (cut to shape)
Marble	Mats
Alabaster	Plates
Plastic	Trays
Fabric	Trivets
Bamboo	Antique stands
Metal	Pedestals

Wood:
Crosscuts of tree trunks should be dried out slowly to avoid cracks. They can be left natural, darkened with linseed oil, polished with furniture wax or varnished, which renders them impervious to water.

The same treatment may be given to wood from a timber yard. It may also be stained, sanded, polished, painted. Close grained wood such as oak, apple, cherry, elm, sycamore and walnut are attractive.

Hardboard and plywood can be cut to shape and painted.

Fabric:

This may be draped or tailored. For a 'slipcover' for a tray or piece of wood, cut any fabric $2\frac{1}{2}''$ wider than the base all round. Turn in the edge twice to make a neat slot in which to thread elastic. Tighten and cut off the elastic. Alternatively use shirring thread. The slipcover may be easily removed and cleaned. It may be made in a variety of fabrics, colours, textures and two fabrics may be combined for a 'see-through' effect.

Angular bases may be permanently covered by mitring the corners and using gummed tape to secure the cover to the base.

Braid may be glued on to the edge of a base or pinned temporarily.

SUPPORTS FOR PLANT MATERIAL

Plant material must be supported in position for desired effects. The collective term for devices which hold plant material in position is 'mechanics'. The simpler the mechanical approach, the purer and less 'contrived' is the finished design.

PINHOLDERS

Also called needlepoint holders, kenzans, frogs. These consist of small vertical pins embedded into lead with the sharp ends pointing upwards and on to which stems can be impaled. Sizes and shapes vary. The best pinholders are heavy with long pins placed closely together.

A pinholder built into a well which holds water, can also be purchased. This eliminates the use of any other container and may be used on a base. A well-type pinholder may be made from a food tin with the addition of a pinholder. The tin should be deep enough to hold water reaching over the top of the pinholder. Dark, matt paint normally subdues the shine of the tin. These well-type pinholders are suitable for smaller quantities of plant material.

Pinholders with pins placed very far apart are for use with plastic foam.

Method of use

Place a pinholder on to a container. If it slips it may be secured with Plasticine or sealing strip rolled into a sausage and pressed firmly on to the base of the pinholder in a ring. Alternatively use four blobs of Plasticine. Press the pinholder firmly down on the container and give a small twist. It is essential that pinholder, container and Plasticine are dry otherwise the pinholder will not adhere. The stems of plant material are pressed on to the pins or between them. Push firmly on vertically or, if an angle is required press gently down to one side. Pinholders suit shallow containers and simple arrangements. They are not suitable for a very slender stem unless it is placed into a section of a hollow, larger stem for extra support. When a large quantity of plant material is used, a second support to the pinholder is normally necessary.

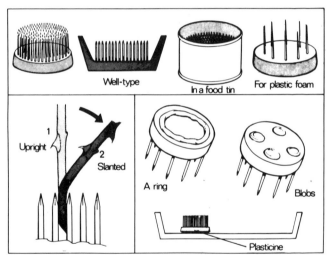

Top: Pinholders; *Left:* Impaling a stem; *Right:* securing with plasticine.

WIRE NETTING

This is also called chicken wire. When crumpled it gives support to stems. These may be placed at a horizontal angle providing stem ends of fresh plant material are in water.

2″ mesh is normally used for deep containers and 1″ and ½″ for use as a 'cap' over the top of a pinholder or plastic foam. It is not crumpled over plastic foam but used flat, as a second support for stems should the foam give way. Plastic-coated wire netting is difficult to crumple.

Method of use

For a deep container cut the netting as wide as the container and approximately three times its depth. Remove the thick selvedge. Bend into a U shape with the cut ends upwards and crumple down into the container so that the cavity of the container is filled but not so tightly that stems cannot be inserted. Some of the netting may be left standing above the container to support stems and the cut ends may be used to wind around stems for extra support.

If the netting wobbles about in the container it can be secured with:

1. An elastic band placed around both it and the container.
2. A length of wire from a reel twisted on to the netting on one side, passed under the container and twisted on to the other side.
3. Lengths of wire from a reel twisted on to the netting and on to handles or around any stem of the container.
4. A stem of plant material inserted through the netting and on to a pinholder.

Wire netting placed as a cap over plastic foam or a pinholder may be similarly secured.

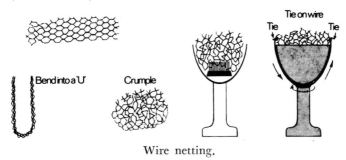

Bend into a 'U' Crumple

Tie on wire
Tie Tie

Wire netting.

PLASTIC FOAM

This is a water-retaining plastic material which is sold in

a variety of shapes and sizes. It is very light until filled with water but a block weighing 2 ounces will weigh 4 pounds after soaking. Stems can be inserted and positioned very accurately at any angle. It is not suitable for very soft stems. It may be used until it is too full of holes to support plant material. In between use the foam should be kept in a plastic bag to keep it moist. It is of valuable use for containers which do not normally hold water as it may be wrapped in polythene. Holes are made in the polythene with a stick or skewer to insert stems.

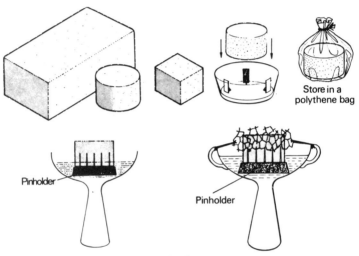

Store in a
polythene bag

Pinholder

Pinholder

Plastic foam.

Method of use
Cut with a knife to a suitable size for the container. If the block stands above the rim of the container, stems can be inserted flowing downwards. If possible the container should be a little larger than the foam so that more water may be added to the surface as it dries out in a warm room. Very large blocks of foam are not necessary even in a big container as they are difficult to hide.

The foam should be soaked before placing in the container, as instructed on the packet. Most foam needs to be dropped into a bowl of water deeper than itself and left until it sinks and is level with the surface of the water. This takes 2–3 minutes for a block of about 3″ square and 10 minutes for larger blocks. No further water is absorbed by longer soaking.

Some foam products, similar in appearance, do not absorb water and are for use with preserved and artificial plant materials. Stems may be inserted directly or pins and hairpins may be used for securing plant material.

OTHER SUPPORTS

STUB WIRE

Wire in varying gauges and lengths which is stiff and can add support to, or take the place of, a stem. A bent stem may have such a wire inserted inside as a splint. Soft stems with heavy flowers such as hyacinth have added strength when a stub wire is inserted.

Method of use
Flower stems   Gently guide the wire into the stem. Cut off at the stem end. When the flower is to be placed into plastic foam 1″ of wire may be left protruding as extra support in the foam. Care must be taken that the stem end also reaches the water supply. A camellia flower head often drops off its stem but can be held on by inserting two wires at right angles through the back of the flower. These are then bent down and twisted around the stem.

Pine Cones   These may be given a false stem. Slip two stub wires parallel to each other into the lower scales of the cone, one on either side of the centre. Twist the two wires together at the sides of the cone and then bend downwards, twisting all the wires together. Several cones may be wired into a cluster.

Leaves   To support a floppy stem, a stub wire may be placed along the mid-rib on the back of the leaf and then held in place with sticky tape. A preserved leaf may be similarly

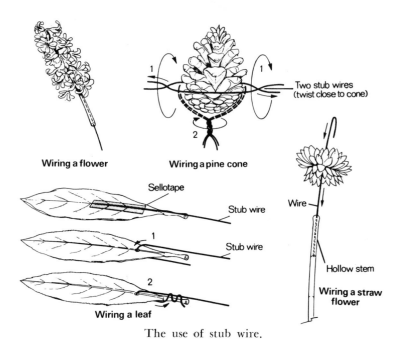

Wiring a flower

Wiring a pine cone

1

1

Two stub wires
(twist close to cone)

2

Sellotape

Stub wire

Wire

1

Stub wire

2

Hollow stem

Wiring a leaf

**Wiring a straw
flower**

The use of stub wire.

given a false stem. Alternatively a stub wire may be threaded through the leaf, both ends of the wire bent down and one twisted around the other.

Flowers without stems Dried flowers such as *Helichrysum* usually have weak stems which must be removed. The flower can be given a false stem with a stub wire pushed through the centre of the flower head. This is often more easily done before the flower dries. Turn over $\frac{1}{4}''$ at the end of the wire and pull it down until this slips into the centre of the flower. The wire stem may be disguised by slipping it into a hollow stem. Alternatively the wire may be covered with florists' binding tape, a soft tape which sticks to itself when the warmth of the hand is applied. Cut off a length and start binding the wire by rolling the tape on at right angles. This holds it in position. Then, holding the tape downwards and slightly at an angle with one hand, twist the wire with the other hand until covered. Press the tape with a warm hand to the wire.

SAND

This may support stems successfully used either wet or dry. It is also useful for supporting a pinholder in a tall container. Fill $\frac{3}{4}$ full of sand and add water until it stands 2″ above a pinholder placed on top of the sand. Alternatively, or in addition, wire netting can be used.

COCKTAIL STICKS

These are useful for holding fruit in position. Press half a stick into one piece of fruit and half into another. Push the fruit together. It is not harmed, as it is by using wire.

DOWEL STICKS or WOODEN SKEWERS

Heavy fruit such as a pineapple may be held in place in plastic foam by two or three pieces of dowel stick pushed into its base. Other fruit such as apples and oranges may be held in position with a length of dowel placed in plastic foam, wire netting or on a pinholder. Grapes may be attached with wire to a dowel and similarly used. Placed on a pinholder, a piece of dowel may act as a splint on to which a floppy stem may be wired or tied. A woody stem may be similarly used.

METAL or PLASTIC CONES

These are used to provide water and give greater height to plant material. The cone is attached with sticky tape or wire to a square garden stick or a length of dowel. The stick is then cut off at a desired length and placed into the mechanics. If the stick projects above the cone for a short distance a stem can be tied on to it. Plastic foam or wire netting may be used in the cone.

TUBES

These may be glass, plastic or metal orchid tubes, or cigar cases. They are used as cones. They may also be used, without a stick, to hold water and plant material placed amongst fruit, preserved plant material or in a pot-et-fleur. They can also be taped to the stems of strong plants.

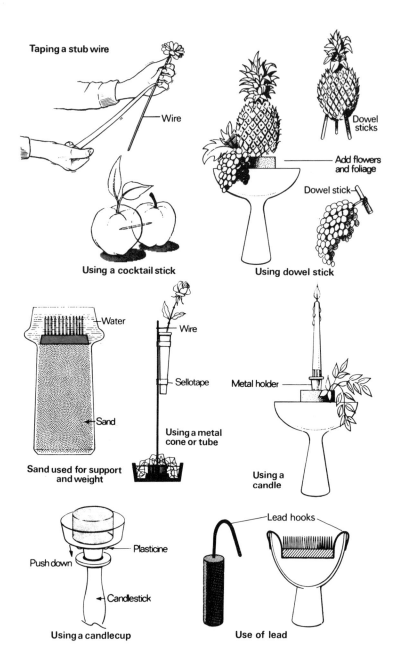

Taping a stub wire

Wire

Using a cocktail stick

Dowel sticks

Add flowers and foliage

Dowel stick

Using dowel stick

Water

Sand

Sand used for support and weight

Wire

Sellotape

Using a metal cone or tube

Metal holder

Using a candle

Plasticine

Push down

Candlestick

Using a candlecup

Lead hooks

Use of lead

CANDLECUPS

These are small containers of plastic or metal which hold water and mechanics. Small knobs at the base fit into the narrow necks of bottles and candlesticks giving a 'pedestal' container. The candlecup may be fixed permanently with adhesive or temporarily with Plasticine.

WOOL

Lengths of wool are useful for binding the ends of stems which split and also for binding several stems together. As the wool is soft it does not cut stems.

CANDLEHOLDERS

Small metal shapes which hold a candle and can be pressed into plastic foam or on to a pinholder.

LEAD

A strip of plumbers' lead is useful to give weight hung over the back of the mechanics if an arrangement should tip forwards. A piece of lead containing a hook may also be bought for this purpose. Two strips of lead (it may be cut with flower cutters) may be placed at right angles and hooked over the rim of a glass container to support a pinholder. The stems do not then show through the glass.

PLASTER OF PARIS OR 'POLYFILLA'

This makes a permanent support for driftwood or for a stick which holds other mechanics.

Method of use

Add water to the powder stirring until similar to thick whipped cream. (When the powder is added to the water, a smoother result is obtained but setting is slower.) Insert wood or stick and hold in position for a few minutes until the plaster sets. If the plaster is placed in a pot, this should be of plastic as china will crack as the plaster sets.

MECHANICS FOR LARGER DESIGNS

1. For great height several tubes may be tied or wired at

intervals and at varying angles to a stake. Staples or nails may be used to hold the wire or string in place on the stake. It is then necessary to insert the stake into a plastic bowl of concrete. The higher the design, the larger and deeper must be the bowl and the concrete. The plastic bowl may be placed inside a large urn or used on a plinth and covered attractively.

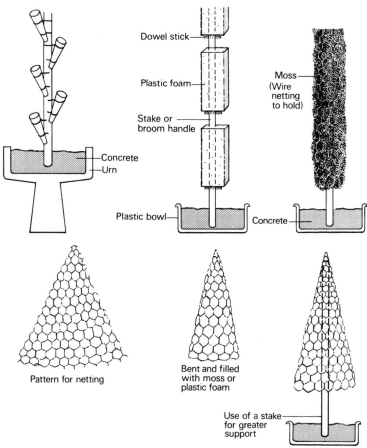

Mechanics for larger designs.

2. A broom handle may be inserted into plaster of Paris in a plastic bowl. Blocks of plastic foam may be threaded on to the stick or moss bound on to it with wire. Wire netting may be placed around foam or moss for added support. If spaces are desired between the blocks of foam, holes should be bored through the broom handle and dowel stick inserted to hold the foam up and prevent it slipping down the handle.

3. A cone shape may be made by cutting a triangle of wire netting. Curve the bottom of it and then bend and attach the sides together with wire. Fill with moss or pieces of plastic foam shaped to fit. For large cones push a stake or stick up the centre and embed in plaster of Paris or concrete in a plastic bowl or pot. Tubes can be buried in the moss or stems placed directly through the netting and into the water-retaining material.

MECHANICS FOR OTHER SHAPES (for fresh plant material)

1. *Swags*
Cover moss or a block of plastic foam with polythene and wrap again in wire netting, 1″ gauge. Insert stems with the aid of a skewer but do not make holes in the underneath or water will leak out. The swag may be hung on a wall with wire attached to the wire netting and to a nail or picture hook on a wall.

2. *Plaques*
Attach the above swag to a shaped board, painted or covered decoratively, by means of nails hammered into the board. Hang on a wall in the same way.

(The mechanics for swags and plaques of preserved plant material are described later.)

3. *Small cone shapes*
These can be made simply with plastic foam roughly cut into a cone and placed on a pinholder in a container.

4. *Garlands*
Cut a long narrow strip of wire netting, 1″ gauge. Place a

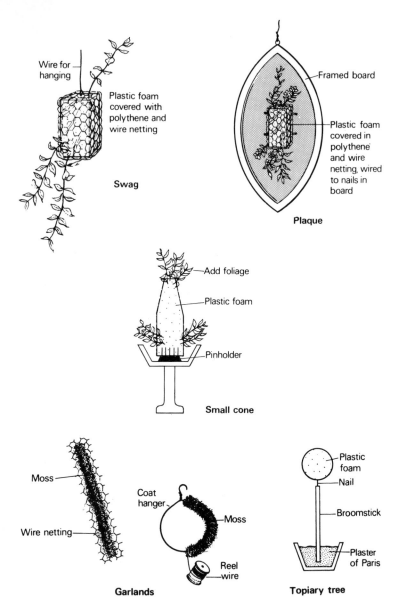

Swag

Wire for hanging

Plastic foam covered with polythene and wire netting

Plaque

Framed board

Plastic foam covered in polythene and wire netting, wired to nails in board

Small cone

Add foliage

Plastic foam

Pinholder

Garlands

Moss

Wire netting

Coat hanger

Moss

Reel wire

Topiary tree

Plastic foam

Nail

Broomstick

Plaster of Paris

Mechanics for other shapes, using fresh plant material.

strip of moss or plastic foam along the centre. Bend the netting over to hold the moss or foam. Polythene may be wrapped over the foam or moss before inserting in the wire netting. When foam is used gaps should be left between pieces to allow the garland to bend. Nylon stockings, rope or heavy wire may also be used as a foundation with moss bound on with reel wire. This makes a slender garland but is not easy to construct. A circular garland may be made on a wire coat hanger bent into a circle and bound with moss. A lampshade ring may similarly be used. The simplest garland is made of short stems of greenery bound together with reel wire.

5. *Topiary trees*

Secure a short piece of broomstick into a plastic pot with plaster of Paris. Nail a long headless nail into the top of the stick. Impale plastic foam or a ball of moss, covered with wire netting, on to the nail. It is important to keep the broomstick short because otherwise the weight of the plastic foam when wet will overbalance the tree.

COVER-UPS FOR MECHANICS

Plant material is often used to hide mechanics which it is not desirable to show. Alternatively the following are suggestions:

pebbles	fabric	coral	coal
rock	windscreen	shells	beads
stones	glass	driftwood	bark
sand	glass chunks	gravel	mosaic
fungi	marble	glass fibre	chippings
moss	chunks	marbles	

ACCESSORIES

This term normally refers to objects other than plant material used as part of the design, but not the vase or container. It includes figurines, shells, plates, ornaments, materials such as copper wire, coral fan and so on. Accessories may be incorporated either in the container or used apart from it. In some schedules of definitions an additional placement of plant material not contained within the arrangement is regarded as an accessory.

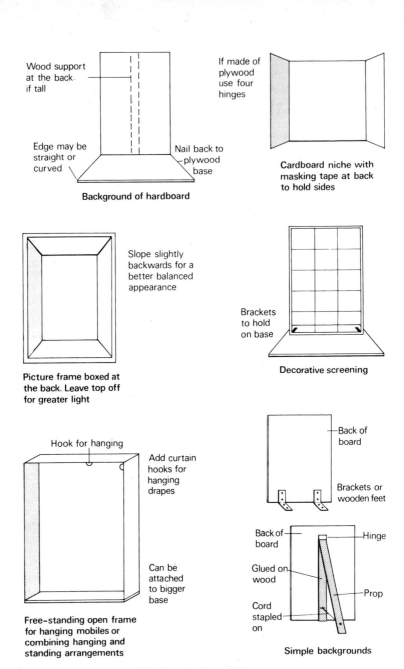

Wood support at the back if tall

Edge may be straight or curved

Nail back to plywood base

Background of hardboard

If made of plywood use four hinges

Cardboard niche with masking tape at back to hold sides

Slope slightly backwards for a better balanced appearance

Picture frame boxed at the back. Leave top off for greater light

Brackets to hold on base

Decorative screening

Hook for hanging

Add curtain hooks for hanging drapes

Can be attached to bigger base

Free-standing open frame for hanging mobiles or combining hanging and standing arrangements

Back of board

Brackets or wooden feet

Back of board

Glued on wood

Cord stapled on

Hinge

Prop

Simple backgrounds

Backgrounds and frames.

The background to a flower arrangement may be the walls or furnishings of a room, hall or church. It may be a niche or alcove in a room or provided at a show. It may be a background supplied by an arranger to complement a particular design.

Suggestions for home-made backgrounds:

Made of:		*Cover with:*	
hardboard	glass	fabric	fablon
plywood	perspex	sandpaper	wood veneer
canvas	cardboard	wallpaper	Snowcem
cork	screening	paper	anaglypta
		plastics	paint (with
		foil	various effects,
			e.g. sponging)

CONDITIONING

This term refers to the preparation of cut plant material so that stems will take up water easily and also to the filling of stems with water.

FOLIAGE

This may be filled by submerging under water for a minimum of two hours as leaves can take in moisture through their surface tissue. Damage to the leaves is not usual although grey foliage loses its greyness as the small hairs become waterlogged and it is therefore better not submerged but placed with the stem ends only in water.

FLOWERS

These are damaged by long submerging. Flower stems are usually conditioned according to the type of stem.
1. Soft stems—cut 1″ off the stem preferably under water.
2. Hard stems—slit 2″ up the stem with a knife. Place in water at once.
3. Woody stems—scrape off 2″ of bark, slit or crush the stem for 2″. Place in water at once.

319

4. Hollow stems—fill with water by means of a funnel. Plug with cotton wool which acts as a wick in water.
5. Milky stems—char with a match, candle or gas flame. Put in water at once. Repeat if the stem is recut.

After initial preparation place in water at once. Then the flowers should be placed in deep water for a minimum of 2 hours in a cool, dim, draughtless place. Shop flowers have usually been conditioned before they are bought but these should still have approximately 1″ of stem cut away under water.

STEM ENDS

Water should enter the stem end easily. It is helpful to slit hard stems for an inch or two using scissors or a knife. In addition, woody stems should have a few inches of bark scraped away. If bark is removed from the outside of woody stems, tissue is exposed which is softer and more permeable. Cut ends of stems begin to 'heal' when left exposed to the air and a protective callus may seal the end and prevent water from entering the stem. This seal can be removed by:
1. Cutting 1″ off the stem, under water.
2. Dipping the end of the stem in boiling water which kills the cells immersed in it and prevents them from becoming a callus. (This is especially beneficial to woody and hard stems such as those of lilac and roses.)
3. Burning the stem end with match, flame or gas-jet, which also kills the cells and enables water to enter the stem more readily. This is similar to the boiling water method but more drastic.

Burning is essential to stems which exude a milky fluid such as euphorbias and poppies. The milky fluid, called latex, which is a solution of rubber, can form an impermeable layer as it dries. Charring the end stops further latex from leaking out and allows water to enter.

Flowers placed near steam or flame should have their heads protected by a cloth or bag.

Wilted flowers Although plant material may have been well conditioned, it may still wilt through lack of water in the stem. This is usually because of an airlock, which

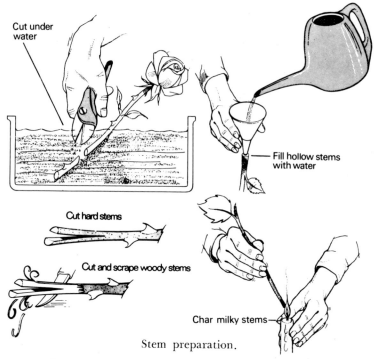

Cut under water

Fill hollow stems with water

Cut hard stems

Cut and scrape woody stems

Char milky stems

Stem preparation.

causes the stem to lose turgidity and flop. When a stem is cut from a plant, air rushes into the cut end at once. The air bubbles increase the longer the stem is out of water, preventing water from entering however much is available. Placing stems in water immediately after cutting reduces the air intake but is not entirely satisfactory. The best way to remove an airlock or a possible one is by cutting it away under water. Atmospheric pressure then causes water to enter and connect up with the normal sap within the tissues. It is usually effective to cut off 1"–2" of stem, dependent upon the time the stem has been out of water. Boiling water will remove some of the air as it expands with the heat and some bubbles will be forced out of the stem end, having nowhere else to go. However this does not remove all the air.

Methods of increasing the water content of wilted stems:
Cut off 1"–2" of the stem to remove an airlock and then
1. Float or submerge the flower and stem horizontally in water for two hours OR

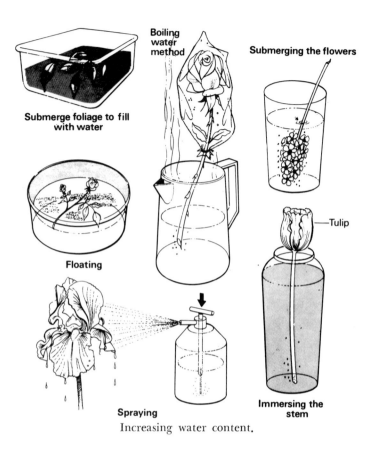

Submerge foliage to fill with water

Boiling water method

Submerging the flowers

Floating

—Tulip

Spraying

Immersing the stem

Increasing water content.

2. Place in 1″ of boiling water and allow to cool OR
3. Immerse the flower head in water for two hours, cutting the stem end after this OR
4. Spray with water to increase the humidity OR
5. Cut the stem the length of a milk bottle filled with warm water and place it in the bottle so that the stem may take in water through the whole length of its outside surface. This works well with a soft stem as it has little thick protective outer covering.

WATER TEMPERATURE

Excessive heat destroys cells and should only be used for stem *ends* when conditioning or reviving. Warm water 'moves' more easily than cold and passes quickly into the cells. Water, pleasantly warm to the hands, may be used for conditioning as it gives a flower a good start and any water shortage is soon made up. Stems may be successfully left in 1" of boiling water for half an hour and then warm water may be added to the jug or bucket, to cover as much of the stem as possible.

BACTERIA

The growth of this should be discouraged as it produces slime to block the water channels in stems, fouls the water and shortens the life of cut flowers. Bacteria grows because of the natural processes of decay and can be reduced by sterilising the ends in boiling water or in a flame. It is also helpful to add a mild disinfectant to the water such as chlorhexidine at the rate of $\frac{1}{4}$ teaspoonful to 1 pint of water. This eliminates the need for changing the water in containers.

PLANT FOOD

Minerals and other substances normally pass, dissolved in water, from the roots of a plant into the stems. When a stem is cut from the plant, the supply of nutrients is cut off. Nutrients may be added to the water in the container to continue the supply, although normally cut flowers do not last long enough to become short of nutrients. Some people recommend the use of 1 level teaspoonful of glucose to 1 pint of water.

Dipping the stem ends in boiling water prevents the leakage of nutrients, retaining them in the stem, and also reduces the growth of bacteria caused by the water in the container working on the substances which have leaked out.

GARDEN PLANT MATERIAL

If this is cut from a plant at the *end of the day* it will contain maximum food reserves, because the plant manufactures food during daylight hours using energy from the sun. This enables the detached part to survive longer. Cells rich in dissolved substances also resist decay better than those with weaker concentrates.

Stems cut from a plant in the *early morning* contain more

water than in the evening. During the hotter part of the day water is lost even to the extent of wilting and at night this deficit is made up. Cutting at the end of the day gives a stem containing more nutrients and less water. Cutting in the early morning gives a stem with more water and less nutrients. Since flower arrangers can provide water more easily than nutrients, the evening is probably the better time to cut. This also gives the night hours for conditioning in a dark place.

DEFOLIATION

By removing all leaves from a stem, the transpiring surfaces are cut down and less water is lost. This is essential for lilac, *Clematis*, *Philadelphus* and other flowers difficult to condition.

Leaves become quickly decayed if kept under water in a container, so should be removed from the lower part of a stem when making an arrangement.

FORCING INTO EARLY FLOWER

Plants can be induced to flower earlier than normal by giving extra warmth. Flower arrangers find this is a useful method of having early flowering branches in the spring. Cut stems after a lengthy period of low temperature and when there are large buds and some signs of life. The nearer to normal flowering time the stems are forced, the more rapidly the flowers will open. Bring indoors, scrape 2″ of bark away and place in 2″ of boiling water. Fill the bucket with warm water and place in a warm place.

Forcing is possible of trees and shrubs which form their flowers within dormant buds but not of those which form flowers during the current year's growth. The following are suitable:

Malus—apple
Ribes nigrum—blackcurrant
Jasminum nudiflorum—
   jasmine
Forsythia
Salix—willow
Lonicera—honeysuckle
Corylus—hazel

Syringa—lilac
Chaenomeles—Japanese
   quince
Magnolia
Pyrus communis—pear
Prunus—plum, cherry,
   peach, almond

324

Camellia: spray often.

Carnation: cut above a 'knob'.

Chrysanthemum: use chlorhexidine to decrease bacteria.

Clematis: immerse whole flower for an hour.

Clematis vitalba (Old Man's Beard): put in glycerine mixture (1 part glycerine to 2 parts hot water) before the flower appears.

Acacia (mimosa, wattle): keep in a polythene bag until immediately before arranging.

Anemone: condition in warm water.

Autumn leaves turning colour: spray with 1 part glycerine mixed with 3 parts water.

Bulbous plants: arrange in shallow water after conditioning, to avoid soggy stems.

Bulrush: spray with hair lacquer or varnish to prevent blowing.

Foliage: soak, then arrange in water containing soluble aspirin (half an aspirin to 1 pint water). This closes the pores and so retains moisture.

Gardenia: keep in airtight bag until used. Handle with wet hands.

Gerbera: easily forms air bubbles in stem, cut under water and stand in 1″ of boiling water. Add warm water.

Hydrangea: immerse flower heads in water for 1 hour.

Hellebore: pick in the fruit stage for longest life.

Holly berries: pick before the birds eat them, stand in a bucket half full of water. Place a polythene bag over the top and tucked in the sides and leave out of doors.

Lily: remove anthers to prevent pollen damage to clothing and petals.

Ranunculus: wrap tightly in newspaper while conditioning to keep stems straight.

Tulip: as above.

Sansevieria lèaf: avoid putting directly in water which causes sogginess. Wrap ends in polythene to keep dry in water.

Syringa (lilac), Philadelphus, Viburnum opulus: defoliate.

Violet: immerse flower head in water overnight as humid conditions are required.

Water-lily: drop melted wax in the centre to hold flower open.

RETARDING FLOWERS

It is possible to retard flowers in a refrigerator. The most suitable temperature is 5.5 C. as anything colder may destroy the cells. Seal the flowers in foil or polythene after an initial soak. Roses, carnations, tulips and lilac are suitable and can be held back for a week although they may not last long when removed from the refrigerator. Peonies and gladioli may be left on a stone floor out of water for several days in tight bud. To start them again, cut the stems and place in warm, deep water when wanted for an arrangement.

TRANSPORTING PLANT MATERIAL

Florists' flowers should be wrapped to protect the heads from draughts or strong sunshine.

Garden flowers may be laid in a cardboard box with a lid and air-holes. Flowers are the best support for each other when packing.

Polythene should not normally enclose flowers, especially in hot weather when they develop too quickly.

Foliage may be successfully packed in polythene bags.

Wild plant material should be dipped in water if possible and then placed in a covered box. Keep out of sunshine which dehydrates them quickly and often beyond revival.

Spiky material such as gladioli, antirrhinum, stock, delphinium, should be carried upright, unless curved tips are required.

A completed arrangement may be transported in a large box with newspaper packed tightly around the container for support.

Fabric becomes less creased if rolled around a cardboard tube.

SKELETONISING PLANT MATERIAL

Recipe 1
Choose mature but not old leaves. Ivy, laurel, magnolia, avocado are suitable.
Boil $\frac{1}{2}$ box (regular size) of Tide in a large pan of water.
When boiling, add leaves and boil for 35 minutes.

Remove and brush gently under a little running water to remove green slime. An old tooth brush is suitable.
Stubborn leaves may be returned to the pan for a while.
Place on newspaper to dry. Press to flatten.
Care should be taken not to tear the leaf when brushing.

Recipe 2
Dissolve 1 ounce of washing soda in 1 quart of boiling water with 2 ounces of slaked quicklime. Boil for 15 minutes, pour off the clear liquid and bring it to boiling point. Add leaves and boil for one hour if necessary adding boiling water to replace that lost by vaporisation. Remove leaves and brush away cellular matter as before.

Recipe 3
Soak mature leaves in 2 tablespoons of chlorox to 1 quart of water for a minimum of one hour. Rinse and wipe away cellular matter. Dry and press. (More suitable for leaves with thin tissue.)

DYEING FRESH FLOWERS

Dyes may be mixed for subtle effects and special flower dyes are available.
1. Stand cut ends in a dye solution until the colour creeps up the stem and into the flowers, about 8–12 hours.
2. Dip in dye solution containing a few drops of washing-up liquid, which increases the spread of the dye. Leave a few minutes or until required colour is obtained. Rinse to avoid streaking.

GLITTERING PLANT MATERIAL

1. Brush plant material thinly with a light clear glue or clear varnish. When almost dry, dip into a saucer of glitter powder (various colours). For selected parts of the plant material, put glue only on the parts to be glittered. Shake when dry to remove excess.
2. Spray with clear varnish or metallic paint and almost at once dip in glitter powder or pour on over the plant material. Do this over a plate or newspaper so that excess powder may be collected and used again.

PRESERVATION OF PLANT MATERIAL

Plant material may be preserved and there are several methods. The results in some cases last for many years and may be used again and again. It may be arranged with or without fresh plant material in containers, for pictures, plaques and swags.

DRYING

When the normal growing period of any plant comes to an end it stops taking up water and this is not replaced as it evaporates. The plant then shrivels and dies. Plants respond differently to this process and those with finely branching, strong, rigid, vascular tissue, supporting thin tissue between, keep their shape well even when completely dry. This is very noticeable when there is also a gradual evaporation of water.

Some plants dry naturally out of doors and remain an attractive shape for a long time but they may suffer damage from weather conditions and better results are obtained by drying them indoors.

Other plants may be dried but also need pressing, to keep them from shrivelling.

Drying by Hanging

Pick flowers and seedheads for hanging up to dry. Foliage is normally better when preserved with glycerine. Flowers should be gathered when in good condition, dry, and not fully opened. Seedheads should be picked when beginning to dry on the plant. Thistles, pampas grass and bulrushes shatter easily and should be picked when half developed.

Tie the stems of the plant material in small bunches so that the flowers or seedheads do not crush each other. Remove any leaves as they do not dry successfully and they increase the moisture content of the air as the water evaporates.

Hang to dry in the dark. Hanging the plant material upside down can give a better shaped flower or seedhead and avoids a drooping appearance. Very slow drying may fade the colour and a warm place with a free circulation of air gives best results.

Store for future use, in the same place or in boxes without lids with tissue paper to minimise crushing or by standing in tall jars out of sunshine and always in a dry place. Dried plant material is often fragile and needs care in storage.

Steam dried plant material which loses its shape by holding over the spout of a steaming kettle for a few seconds and then re-shaping quickly. Flat plant material may be steam-ironed. This suits skeletonised magnolia leaves.

Arrange in dry mechanics or, if needed with fresh plant material, dip the stem ends into melted candle-wax, sealing-wax, or nail polish to render them impervious to water and prevent mould and softness.

Suitable plant material:
  Flowers
  Acanthus (Bear's Breech)
  Achillea (Yarrow)
  Acroclinium
  Allium (Onion and related plants)
  Amaranthus caudatus (Love-lies-bleeding)
  Ammobium (Winged Everlasting)
  Anaphalis (Pearl Everlasting)
  Artemisia ludoviciana
  Calluna (Ling)
  Celosia (Cock's Comb)
  Crocosmia
  Cynara cardunculus (Cardoon)
  Cynara scolymus (Globe artichoke)
  Delphinium
  Delphinium ajacis (Larkspur)
  Echinops ritro (Globe thistle)
  Erica (Heather)
  Eryngium maritimum (Sea holly)
  Gomphrena globosa (Globe amaranth)
  Gypsophila paniculata (Baby's Breath)
  Helichrysum
  Helipterum

Hydrangea macrophylla (Hydrangea)
Lavendula (Lavender)
Liatris
Limonium sinuatum (Statice)
Moluccella laevis (Bells of Ireland)
Polygonum (Knotweed)
Protea
Rhodanthe
Salix (Pussy Willow)
Salvia horminum (Clary)
Scabiosa atropurpurea (Scabious)
Sedum (Stonecrop)
Solidago canadensis (Golden Rod)
Spiraea (Spirea)
Xeranthemum
Zinnia elegans (Zinnia)

Fruits and Seedheads
Agapanthus (African Lily)
Allium (Onion and related plants)
Althaea (Hollyhock)
Angelica (Holy Ghost)
Aquilegia (Columbine)
Clematis
Dipsacus fullonum (Teasel)
Hemerocallis (Day-lily)
Iris
Lunaria (Honesty)
Montbretia
Nicandra physaloides (Shoo-fly plant)
Nigella damascena (Love-in-a-Mist)
Papaver orientale (Oriental Poppy)
Physalis franchetii (Chinese Lantern)
Rumex (Dock)
Verbascum (Mullein)

Grasses
Briza maxima (Quaking Grass)
Bromus (Ornamental Oats)

Coix lachryma (Job's Tears)
Cortaderia (Pampas Grass)
Eragrostis elegans (Love Grass)
Hordeum jubatum (Squirrel's Tail Grass)
Koelaria (Blue Meadow Grass)
Lagurus ovatus (Hare's Tail Grass)
Panicum violaceum (Millet)
Setaria italica (Foxtail Millet)
Tricholaena rosea
Triticum (Ornamental Wheat)

DRYING BY PRESSING

Hanging plant material to dry keeps the three-dimensional shape whereas pressed plant material is flat. Pressing reduces the water content but prevents the parts from shrivelling at the same time, which happens with a lot of plant material. This is a suitable method to use for foliage, which becomes shapeless and shrivelled by the hanging method. It is not suitable for fleshy, succulent plants with high moisture content and is not attractive used for very three-dimensional plant material.

Pick on a dry day and arrange on blotting paper or newspaper, covering with a second piece of paper.

Press in a flower press or under books, under bricks or a heavy carpet, for at least three weeks in a warm room. Change the paper if it becomes damp. Really flat plant material, desired for a picture under glass, should be pressed for at least three months preferably for one year. The longer it is left, the more paper-thin it becomes and the colours do not fade as readily when exposed to light.

Store in a dry place in a box. It is possible for dry plant material to re-absorb moisture otherwise.

Restore coarse, pressed leaves which have become dry and brittle by dipping in salad oil and pressing with an iron, between blotting paper or newspaper.

331

Dismantle three-dimensional plant material such as a daffodil, before pressing and dry the parts separately. These can be re-assembled for a picture. Stalks are better pressed separately.

Suitable Plant Material

  Flowers
  Acacia (Mimosa)
  Anthemis (Camomile)
  Astrantia (Hatties Pincushion)
  Auricula
  Bellis perennis (Lawn Daisy)
  Calendula petals (Marigold)
  Clematis—all, including wild and *C. montana*
  Clover
  Coreopsis (Tickseed)
  Cornus (Dogwood)
  Cosmos
  Cytisus (Broom)
  Delphinium
  Erica (Heather)
  Eschscholzia (Californian Poppy)
  Heuchera sanguinea
  Hydrangea
  Laburnum
  Limnanthes (Meadow Foam)
  Limonium (Statice)
  Lonicera (Honeysuckle)
  Lunaria (Honesty)
  Mimulus (Monkey flowers)
  Montbretia
  Narcissus family (dismantled)
  Nicotiana (Tobacco Plant)
  Papaver nudicaule (Iceland Poppy)
  Polyanthus
  Primula (Primrose)
  Ranunculus (Buttercup)
  Ranunculus ficaria (Celandine)
  Saxifraga
  Solidago canadensis (Golden Rod)

Trifolium (Trefoil)
Rose petals
Tulipa (Tulip)
Venidio arctotis (Suttons Sunshine flower)
Vicia (Vetch)
Viola (Violet, Pansy)

Leaves
Acer (Maple)
Adiantum (Maidenhair Fern)
Ampelopsis (Virginia Creeper)
Castanea (Sweet chestnut)
Cineraria maritima (White Diamond)
Clematis montana
Echinops (Globe Thistle)
Fagus (Beech)
Ferns
Fraxinus (Ash)
Geranium robertianum (Herb-Robert)
Gladioli
Grasses
Hedera (Ivy)
Hellebore (Lenten Rose)
Iris
Lonicera (Honeysuckle)
Montbretia
Populus tremulus (Aspen)
Prunus (Cherry, Plum, Peach)
Quercus (Oak)
Rhus (Sumach)
Rubus (Blackberry)
Senecio
Sorbus aria (Whitebeam)

Stalks
Anthemis (Camomile)
Clematis montana
Clover
Primula (Primrose)
Ranunculus (Buttercup)

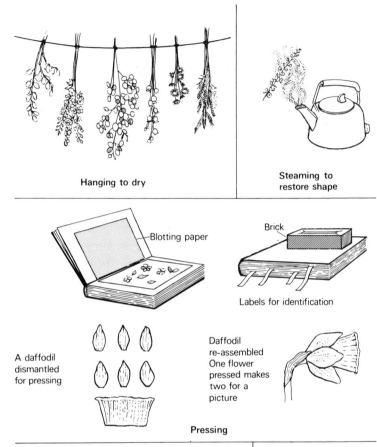

Hanging to dry

Steaming to
restore shape

Blotting paper

Brick

Labels for identification

A daffodil
dismantled
for pressing

Daffodil
re-assembled
One flower
pressed makes
two for a
picture

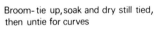

Pressing

Broom- tie up, soak and dry still tied,
then untie for curves

Dry hydrangea in
$\frac{1}{2}$ inch of water

Preservation by drying.

Centres
Astrantia (Masterwort)
Calendula (Marigold)
Papaver (Poppy)

IRONING

Some plant material responds to rapid pressing with a warm iron. Place between blotting paper or newspaper. Press for about five minutes depending on the thickness of the plant material. This is not as longlasting as slow pressing.

Suitable Plant Material
   Leaves
   Aesculus (Horse-chestnut)
   Crocosmia (Montbretia)
   Fagus (Beech)
   Gladioli
   Grasses
   Rhus (Sumach)
   Rushes
   Sedges
   Croton, maple and oak leaves may be dipped in paraffin wax (melted) and then ironed inside sheets of newspaper.

DRYING IN WATER

Hydrangeas dry well and keep a good colour if dried while the stems are standing in $\frac{1}{2}''$ of water in a jar. The water should not be topped up. Pick as the flower is beginning to dry on the plant. Heather also dries better with this method.

DRYING IN HEAT

Some single fruits dry in an airing cupboard. Gourds dry well in this manner but must be left for approximately 3 months until all the water has evaporated through the hard almost impervious outer covering. When dry they will be very light in weight and usually beige in colour. Broom will dry in interesting curves if placed in a hot airing cupboard for two days. Before doing this it should be tied into circles, soaked for two hours in water and then kept tied up until quite dry.

335

Suitable Plant Material
Acorns
Capsicums
Cucurbita sp.
Pomegranates
Rose hips
Small oranges

DRYING WITH DESICCANTS

Plant material may also be dried by means of substances which withdraw the water, and retain it. Suitable desiccants are silica gel, borax, alum and sand. The plant material is arranged carefully to keep its shape, buried in the substance and left undisturbed for a varying length of time depending on the type of plant material and desiccant used. The preserved results will last indefinitely if care is taken but they are often very fragile. They should not be left in strong sunlight which fades them or be exposed to high humidity, as they can re-absorb moisture.

Pick plant material on a dry day. Only very good specimens in peak condition should be selected. Normally choose plant material that is not full-blown. Cut stems of 1″-2″ in length.

Embed by placing 1″-2″ of desiccant on the bottom of a tin. Place the stem down in it and then cover the plant material gently, but completely, 'dressing' it to shape with a pointed stick or a brush. Separate each petal of a flower so that the desiccant enters every cavity. The contours of a flower must have proper support with the desiccant equally distributed around, below and above the petals to prevent the cell fibres from crumbling while dehydration takes place. It is necessary for the desiccant to have a certain amount of weight, suited to the tissue of the flower.

Place a lid on the tin when there is about 1″-2″ of desiccant covering all parts of the flower and tape the lid firmly to make an airtight seal. Keep the tin in a warm, dry place. Experience will tell how long different varieties of flowers take in different desiccants (an indication is given below).

Too rapid or hot drying may give stiff, crisp petals. A wrinkled appearance means that there has been insufficient weight on the petals and a heavier desiccant (or more of it) is needed. If damp spots remain, the desiccant has not covered every part of the flower. Normally it is wise to allow only one flower to a container. If several pieces are embedded together, they should not touch each other.

Remove from the box by pouring the desiccant off slowly and without reversing the motion, which could damage the flower. Let the flower drop into the hand. Dust with a brush to remove any grains left. Loose petals may be glued on with a tiny spot of clear glue and this is often necessary for reinforcement. A fine paintbrush or a nail-polish brush is a suitable tool for this. Dull petals may be stroked with oil for greater sheen.

Stems may be lengthened by putting a little glue on the end and then slipping into a hollow stem of another plant. This must also be dry. It may be painted green to look more natural. Alternatively place stub wire against or inside the flower stem and bind with florists' tape. This gives a stem which can be curved.

Store in an airtight polythene bag, or a tin containing a few grains of desiccant or place in hollow, dried stems standing upright in a container of sand. Stuff tissue paper into bell-shapes. Keep away from strong light to prevent the colours fading. The stability of colour depends on the colour and on the flower. Most green, yellows and oranges fade more quickly than reds and violets. These tend to get darker. Tints vary but dark shades are slow to fade.

Clean if necessary with a light brush or sift sand gently over the flower or dip in dry-cleaning fluid.

DESICCANTS

Experience will tell the most suitable. All extract water gently from plant material so that the shape is kept and there

337

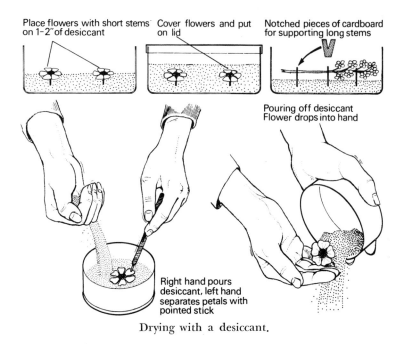

Place flowers with short stems on 1-2" of desiccant

Cover flowers and put on lid

Notched pieces of cardboard for supporting long stems

Right hand pours desiccant, left hand separates petals with pointed stick

Pouring off desiccant Flower drops into hand

Drying with a desiccant.

is little shrivelling as would happen normally. Weight and speed of drying vary.

Silica gel

This is a granular material which can absorb 50% of its own weight in moisture. It is the heaviest desiccant but may be bought ground more finely or crushed with a rolling pin. It is the quickest to dry plant material taking half the time of other desiccants. After use it must be dried in a 250° oven. An indicator of litmus paper sold with it, turns blue when the substance is dry and ready for use. As silica gel retains the heat it should not be handled for some time.

Borax and/or alum

These are the lightest and are suitable for delicate flowers. They take from 1–6 weeks to dry plant material depending on the coarseness of the tissue and the warmth of the room. Borax tends to be adhesive and gives less support to petals but it can be mixed with alum or sand—2 parts of alum or sand to 1 of borax. It does not penetrate easily into cavities and care should be taken to see that the powder covers every petal. Alum may be used alone.

Sand

This has been used to dry flowers for centuries. It penetrates the flower cavities readily because it flows easily. It gives good support to flower petals. Better colours result from adding 1 tablespoon of bicarbonate of soda to 15 pounds of sand. A 1 pound coffee tin holds 4 pounds of sand, sufficient for one rose.

Sand needs cleaning before use:

Fill a bucket $\frac{3}{4}$ full of sand, add water to the top.
Remove floating debris, pour off water.
Add 1 teaspoonful of detergent, fill again with water.
Stir, pour off water.
Rinse by turning sand in clear water, several times.
Dry in 250° oven, 4–5 hours or in the sun, 2–3 hours.
Sift before use.

It need not be cleaned again.

Suitable plant material

The approximate number of weeks for drying in sand is given next to the plant material. As a general rule borax and borax mixed with sand take half the time indicated. Silica gel takes up to a maximum of one week. Unless otherwise stated, the plant material should be placed face upwards.

Althaea (Hollyhock) (2). Use single flowers, easy
Anemone (2)
Aquilegia (Columbine) (2). Dry when young
Azalea (2)
Calendula (Marigold) (2). Face down for large doubles
Camellia (2)
Campanula (Canterbury Bell) (3). Dry individually
Chrysanthemum (3). Shatter easily, especially large ones. glue needed
Clematis (3). Face down

Cosmos (2). Face down
Crocus (3). Easily re-absorbs moisture
Dahlia (2)
Delphinium (2). Horizontal
Delphinium consolida (Larkspur)
Dianthus barbatus (Sweet William) (2). Entire cluster
Dianthus carophyllus (Carnation) (2)
Foliage—all varieties (2). 1 for other media
Gerbera jamesonii (Transvaal Daisy) (2)
Gladiolus (2). Individual florets. Fades
Gloriosa (Glory Lily) (2)
Helianthus (Sunflower) (2)
Hellebore (2)
Hemerocallis (Day-lily) (3). Yellows are good.
Hydrangea (1). Green is good
Moluccella laevis (Bells of Ireland) (2). Face down
Narcissus (Daffodil) (3). Re-absorbs moisture easily
Nymphaea (Water-Lily) (2). Easy
Orchis (Orchid) (4). Cattleya mossiae is the best
Paeonia (Peony) (2). Easy
Petunia (3). Good for white, not red
Primula (Primrose) (2)
Ranunculus (Buttercup) 10 days
Rose (2). All do well.
Saintpaulia (African Violet) (2)
Scabiosa (Scabious) (2). Glue centre
Syringa (Lilac) (2). Good, large container needed
Tulipa (Tulip) (3) Darkens
Viburnum opulus sterile (Snowball Tree) (2). When green
Viola (Violet) (2)
Viola wittrockiana (Pansy) (3)
Zinnia (2)

PRESERVING WITH GLYCERINE

Plant material may be preserved with glycerine to give a
more supple, less brittle result than the drying methods of
preservation. The glycerine is mixed with water and taken up
by the stem. The water evaporates but the glycerine remains

in the cells of the plant as it is less volatile. The natural colour of the plant is not normally kept and it turns brown, dark green or blue-grey, but in many variations of these colours. The results are tough and long-lasting, in some cases almost indestructible.

The plant material must be treated while it is still absorbing moisture and before any part begins to dry, as the glycerine must be taken up by the stem and is carried to every part of the cutting in order to give complete preservation. Foliage, both branches and single leaves, preserve very well by this method. A few flowers and seedheads may be treated.

Recipe
Pour into a jar 1 part of glycerine and 2 parts of hot water. Stir well.

¼ teaspoon of chlorhexidine may be added to prevent mould. (*Note:* glycerine can be mixed with cold water but combines more rapidly and readily with hot. Stirring is essential as otherwise the glycerine sinks to the bottom of the jar. The plant material cannot take it up undiluted with water.) This mixture may be used over and over again.

Plant Material
This must be in good condition and not beginning to dry out. When a plant prepares to lose its leaves, a layer of protective cork grows across the base of the leaf stalk and to the outside of this, a layer of very weak tissue which eventually disintegrates, letting the leaf fall off. It leaves behind a leaf scar, which is protected. Abscission layers, as they are called, are formed *before* the leaf gets dry and they will prevent glycerine from entering. A general rule is to pick when the plant is at its best—mature, but not old. Young foliage does not take up any moisture easily. July is a good month for many plants. Remove damaged and unwanted leaves as it is wasteful to use glycerine on these.

Stem Ends
The glycerine/water solution should reach 1″–2″ up the stem of the plant material and must be kept topped up if

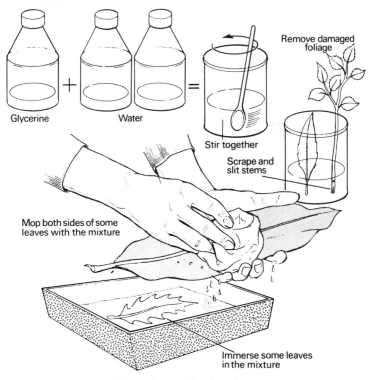

Glycerine + Water = Stir together

Remove damaged foliage

Scrape and slit stems

Mop both sides of some leaves with the mixture

Immerse some leaves in the mixture

Preserving with glycerine.

absorbed before preservation is complete. Any length of stem may be placed in the solution, including branches of beech 5 feet tall. Cut all stem ends before placing in the mixture as for conditioning. Scrape off any bark for 2″ and split the ends of hard and woody stems, which may be put in the glycerine while still hot, as this is helpful to rapid absorption.

Colour
Eventually the foliage will change colour and this is an indication of complete preservation. Lighter results may be obtained by placing the plant material in the sun *after* preservation, for a week or two.

Mopping
Some plant material with heavy tissue absorbs moisture slowly through the stem. As a result the tips of the leaves may dry out giving a half-preserved, half-brittle result. This

may be avoided by mopping the whole leaf on both sides with the glycerine/water solution before standing the stem in it. Cotton wool or paper tissue can be used. This is very necessary when preserving aspidistra and large *Fatsia japonica* leaves.

Immersion
Smaller, heavy-tissued foliage may be submerged in the mixture in a shallow dish. This suits ivy, smaller leaves of *Fatsia japonica, Bergenia,* fig and other foliage which seems difficult to preserve.

Timing
The time taken to preserve plant material varies according to the type of plant and the season, from beech which may take only a few days to aspidistra which normally takes 3 months. The safest guide is the colour of the plant material which should be a uniform brown, dark green or blue-grey. Interesting colour effects may result from deliberately removing foliage from the mixture, before it is quite preserved. Sometimes beech which has thin tissue, may be left in too long and then beads of glycerine appear on the surface. This should be blotted off with paper tissue or the leaves may be pressed gently between newspaper.

Length of Life
Preserved foliage with very strong tissue such as *Fatsia japonica* and laurel will last indefinitely and is very tough. Beech, which has weak tissue, may last only one winter in a warm room before shrivelling although it has been known to last many years.

Reaction to water
Plant material preserved by the glycerine method is not harmed by being placed in water or water-retaining substances, because glycerine has penetrated into all the tiny cells and remains there, only the water content of the glycerine/water solution having evaporated from the leaves. Neither does it harm the plant material to wash it. It is ideal for combining with fresh plant material in the same container.

343

FOLIAGE

Timing is given in approximate weeks. Treat in mid-summer unless otherwise stated.

Anthurium	3–4, mop, any time
Adiantum (Maidenhair fern)	2–3, any time
Aspidistra	12, any time, mop,
Atriplex	$\frac{1}{2}$
Aucuba japonica (Spotted Laurel)	3–4, very dark
Begonia rex	1, needs false stem
Bergenia (Megasea)	3–4, submerge, very dark
Buxus (Box)	3–4, golden
Camellia	4, shiny, dark, strong
Castanea sativa (Sweet Chestnut)	$1\frac{1}{2}$, wire leaves singly
Choisya ternata (Choisya)	4–5
Cotoneaster	Varies according to variety
Dracaena	12, mop
Elaeagnus pungens	4–6, variegation disappears
Eucalyptus (Gum tree)	2–3, grey-violet
Fagus (Beech)	1, green gives a better colour than copper
Fatshedera	4–6, mop
Fatsia japonica	2–10, mop or submerge
Ferns	2–3, when spores are on back
Ficus elastica (Rubber plant)	4, mop, any time
Grevillea robusta	2, dark brown, any time
Hedera (Ivy)	3, submerge or mop, berries will take glycerine
Helleborus corsicus (Hellebore)	3, light brown
Laurus nobilis (Laurel)	4, dark
Liriodendron tulipifera (Tulip tree)	2–3, light
Magnolia grandiflora (Magnolia)	3–4, dark
Mahonia	3–6, dark and light

344

Paeonia (Peony)	2, black, limp
Pittosporum tenuifolium	2
Polygonatum odoratum (Solomons Seal)	1, after flowering
Pyrus communis (Pear)	1–2
Quercus (Oak)	2, acorns and oak—apples stay on
Rhododendron	2, single leaves
Rose	2, dark green, use woody stem
Sorbus aria (Whitebeam)	1½, grey on one side

FLOWERS

Clematis vitalba (Old man's beard)	2, before flowers open
Eryngium alpinum maritimum (Sea-holly)	2–3
Garrya eliptica (tassels)	3
Hydrangea	2, woody stem needed
Moluccella laevis (bracts)	3, beige

SEEDHEADS

Acer platanus (Sycamore)	2
Castanea (Chestnut)	3
Dipsacus fullonum (Teasles)	3
Iris	2
Plantago (Plantain)	2

MECHANICS FOR PRESERVED PLANT MATERIAL

Dried plant material may be supported with Plasticine, dry plastic foam, a pinholder or more permanently with plaster of Paris or a slower drying cement. If the stem ends are dipped into melted candle-wax, sealing-wax or nail polish, dried plant material may be used in water or water-retaining materials.

Glycerined plant material may be supported in the same ways as dried or as fresh plant material. To avoid mildew the stem ends may be treated as above.

Pressed Flower Pictures

Arrange the entire design before sticking, as this will be permanent and it can be difficult and messy to remove plant material. There are several methods:

1. Attach small pieces of double-sided sticky tape to the undersides of plant material and press on to paper or on to the overlapped plant material. The paper should then be placed on hardboard and covered with glass held in place by a frame or clips.

2. The plant material may be glued on to paper with tiny spots of latex or rubber adhesive to a paper or fabric-covered board. The correct type of adhesive is important as a strong glue may eventually show through the plant material.

No mount should be used with a flower picture, as the glass should touch and press down on the plant material. A backing is needed for adequate pressure. A frame or special glass clips may be used to hold the glass in place. If a design is left in the middle of arranging or gluing it is advisable to place a piece of blotting paper or newspaper over it and a heavy book to prevent the light plant material from blowing out of place. The smaller sizes of plant material are more useful than larger sizes.

Plaques

These use three-dimensional plant material and are not covered with glass. The background displays the design of plant material and it may be any shape and framed or not.

1. (a) Cover a piece of hardboard with fabric. Mitre the corners of the fabric and glue on to the back of the board. Stick gummed paper around the rough edges. Place two curtain screws on the back for hanging up with picture cord. Attach plant material to the right side with clear glue if the plant material is heavy or rubber adhesive if light.

(b) Cover a board in the same way, add a pile of cement in one or more places and insert the stems of plant material into the cement which takes about half an hour to dry. Stems can be removed during this time.

(c) Cover pegboard instead of hardboard and attach plant

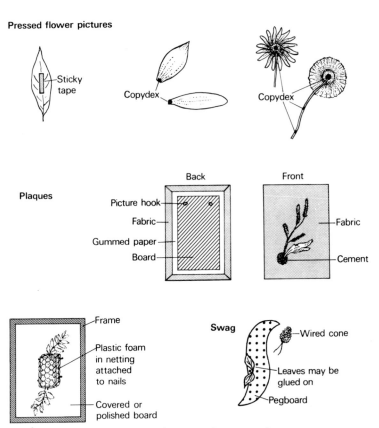

Pressed flower pictures

Sticky tape

Copydex

Copydex

Plaques

Back

Picture hook

Fabric

Gummed paper

Board

Front

Fabric

Cement

Frame

Plastic foam in netting attached to nails

Covered or polished board

Swag

Wired cone

Leaves may be glued on

Pegboard

Mechanics for pictures, plaques and swags.

material with wires pushed through the fabric and the holes in the pegboard.

2. Sand, stain and polish a piece of wood of any shape. Frame if desired. Glue plant material on with a strong clear glue.

3. Paint a shaped piece of hardboard with matt, emulsion paint. Glue on plant material with strong glue.

4. Attach a piece of dry plastic foam to a covered or painted piece of hardboard, pegboard or natural, polished wood by covering the foam with wire netting with a small mesh. Wire with reel wire to a few nails knocked into the wood. Push stems into the foam through the netting.

Swags

The background is not visible in a swag.

1. Cut pegboard to shape. There is no need to cover it. Wire plant material through the holes and glue some on the top. Attach a long wire through the holes to hang up.

2. Cover dry plastic foam with wire netting. Attach a long piece of wire for hanging. Push dried stems through the netting and into the foam.

3. Glue plant material to a piece of hardboard. For more depth, further plant material may be glued on top.

Plaques and swags of preserved plant material may be sprayed with varnish for protection, but this may give a hard shiny effect. They can also be highlighted with plain or metallic spray paints.

WEATHERED WOOD

This is wood that has been weathered by the elements. It is often called driftwood although not necessarily tossed out of water. It includes large and small chunks from trunks and large branches, crosscuts of tree trunks, bark, tree stumps, roots, leafless branches with or without bark. It is essential that wood collected is mostly hard as soft rotting wood is not worth treatment.

Preparation

Scrub with detergent and water to remove dirt and insect life. Disinfectant may be necessary.

Grey wood should be washed very gently as the grey colour is only on the surface and is easily removed.

Dry in the sunshine, airing cupboard or any warm, dry place. Roots seldom need more attention than this.

Remove

(a) Pockets of soft wood with knife or screw-driver.

(b) Undesired bark and broken branches with a knife, secateurs or saw. Bark may be more easily scraped off after soaking in water for 24 hours.

Brush with a wire brush with the exception of grey wood or wood with special markings or textures that might be removed by brushing.

Sandpaper if a very smooth finish is desired (but this can give a dull appearance). A sanding machine gives a very smooth look but is drastic and may give a lifeless look to the wood.

Altering the Shape
Prune branches and roots with secateurs.

Saw off some parts if the shape can be improved. It is better not to saw off too much as a scar is left which is obvious, unless it is coloured to match the remaining wood. Before any major shape changes it is wise to look at the wood for several days at all angles.

Level the wood so that it stands in the correct position. A sawing line can be made by lowering the wood into a bucket of water while holding it at the correct angle. A tide-mark should be left as a guide for sawing or a chalk line may be made just above the water level.

Polishing
Wax for a gentle shine, with furniture wax or shoe polish. Brush the wax on, leave the wood 24 hours to soak it up (it should be applied liberally), brush again and finish with a soft cloth. Waxing protects as well as giving a sheen.

Varnish gives greater protection against water stains but also gives a harder appearance to the surface.

Note: Grey wood should be neither waxed nor varnished if the greyness is to be kept.

Colouring
Wood normally needs no additional colouring as it is beautiful in itself. If special effects are required, colour may be added. There are several methods:

Polish with coloured shoe polish.

Stain with wood stain. Wax may be used on top of this.

Paint
   (a) With a brush and matt paint. This can give a dull lifeless appearance (which may be desired). More interest may result from wiping some paint off while it is still wet.
   (b) Spray with spray paint (matt or shiny) so that the wood shows through. Gold, silver and copper highlights may be added.

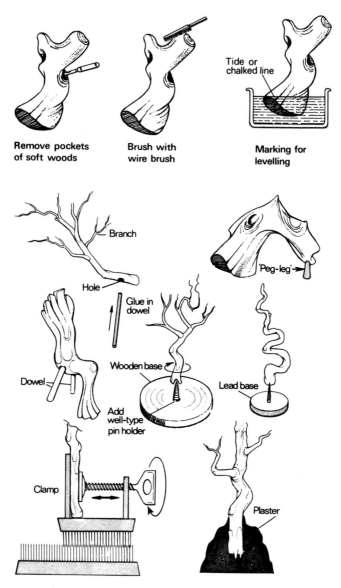

Remove pockets of soft woods

Brush with wire brush

Marking for levelling

Tide or chalked line

Branch

'Peg-leg'

Hole

Glue in dowel

Dowel

Wooden base

Lead base

Add well-type pin holder

Clamp

Plaster

Treatment and mechanics for weathered wood.

Darken with linseed oil which also preserves the wood. Wax may be used on top of this.

Grey by soaking for 24 hours in a bucket of water containing $\frac{1}{2}$ pound of salt. Dry in the sun or an airing cupboard. This process may need repeating.

Blacken with a blow lamp, in a bonfire or with paint or black shoe polish. Wax may be applied afterwards.

Bleach by soaking overnight in a bucket of water containing half a bottle of bleach. This yellows the wood slightly. Oxalic acid crystals, 1 tablespoon to 1 quart of water, will give a pinker appearance. Soak in water for ten minutes and then rinse with hot water.

Touch up with coloured chalks rubbed into the wood.

MECHANICS

A Pinholder is suitable for branches, roots, some chunks if the wood is fairly soft.

Dowel stick may be glued into a hole of the same size drilled in the wood. The dowel stick can be pushed into sand or plastic foam to support the wood. Several pieces may be needed in one piece of wood. Short lengths of dowel stick may be secured in a pinholder for similar support.

Plastic foam supports lightweight branches and roots.

A clamp built into an 'upside-down' pinholder which can fit firmly on to a regular pinholder.

A screw

(a) built into the centre of a heavy piece of lead. This is good for heavy branches and vines. A hole should be made with a drill in the base of the branch, care being taken that the hole is made at the right angle.

(b) fixed through a base pointing upwards. The branch or chunk of wood is twisted on to the screw, which should be countersunk to avoid scratching furniture. Felt may be glued on to the base to cover the screw head also.

Wooden legs can be glued, nailed or screwed on to a large chunk of wood to support it at a desired angle.

Glue several pieces of the same type of wood together to make one more interesting piece.

Plaster of Paris or 'Polyfilla' is good for supporting heavy branches which are not secure in a clamp. Make a lump of plaster (see page 313). Hold the branch in position until it sets. A hollow may be made so that a pinholder can be placed close to the wood. The plaster may be covered with stones, moss and other cover-ups.

Plasticine is suitable for very light branches only and even then cannot be relied upon to support wood safely.

HOW TO MAKE A COLOUR CIRCLE

The making of a colour circle has value as it leads to a greater understanding of colour and its nature. The following circle takes 5–8 daylight hours to complete and is similar to the one on page 181 but larger in size.

MATERIALS AND EQUIPMENT

1 sheet of drawing paper wider than 22″. This can be Double Elephant 40″ × 27″ or Imperial $30\frac{1}{2}$″ × $22\frac{1}{2}$″

Clean water (working near a tap is useful)

Paste or glue

Clean rag

A sharp pair of scissors

A sharp pencil

A small pair of compasses and a large pair. If the latter is not available, a piece of strong cardboard $\frac{3}{4}$″ × 14″

A ruler

A protractor

A paint brush size 7 (a sable one is unnecessary)

A patty pan with 6 pans at least

Tubes of Designers Gouache in:

Titanium white, Ivory black, Spectrum yellow, Cobalt blue, Periwinkle blue, Bengal rose. Alternative colours may be used but trial is advised before using. (Note: Bengal rose may be thought too 'pink', in which case use a scarlet-red for the mixing of orange and crimson-red for the violet.)

METHOD

1. Mark the centre of the paper with a dot.
2. Use the large pair of compasses and from the marked centre draw circles of diameters 22″, $16\frac{1}{2}$″, 11″, $5\frac{1}{2}$″ (radii

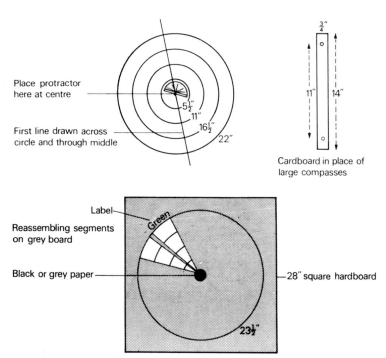

Place protractor here at centre

First line drawn across circle and through middle

$5\frac{1}{2}''$
$11''$
$16\frac{1}{2}''$
$22''$

$\frac{3}{4}''$
$11''$ $14''$

Cardboard in place of large compasses

Label

Reassembling segments on grey board

Green

Black or grey paper

28″ square hardboard

$23\frac{1}{2}''$

Construction of a colour circle.

of 11″, $8\frac{1}{4}''$, $5\frac{1}{2}''$, $2\frac{3}{4}''$). If large compasses are not available, use instead the long piece of cardboard by making two holes in it 11″ apart with a sharp point. Draw the required 22″ circle by placing the sharp point of the small compasses through one hole, on to the marked centre of the paper and a very sharp pencil through the other hole. Holding these firmly in place ask another person to revolve the paper. A 22″ circle should result.

Using the same method, make a further circle of radius $8\frac{1}{4}''$. Then make circles of $5\frac{1}{2}''$ and $2\frac{3}{4}''$ radii with the smaller compasses.

3. Draw a diameter across the outside circle making sure that it passes through the centre of the circle.

4. With a protractor placed on this line, at the centre of the circle, mark 30, 60, 90, 120, 150 degrees with dots and draw a line through the centre of the circle and each of these dots right across the outside circle.

353

5. Proceed to paint. Alternatively those not used to painting may prefer the following method:

Cut carefully around the outside 22″ diameter circle. Then cut out each pie-shaped segment from the outside of the circle to the centre. There should be 12. The segments will be re-assembled later. If mistakes are made in painting a new segment may be cut from paper by drawing round the old segment, cutting out and re-painting.

PAINTING

6. Paint the segments with clear water and allow to dry. The gouache goes on more smoothly.

7. Mix in two patty pans a quantity of Bengal rose or its alternative (it should be a slightly blue-red). See that the mixture is well saturated with paint and not watery. Colour the outside band of one segment with this. This is the hue of red.

To one pan of red, add white paint to make a tint. When the hue is dry, paint the adjoining band. To the same whitened mixture add a *little* black, which makes a tone. Paint the third band with this. To the s*econd* pan of red paint, add a *little* black and paint the final band to give a shade.

8. Repeat the whole sequence with Cobalt blue and then with Spectrum yellow, painting segments equidistant from each other and from the red. The primary colours will now be painted.

9. Mix Spectrum yellow and Bengal rose together to make orange and place a little into each of 6 patty pans.

Use two pans of orange to paint a segment between the red and yellow primary hues. Make a hue, a tint, a tone and a shade as for the primary colours (see 7).

Use two more pans of orange mixed with a little more yellow to paint the segment between yellow and orange, with yellow-orange. Paint a hue, a tint, a tone and a shade as before.

Use the remaining two pans of orange to make red-orange by adding a *little* more red. Paint the segment between orange and red with this.

10. Mix Periwinkle blue and Bengal rose together to make

violet in six pans. Paint the segments of violet and then red-violet and blue-violet (as in 9 for the oranges).

11. Mix Spectrum yellow and Cobalt blue together to make green. Paint the segments of green, blue-green and yellow-green.

The secondary and tertiary colours are now painted and the circle is complete.

MOUNTING

Paint a 28" square of hardboard or heavy cardboard with mid-grey emulsion paint. (Colours appear the nearest to normal against grey.) Glue on the painted circle with yellow at the top (being the most luminous colour it appears more natural at the top). A sharp grey or black line may be drawn between the segments for clarity.

If the segments have been cut out reassemble them in order (as on the colour circle, p.181 and using a $23\frac{1}{2}$" circle drawn on the mounting board as a guide line, glue on with the outer edge of each segment placed on the guide-line.

Leave a narrow grey space between each segment for clarity. Cover the central points, for neatness, with a small circle of black paper.

Label the colours.

To make the board free-standing a hinged prop can be added to the back.

Cover with a sheet of Neo-film or Neer glass tacked to the top of the board or with matt self-adhesive Filmomatt. This must be put on with great care to avoid 'bubbles' but gives a more permanent protection, although it cannot be removed again and very slightly dulls the colours.

Notes for Success

    (a) More white is needed to make a tint, than black to make a shade.

    (b) Use little water except with violet.

    (c) Red is a powerful pigment, yellow is weaker.

    (d) The colours may run into each other unless dry.

    (e) Grade the colours carefully if the segments have been cut out, e.g. Yellow-green means a green with a yellowish appearance and it should be placed between the green and yellow.

Making a pot-et-fleur.

Absolute accuracy in colour mixing is unnecessary for a flower arranger's colour circle.

MAKING A POT-ET-FLEUR

EQUIPMENT

A container deep enough to allow watering of plants.
Washed gravel, chippings or pieces of old crockery.
A bag of John Innes Compost No. 2.
Several pieces of charcoal.

METHOD

Place a 1″ layer of washed gravel (or alternative) in the bottom of the container. Break up the charcoal and spread over the gravel. Add John Innes Compost to a depth of about 2″. Remove the plants from their pots by turning upside down and rapping the edge of the pot against something hard. The plant should drop into the hand (do not water before doing this). Place the plants complete with root balls, on the compost and arrange as desired.

When satisfied with the design, fill the spaces between the plants with compost to within 1″ of the top of the container. Plants may be put in at angles and need not be positioned upright.

When needed, add the mechanics for cut flowers.

Cultural requirements are the same as those for house plants.

PLANTS LEFT IN POTS

When plants are not removed from their own pots, gravel and charcoal are used as above. Moist peat may be used to fill in between the pots and to cover the pots in place of compost.

HOME-MADE CONTAINERS

1. LOW CONTAINER

Equipment

A sheet of lead (from a plumber)

Tin.snips or strong scissors

Wooden mallet or padded hammer

A block of wood approximately $3'' \times 2'' \times 2''$

A paper pattern of a regular or irregular shape which will be the shape of the container's base.

Method

Cut the lead to the shape of the paper pattern leaving an extra $1\frac{1}{2}''$ (minimum) margin all round for the sides of the container. Turn up the edge of the lead to the depth of the allowed margin, by knocking it up with the mallet against the small block of wood.

Edges may be trimmed or bevelled with a file. Steel wool erases any marks and gives a slight sheen.

The lead may easily be reshaped.

2. TALL CONTAINER

Equipment

A tall round tin with one end removed *or*

A plastic washing-up liquid container with the top removed with scissors.

Covering as required from choice below.

Method

For weight, melt lead and pour in $1''$ *or* use $2''$ concrete or plaster of Paris *or* use wet sand when container is completed (see page 311).

Cover with any of the following:

(a) Bamboo cane split in half and glued on with an impact glue. The cane may be stained.

(b) Mosaic tile put on with grout (mortar used to fill cracks) supplied with mosaic tile.

(c) Fablon cut to fit plus a $\frac{1}{2}''$ margin to overlap at the top and bottom. Clip these overlaps for almost $\frac{1}{2}''$ and turn inside the top of the tin and over the bottom. Braid may be used around the edges.

(d) A straw mat cut to fit and glued on.

(e) Snowcem moulded on to the surface roughly. This may be painted.

(f) Heavy string wrapped on to the glued surface. Glue a little at a time.

A textured effect may be obtained by rolling any damp or lightly glued surface in seeds, coffee grounds, vermiculite, ground-up egg-shells, sand. Sand and paint may also be mixed together for a rough surface. These surfaces may be painted with emulsion paint or rubbed with shoe polish for varying effects.

3. OPAQUE BOTTLE

Swirl oil paint inside the bottle until all is covered. Pour off excess.

4. MODERN PEDESTAL CONTAINER

Equipment
    1 plastic plant saucer or a 'pot' saucer
    1 plastic plant pot without holes in the bottom *or*
    A plastic beaker with a lid or a 'pot' plant pot
    Paint
    Contact glue

Method
Glue the saucer to the inverted plant pot and paint both. For greater weight, fill a beaker with sand or plaster of Paris. Cover with the lid before glueing on to the saucer. See No. 2 for textural effects.

5. 'TRADITIONAL' CONTAINER

Equipment
    12" length of broom handle
    1 small packet of Polyfilla
    Paint (antique gold is attractive)
    3 6" baking tins *or* 2 baking tins and a wooden base
    Screws and screwdriver.

Method

Screw the end of the broom handle to the centre of one baking tin placed upside down *or* to the wooden base. Screw another baking tin the correct way up to the top of the broom handle. This is the container on a pedestal and base. The third baking tin is placed inside the top one to make it into a water-tight container.

Mix Polyfilla to a thick paste in a bowl and apply with the hands to the broom handle and base, making an irregular surface.

Before the Polyfilla sets add any decoration, e.g. plastic angels, artificial fruit or flowers.

When set, spray or brush with paint. The shine may be dulled with shoe polish. All the container should be painted.

6. A MODERN CONTAINER OF PLASTER OF PARIS

The basis for this is cast slabs of plaster joined together.

Equipment
    Heavy foil
    Plaster of Paris—one bag
    Modrok plaster bandage (or Dragon-silk)
    File, sandpaper or rasp
    Plasticine
    Heavy wire.

Method

Make a mould for each side of the container by cutting out pieces of heavy metal foil to the required size, adding $\frac{1}{2}''$ all round for the depth of the plaster slab. Turn up the sides of the foil, mitring the corners. Make sure there are no gaps or holes. A wood mould can be used instead. Oiling the mould is helpful.

The Mixture

Sprinkle plaster of Paris on top of water in a plastic bowl until it forms mounds just below the surface. Stir quickly and tap the sides of the bowl to remove bubbles from the bottom. Pour into the moulds. Do this quickly. $\frac{1}{2}$ pint of size to $\frac{1}{2}$ bucket of water can strengthen the plaster and slow the

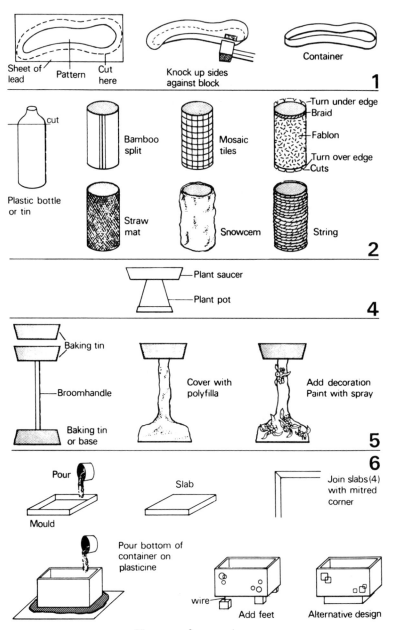

1

Sheet of lead / Pattern / Cut here

Knock up sides against block

Container

2

Plastic bottle or tin

cut

Bamboo split

Mosaic tiles

Turn under edge
Braid
Fablon
Turn over edge
Cuts

Straw mat

Snowcem

String

4

Plant saucer

Plant pot

5

Baking tin

Broomhandle

Baking tin or base

Cover with polyfilla

Add decoration
Paint with spray

6

Pour

Mould

Slab

Join slabs (4) with mitred corner

Pour bottom of container on plasticine

wire

Add feet

Alternative design

Home-made containers.

setting process. Modrok plaster bandages may be cut to fit and placed on top for greater strength. Leave plaster 20 minutes to harden before removing from the moulds.

Joining the sides

Mitre edges with a file, sandpaper or rasp. Scratch the inside surfaces slightly and dampen them. Press together. Dip a length of Modrok plaster bandage into a saucer of water and push into the mitred corner down the whole length. Then place two or three strips crosswise. When the strips have set mix a small amount of plaster with water until creamy and with a knife press this on to the seam to neaten and strengthen.

Casting the bottom of the container

Place a flattened piece of Plasticine on to a flat surface and press the container on to it. Pour a small amount of plaster into the container and on to the Plasticine. Leave until set and then remove. For greater strength, scratch grooves in the inner sides of the container at the bottom so that as the plaster is poured in it enters the grooves.

To make feet

Flatten a piece of Plasticine on to a flat surface. Make holes in it the size of the required feet (a small tube makes round feet). Pour plaster in to the holes and push a length of wire in at once. Twist the wire and leave $\frac{1}{2}''$ sticking up and out of the plaster. Drill small holes in the bottom of the container where the feet are to go. Dampen these and pour in a little plaster. Push the feet on to the bottom at once so that the wires go into the hole. Leave to set.

Waterproofing

Paint with polyurethane varnish.

Colour

Kingston paint stains added to the water or any acrylic paint on the surface.

Rough Edges

Remove with rasp, file, sandpaper or steel-wool.

Alternative Method
Make a framework of wire mesh and cover with layers of dampened plaster bandages. Smooth plaster of Paris over the top.

Patterned Surface
Draw the desired design on paper. Place on to the bottom of the foil mould. Draw over the design with a sharp pencil. This makes marks on the foil which will transfer to the plaster.

FLOWER ARRANGEMENTS AND PHOTOGRAPHY

As flower arrangements have such transient beauty, it is useful to make permanent records by means of photography. Not only may these photographs be appreciated for their artistic value but they can form an excellent record of past work. They are also a useful source for publications such as calendars, magazines, cards and books.

For the serious student, photographs are an excellent method of assessing arrangements. Design faults, not so obvious in the actual flower arrangement, are usually clearly revealed in a photograph and this is especially true of black and white work.

Flower arrangement photography is specialised work and when an arranger engages a professional photographer he will require some help and guidance from her. There are some points which the flower arranger can look after, without a technical knowledge of photography, which will contribute to a better picture.

BACKGROUNDS

(a) The natural furnishings and furniture of a home usually prove successful. Homes, churches, country houses and cathedrals can provide excellent backgrounds of papered or painted walls, curtains, stonework or wood panelling. When composing the surroundings which will be seen in the final picture, care should be taken that objects such as furniture and paintings are well integrated into the complete design and make a balanced composition. For example, folds of curtains should hang well, chairs straightened and all other such details carefully checked, by continually looking in the view-finder to study the final picture.

(b) Artificial backgrounds must be very well groomed. Creasing, ruckling and markings become exaggerated in the photograph. Jazzy patterns and blank white backgrounds tend to overpower rather than enhance the flower arrangement.

Materials for backgrounds can be strong, uncreased paper, backed hessian, display felt (which being 72″ wide gives a good margin of background), straw matting, coloured sheets, a slide screen, painted and papered boards or curtains hung on a clothes maiden.

A horizontal, dividing line on the photograph which is caused by placing the table against a wall, can be eliminated. Place the paper or fabric both behind and below the arrangement in a continuous flow, curving it gently over the point where the table meets the wall. The paper or fabric can be tacked to the wall, to a batten on the wall or held on curtain hooks or brackets with a cane.

Textural effects, if not too strong, may be effective on backgrounds and relieve plainness. Interest may also be obtained with lighting to give a change of value.

Backgrounds are the frame for the design and must be sufficiently wide for the camera to photograph the arrangement with a margin of background all around. No objects should unintentionally be seen on any side of the background in the completed picture and there should be a continuous background running from top to bottom and from side to side. Far more coverage is necessary than would be expected.

CAMERA POSITION

A design photographs best from the front, from where the arranger designed it to be seen.

The height of the camera is important and the *arranger's* eye-level is usually the best position. A camera placed above or below this position will give distortion and undesired emphasis to some parts of the design. It should also be decided if the inside of the container is to be seen or if the camera should be positioned so that the inside is hidden by the front of the container.

It is extremely easy for an amateur to cut off the top or the bottom of a design, which spoils an otherwise excellent photograph, so plenty of margin should be allowed in the viewfinder. On the other hand the margin should not predominate and the arrangement should pleasingly fill the rectangular space. Containers with symmetrical handles should be taken so that they present a straight face to the camera. Bases, unless deliberately desired at an angle, should be parallel to the bottom of the rectangle.

LIGHTING

This is best left to the photographer but the flower arranger should see that strong artificial light is turned on for as short a time as possible because the heat soon causes the plant material to wilt.

The flower arranger who wishes to try photographing her own arrangements will need three lights for success normally. A suggestion is to use a strong light near and to one side of the camera to give front lighting to the design and show details. A second light to the side of the design will give moulding and a more three-dimensional quality. This might be at an angle of 45° from the arrangement with a downward angle also at 45°. The third light can eliminate shadows on the background if directed on to the background. It also gives tonal variety to it, which is more interesting in the final picture. If this light is placed on the floor below the table a glow is given at the base of the design.

Black and white photographs may be taken successfully in strong daylight (not direct sunlight) without flash or artificial light. This method can eliminate heavy shadows.

Advice must be taken on the correct type of film for the lighting used.

CHOICE OF COLOUR FOR DESIGN AND BACKGROUND

Colours appear in black and white photography in terms of grey. A comparison of colours in relation to the grey scale is useful but it is emphasised that this refers to pure hues

365

without modification. Colours modified in any way may have a different position on the grey scale.

White	1	
	2	
	3	Yellow
	4	Orange
	5	
Greys	6	
	7	Green
	8	Red
	9	Blue
	10	Violet
	11	
Black	12	

Maximum picture impact in black and white photography comes from placing light-toned flowers and containers against dark backgrounds and vice-versa. Difficulty may arise over choice of background if light-toned flowers are used in a dark container.

In colour work background colours at full saturation can over-whelm the colours of the plant material and those of the same colour as the plant material, even if a different value, may prove difficult as a slight variation of the colours in printing can cause the flowers to merge into the background.

DESIGN OF THE FLOWER ARRANGEMENT

Designing *for* photography is different from designing for flower arrangements normally, in that far less plant material is needed. Clear spaces are needed so that the forms are seen. Three dimensions are not as necessary and flowers recessed may merge into the foreground flowers and cause confusion. For black and white work even less plant material than for colour work is effective and it can be arranged in two-dimensions. Good spacing is essential in black and white photography which means that modern designs often give the best photographs. When preparing for a photograph it can be helpful to arrange against a light, such as a window, so that the silhouette is seen and before taking an expensive colour photograph it is helpful to take one with an instant developing camera so that faults may be corrected in the design.

A study of many photographs of flower arrangements is very helpful and they should be observed with regard to lighting, background, use of colour and the composition of the design.

MATERIALS

Consult Yellow Pages for local suppliers

TOOLS AND MECHANICS

Tools and mechanics developed especially for flower arrangement and described in part 4 are obtainable from florists' shops, garden centres, ironmongers and flower club sales tables. By mail order from: Floraproducts, Stanley Gibbons Magazines Ltd, Drury House, Russell Street, London WC2B 5HD.

ADHESIVES

From paint and wallpaper shops, ironmongers, DIY shops, stationers' art shops.

For paper:
Wallpaper paste, wheat paste, cow gum, rubber cement. Aerosol fixatives for drawings and pastels.

For other media:
Contact cement, epoxy cement, white glue, rubber cement, acrylic medium, spray adhesives (e.g. Evostik, Copydex, Weldwood, Bostik, Uhu, Marvin. P.V.A. for plastics).

For mending containers:
Epoxy resin high stress adhesive (e.g. Araldite).

PAINT

From art shops, paint shops, the Visual Aid Centre, 78 High Holborn, London W.C.1, chemist shops.

Acrylic paints
Plastic paints, water based, usable on any non-oily surface

such as paper, masonry, plastic, wood, acetate, fabric, masonite, canvas, clay, Plasticine. They may be called vinyl, emulsion, polymer. The emulsion is the plastic paint in liquid form with water as a base in which the particles are suspended. After painting a surface, the water evaporates and the small units join together to form a continuous, waterproof, flexible film. These paints are resilient and can be cleaned up with water (e.g. Cryla, P.V.A. colours, sold in tubes).

Poster paint
Water based, low cost paint which is quick drying. Not always permanent. Sold in jars. Fluorescent poster paint is brilliant and visible from a greater distance than other paints.

Water colour
Transparent paint, water based. Sold in tubes and small blocks. Does not cover as solidly as opaque water colour, i.e. poster and gouache.

Gouache
Opaque water-based paint which spreads easily and smoothly, covers well, dries quickly. May crack if very thickly applied. Sold in tubes (e.g. Designers Gouache).

Powder colour
Also called dry colour. It is a pigment in powder form which may be mixed with water or polymer medium, polycell, white glue (e.g. Marvin). Very inexpensive. (Reeves powder colour: Tempera in blocks and tins).

Paint for acetate film
Thinned with water but waterproof when dry, fast to light (e.g. Reeves Filmagraph colours).

Oil colour
Slow-drying, oil-based. Needs turpentine or its substitute to clean up after using.

Finger-paint mix
Make with powder colour and paste.

Metallic paint
Obtainable in an aerosol container, quick drying. Also obtainable as a metallic powder to mix with bronzing liquid. This is applied with a brush and is cheaper but slower drying. Greater range of colours.
Gold leaf for gilding in painting and collage. This is fragile and difficult to manipulate. It is applied with gold size.
Metallic paste applied with cloth or fingers, suitable for many different surfaces and gives an excellent finish (e.g. Rowneys Goldfinger).
Liquid leaf for gilding, flammable and needs a special thinner.

Enamel paint
For art work (e.g. Humbrol Art Enamels).

Dyes
Cold water dyes for tie and dye processes (e.g. Dylon). Also used for Batik work. Wood stains and dyes.

WOOD
From timber merchants, carpentry and D.I.Y. shops. Pegboard, hardboard, chipboard, plywood, masonite, selected wood for bases.

STONE
From stone masons.
Marble, alabaster, Bath stone which is soft for carving.

TRANSPARENT COVERINGS
From art shops, stationers, the Visual Aid Centre. Polythene sheeting for show benches in a number of widths, in rolls from Lakeland Plastics, Alexandra Buildings, Station Precinct, Windermere, Cumbria and Transatlantic Plastics, 382 Sutton Common Road, Sutton, Surrey.

Stiff sheet, not adhesive
Plastic substitute for glass (e.g. Neerglass, Neo-film).

Shiny, adhesive
Self adhesive in colours and colourless, a P.V.C. film (e.g.

Transpaseal). The same with greater strength, both in colours and colourless (e.g. Filmolux).

Matt, adhesive
No shine at all and almost invisible. Dulls colours slightly (e.g. Filmomatt).
All self-adhesive film needs great care in applying to avoid bubbles of air and creasing. It is not removable without damaging the work covered.

DRAWING AIDS
From art shops, stationers, the Visual Aid Centre.
Templates to draw curves and other shapes. Charcoal sticks in soft, hard, and medium textures and various sizes. Stencils for lettering, felt-tip markers and fine-line markers in black and colours. Water colour drawing pens, lettering pens. Ready made lettering (e.g. Letraset).

PAPER AND BOARDS
From stationers, art shops, Paperchase, 213 Tottenham Court Road, London W1, the Visual Aid Centre.
Paper, hand-made and machine-made, usually in categories of smooth (Hot-pressed H.P.), medium (not hot-pressed, NOT) and rough (Rough). All sizes including sketching pads. Newsprint pads and paper for rough sketching which are cheap although not permanent. Water colour paper, pastel papers in a range of related colours, fluorescent papers in glowing colours, sugar paper in blue, buff and grey, poster paper, tissue paper, gummed papers, foils, French marbled papers, heavy papers in a hue, tints, shades of colours (e.g. Color-aid papers).
Wide paper for photography (e.g. Colorama). Wallpapers.
Cardboard for mounting and drawing in many weights, sizes and colours.
Savage background papers, 50 colours, 9′ or 4′ 6″ wide, from Pelling & Cross Ltd, 104 Baker Street, London W1M 2AR and also regional agents.

CHEMICALS
Boots Ltd will obtain in small quantities.

Alec Tiranti Ltd., 21 Goodge Place, London W1, and the Fulham Pottery, 184 New Kings Road, Fulham, London S.W.6 (clay), artists suppliers.

Clay, resins, potters' and wood carvers' tools and equipment. Modelling compound which sets rock hard but can be broken down and re-used (e.g. Sofenbak). Prepared papier-mâché. Plaster impregnated gauze for modelling (e.g. Mod-roc, Reeves). Modelling material which, if to be retained, can be baked on completion in a domestic oven to 140°. It then becomes a hard resilient solid which may be carved with a sharp knife (e.g. Plastaset, Reeves). Self-hardening clay (e.g. Plastone). Clay may be bought in powder form or in plastic condition, in grey or terra-cotta. This clay needs firing at 1030° to 1100°. Plasticine which does not harden.

FABRICS

From haberdashers and display firms.

Felt in many colours 71″ wide, from Felt and Hessian Shop, 34 Greville Street, London EC1.

Cork carpet in rolls, 39″ wide. Furnishing and dressmaking fabrics. Plastic, 51″ wide, 50 colours. Dyed hessian, 72″ wide. Stainless steel sheets 2′ 6″ × 2′. Paper backed hessian, self-adhesive hessian and hessian 71″ wide.

Fine lawn and cotton.

Cotton sheeting 70″ and 90″ wide, polyester and easycare sheeting 70″, 90″ and 108″ wide, butter muslin, unbleached cotton sheeting 40″, 73″ and 93″, all useful for shows and exhibitions, from Limericks, 110 Hamlet Court Road, Westcliff-on-Sea, Essex.

BAMBOO

Display firms, garden centres and cane furniture shops.

Cane-sheeting. Wood weave panels. Bamboo curtaining. Grass mats of various kinds.

Display magazine gives addresses of display firms.

HANDICRAFT MATERIALS

Many of these may be obtained from Dryad Handicrafts, Northgates, Leicester and The Needlewoman, Regent Street, London.

This may be obtained with the correct grain for drying plant material from Floradesac Ltd., 2 Market Place, Tetbury, Gloucestershire GL8 8DA, under the name of 'Flora-D-Hydrate'.

PHOTOGRAPHIC PRODUCTS

Kenro Photographic Products, High Street, Kempsford, Gloucestershire GL7 4EQ.

HELPFUL READING

MAGAZINES

Flora, published bi-monthly by Stanley Gibbons Magazines.
The Flower Arranger, quarterly publication of NAFAS.
Both provide a book service which is useful to readers without a local bookshop.

FLOWER ARRANGEMENT

A History of Flower Arrangement, Julia Berrall (Thames & Hudson).
Chinese Flower Arrangement, H. L. Li (Van Nostrand). o.p.
Church Flowers, Month by Month, Jean Taylor (Mowbray).
Complete Guide to Flower and Foliage Arrangement, Iris Webb (Webb & Bower).
Conway's Encyclopaedia of Flower Arrangement, J. G. Conway (Routledge and Kegan Paul).
Creativity in Flower Arrangement, Frances Bode (Hearthside Press).
Design for Flower Arrangers (revised), Dorothy Riester (Van Nostrand).
Design with Plant Material, Marian Aaronson (Grower Books).
Flower Arrangement—Free Style, Edith Brack (Whitethorn Press).
Flower Arrangements and their Settings, George Smith (Studio Vista).
Flower Arranging in House and Garden, George Smith (Pelham Books).
Flowers in Church, Jean Taylor (Mowbray).

Flowers in the Modern Manner, Marian Aaronson (Grower Books).

Flowers, Space and Motion, Helen Van Pelt Wilson (Simon & Schuster).

Guide to Period Flower Arranging, NAFAS.

Japanese Flower Arrangement, Norman Sparnon (John Weatherhill Inc).

Modern Abstract Flower Arrangement, Emma Cyphers (Hearthside Press).

Modern Flower Arranging, Edith Brack (Batsford).

Nature, Art and Flower Arrangement, Emma Cyphers (Hearthside Press).

New Structures in Flower Arrangement, Frances Bode (Hearthside Press).

Period Arrangements, Margaret Marcus (Barrows). o.p.

Plants and Flowers for Lasting Decoration, Jean Taylor (Batsford).

Practical Flower Arranging, Jean Taylor (Hamlyn).

The Art of Flower Arranging, Marian Aaronson (Grower Books).

The Art of Flower Arrangement, Beverley Nichols (Collins). o.p.

The Art of Flower Arrangement, N. de Kalb Edwards (Thames & Hudson).

The Art of Japanese Flower Arranging, Stella Coe (Jenkins).

The Complete Book of Flower Preservation, Geneal Condon (Robert Hale).

The Craft of Flower Arrangement, Jean Taylor (Stanley Paul).

The Driftwood Book, Mary Thompson (Van Nostrand).

The Eye of the Flower Arranger, Lim Bian Yam (Collingridge). o.p.

The Poetry of Leaves, Norman Sparnon (Weatherhill).

PLANT MATERIAL

A Gardener's Dictionary of Plant Names, A. W. Smith and W. T. Stearn (Cassell).

Botany for Flower Arrangers, John Tampion and Joan Reynolds (Pelham Books).

Flower Arranging from your Garden, Sheila Macqueen (Ward Lock).

Garden Foliage for Flower Arrangement, Sybil Emberton (Faber).

Houseplants Made Easy, Jean Taylor (Independent Television Publications).

Perennial Garden Plants or The Modern Florilegium, Graham Stuart (Dent).
Plant Marvels in Miniature, C. Postma (Harrap).
Reader's Digest Encyclopaedia of Garden Plants and Flowers.
Shrub Gardening for Flower Arrangement, Sybil Emberton (Faber).
The Concise British Flora, W. Keble Martin (Ebury Press and Michael Joseph).
The Dictionary of Roses, S. Millar Gault and P. M. Synge (Michael Joseph).

RELATED BOOKS

The Shell Nature Book, (Phoenix House).
Wild Flowers for your Garden, Stephen Dealler (Batsford).
Wild Flowers of Britain, Roger Phillips (Ward Lock).
200 Houseplants in Colour, G. Kromdijk (Lutterworth).
A Basic Course in Art, L. W. Lawley (Lund Humphries).
Adventures of Modern Art, Bihalji-Merih (Harry N. Abrams).
An Introduction to Art and Craft, Rita Greer (Pitman).
Art and Visual Perception, Rudolf Arnheim (Faber).
Basic Design, Kenneth F. Bates (The World Publishing Co.).
Basic Design: The Dynamics of Visual Form, Maurice de Sausmarez (Studio Vista).
Collage and Found Art, Done Meilach and Elvie Ten Hoor (Studio Vista).
Colour and Form, Gottfried Tritten (Batsford).
Colours and What They Can Do, Louis Cheskin (Blandford).
Creative Art from Anything, Done Meilach (Pitman).
Creative Crafts in Education, Seonaid Robertson (Routledge and Kegan Paul.)
European Flower Painters, Peter Mitchell (Black).
Form and Space, Edward Trier (Thames & Hudson).
Historical Colour Guide, Elizabeth Burris-Meyer (William Helburn Inc.).
Introducing Seed Collage, Caryl & Gordon Sims (Batsford)
Larousse Encyclopaedia of Prehistoric and Ancient Art, Rene Huyghe (Prometheus Press) and others in this series.
Making Pottery Without a Wheel, F. Carlton Bell & J. Lovoos (Van Nostrand).
Modern Sculpture, Herbert Reed (Thames & Hudson).

150 Techniques in Art, Hans Meyers (Batsford).

Patterns in Nature, Peter S. Stevens (Atlantic Little Brown).

Patterns in Space, Richard Slade (Faber).

Pressed Flower Pictures, Pamela McDowell (Lutterworth).

The Art of Colour and Design, Maitland Graves (McGraw).

The Craft of Photography, Roy Hayward (Stanley Paul).

The Enjoyment and Use of Colour, Walter Sargent (Charles Scribner).

The Magic World of Flower Arrangement, Myra J. Brooks (Barrows).

The Modern World (Landmarks of the World Art Series), Norbert Lynton (Hamlyn).

The Nature of Design, David Pye (Studio Vista).

The Potters Craft, Bernard Leach.

The NAFAS Guide to Colour Theory (pamphlet), (The National Association of Flower Arrangement Societies).

The Technique of Collage, Helen Hutton (Batsford).

Vision and Design, Roger Fry (Pelican).

Some books listed here may be permanently, or temporarily, out of print, but can usually be borrowed from public libraries.

Index

Compiled by F. D. Buck

Page references in italic indicate an illustration